RICHARD G. LUGAR,

STATESMAN OF THE SENATE

RICHARD G. LUGAR,

STATESMAN OF THE SENATE

Crafting Foreign Policy
from Capitol Hill

JOHN T. SHAW

INDIANA UNIVERSITY PRESS

Bloomington & Indianapolis

This book is a publication of

Indiana University Press
601 North Morton Street
Bloomington, Indiana 47404-3797 USA

iupress.indiana.edu

Telephone orders   800-842-6796
Fax orders   812-855-7931

⊖ The paper used in this publication meets the minimum
requirements of the American National Standard for
Information Sciences—Permanence of Paper for Printed
Library Materials, ANSI Z39.48-1992.

Manufactured in the United States of America

Cataloging information is available from the Library of Congress.

1 2 3 4 5 17 16 15 14 13 12

For Mindy

The Legislator is an indispensible guardian of our freedom. It is true that great executives have played a powerful role in the development of civilization, but such leaders appear sporadically by chance. They do not always appear when they are most needed. The great executives have given inspiration and push to the advancement of human society, but it is the legislator who has given stability and continuity to that slow and painful progress.

J. WILLIAM FULBRIGHT,
"The Legislator: Duties, Functions and Hardships of Public Officials," speech delivered at the University of Chicago, February 19, 1946

CONTENTS

PREFACE

Richard G. Lugar has been one of the most influential U.S. senators in the realm of foreign policy for more than a quarter of a century.
While he has not always attracted as much attention as some of his Senate colleagues, Lugar's accomplishments place him in the upper echelon
of his contemporaries. He will, I believe, be remembered in the top tier
of Senate foreign policy heavyweights, in the company of such historically significant senators as Arthur Vandenberg, Henry Jackson, and
J. William Fulbright. Assessing his current work and long-term legacy
requires that an analyst confront important and difficult questions:
Can a politician also be a statesman? What is the relationship between
statesmanship and effectiveness in Congress? Is statesmanship still an
effective operating strategy in this charged and polarized political environment? What are the costs and benefits for a lawmaker in adopting
the role of a statesman?

I've covered Capitol Hill for more than 20 years as a congressional
reporter and have had the opportunity to observe many senators closely,
including Robert Dole, George Mitchell, Daniel Patrick Moynihan,
John Danforth, Edward Kennedy, Al Gore, Mark Hatfield, John Chafee,
Lloyd Bentsen, Bill Bradley, John Warner, and Sam Nunn. Lugar has
long intrigued me as a throwback to an earlier era when many senators
developed expertise in particular areas and embraced the rewards and
responsibilities of national leadership. They were effective politicians
who were also able and willing to take the long view. Now, in an increasingly polarized, hyper-partisan Washington, senators who place their
primary emphasis on advancing the national good are rare. A lifelong

and loyal Republican, Lugar is usually willing to put his party label aside and work with members of both parties to tackle the nation's most serious problems. His most significant collaborations have been with Democrats such as Sam Nunn, Joe Biden, and Barack Obama.

When *Time* magazine ran profiles of the ten most effective senators several years ago, Lugar was included and called simply "The Wise Man." The article described him as principled, tough, cool-headed, and ahead of the curve on many policy matters. "He is a quiet, intelligent, steady force," former senator Bob Kerrey, a long-time Lugar colleague, told *Time*. "He's unmovable when he reaches a conclusion about what ought to be done."[1]

During his tenure in the Senate, Lugar has achieved some important successes, including creation of the landmark Nunn-Lugar Cooperative Threat Reduction Program that has made the United States and the world more secure. He has pushed for the United States to be a powerful actor on the world stage, part of a community of nations that respects the rule of law and international norms. There have also been setbacks. Lugar chaired the Foreign Relations Committee when the Iraq war was launched in 2003 and continued to head up the panel during the critical years of the war. Some, including several of Lugar's strongest supporters, believe that the senator should have been far more forceful in outlining his concerns about the war. They believe that Lugar, almost uniquely, had the stature to challenge the Bush administration to reassess its plans for the war in Iraq. Instead, he opted for expressing reservations in private meetings—reservations that were largely brushed aside. Though he was well informed and even prescient about the war's risks, he had only a modest impact on the administration's Iraq policy. One question that we will consider is whether a more combative style, such as that used by Senate Foreign Relations Committee Chairman J. William Fulbright during the Vietnam War, would have been more effective. Students of the current Senate question whether Lugar's careful, methodical approach to developing policy can still persuade fellow lawmakers in a political environment that is so polarized and combative.

There are some paradoxes, or at least interesting complexities, surrounding Lugar. He is a conservative Republican who breaks from prevailing party views in such areas as environmental protection, conservation, federal nutrition programs, international law, global institutions such as the United Nations, aggressive HIV/AIDS programs, robust diplomacy, and generous foreign aid. Though modest and self-deprecating, he has a lawmaker's penchant for naming things after himself, or at least allowing others to do so. His national security program is known as the Lugar Doctrine, his ideas on energy, the Lugar Energy Initiative. He has named scores of awards and internships after himself. There is even the Richard G. Lugar School Food Service Employee of the Year award, given by Indiana's Department of Education to the school food service employee who demonstrates the most outstanding professionalism.

Though Lugar remains involved in Congress's legislative struggles, he also has a broader conception of the role of the senator as a kind of statesman who undertakes long-term projects for the national good, even if they have few short-term benefits. In this capacity, Lugar builds networks outside of government, delivers detailed policy speeches, meets with key international leaders, and travels extensively—and without apology. His schedule looks more like that of a deputy foreign minister than a senator. He probably knows more about the internal politics of Russia, Ukraine, and Albania than anyone else in Congress. Lugar has a clear view of how Congress can shape foreign policy. The president, he argues, is the natural leader on foreign policy. But he is convinced that Congress can, and should, play a constructive role in shaping the agenda and solving problems. Lugar has shown how to do so for more than three decades. Consequently, the best way to measure Lugar's success is not just in the number of bills he has written and passed but also the ways in which he influences debates about American foreign policy.

Lugar's success as a senator rests on several characteristics of his working style, including the fact that he has developed a formidable political operation at home that gives him considerable running room on Capitol Hill. Being an icon in Indiana has allowed him to be a player in Washington.

Second, Lugar focuses his energies on large, long-term projects. Senators can spend all of their days attending hearings and press conferences, meeting with constituents, and voting—and actually accomplish very little. Lugar is interested in a wide range of international issues but focuses acutely on what he calls the existential issues facing the United

States: the need for American energy independence, controlling the
spread of weapons of mass destruction and reducing the nuclear arsenals in the world. He is also increasingly passionate about tackling the
global food crisis.

Third, mindful of his long-term goals, Lugar is often effective at
locking in incremental gains. He knows that in Congress there are far
more routine bills than landmark ones and it is imperative to attach
parts of your agenda to legislation that is moving through Congress.

Finally, he has a knack for bipartisanship. A conciliator by nature,
Lugar knows that in the modern Senate almost nothing gets done unless there are 60 votes. This underscores the necessity of broad-based
bipartisan support, and over the years Lugar has developed important
and intriguing partnerships with Democrats. But Lugar's penchant for
bipartisanship has made his position in the Republican party more complex. Many of his younger, more aggressively conservative colleagues
view bipartisan collaboration as a sellout. They see Lugar's conciliatory
approach as a weakness, not a strength.

I approached Senator Lugar in the summer of 2006 about writing
a book that would examine his career, focusing on his role in helping
to shape American foreign policy from Capitol Hill. Such a study, I
told him, would require both considerable access and complete independence. He agreed to participate in the project, and for 5 years gave
me special access to his work. I've observed him in Washington, inter-
viewed him regularly, and spoken with his wife, Charlene, as well as with
numerous aides and dozens of his colleagues. I've had the opportunity
to watch him with his constituents in Indiana and travel abroad with
him to Russia, Ukraine, and Albania.

I have been able to observe Lugar during several distinct phases in
his career. When I began this project he was the Republican chairman
of the Senate Foreign Relations Committee serving under a Republican
president, George W. Bush. The chairmanship of the committee and
Lugar's desire to cooperate with a Republican president influenced his
agenda and placed clear constraints on his work. Then Democrats won
control of both the House and Senate in the 2006 mid-term congressional elections. For Lugar, this meant relinquishing the prized chairmanship while remaining the panel's top Republican. With Bush still

in the White House, Lugar had a responsibility to defend the president while also working with Democrats on foreign policy challenges on Capitol Hill. With the election of Barack Obama as president in 2008 and the continuing Democratic control of Congress, Lugar assumed the role of a leader of the loyal opposition on foreign policy. His challenge has been to help Republicans articulate a credible foreign policy while also helping the country and his former colleagues President Obama and Vice President Biden deal with the troubled world. By the spring of 2011, Lugar faced a changed political environment in Indiana. While still widely admired and respected by his fellow Hoosiers, several conservative Republican groups announced they would try to defeat him in the 2012 GOP primary. Lugar responded aggressively by raising campaign funds, emphasizing his long history in the Republican party and his close cooperation with the Reagan administration.

This is a book of both reporting and research. Over the past several years, I've been fortunate to be with the senator in dozens of situations. We've eaten lunch together in the Senate dining room and at a McDonald's in Hammond, Indiana. I've seen him at house parties in Indianapolis, walking the streets of Odessa in Ukraine, and hosting Angelina Jolie and Tony Blair at the Senate Foreign Relations Committee's elegant reception room. I've watched him lobby for a bold farm reform amendment, deliver important speeches on the Senate floor, and lecture on global affairs at think tanks and policy conferences. I've listened to his speeches, read his essays, met with him and his top staffers. I've also studied the literature related to Congress and foreign policy in an attempt to place Lugar's work in a broader context.

This book is not a biography of Richard Lugar but rather a case study of how Lugar has influenced U.S. foreign policy from his position in the Senate. I begin with several snapshots of his work in Washington, Indiana, and overseas. The second chapter provides a biographical sketch of the senator, describing his personal and political roots in Indiana. I discuss his work as mayor of Indianapolis to reorganize city and county government because it was a pivotal political and governmental experience for him. In the following chapters, I provide background on Congress's institutional powers pertaining to foreign policy and then describe a number of areas in which Senator Lugar has been involved in substantial and consequential ways: the Nunn-Lugar program, energy policy, the wars in Iraq and Afghanistan, foreign aid reform, the global food crisis, the Law of the Sea Treaty, and the New START treaty. I discuss the senator's efforts to remain connected with the people—and the voters—of Indiana. And I conclude with an assessment of Richard Lugar's legacy in shaping American foreign policy.

I should note that the various issues I explore are ones that Lugar worked on actively during the five years that I observed him. Consequently, I will only discuss briefly several matters of great importance to Lugar's legacy such as his work in South Africa and the Philippines in the mid-1980s. No doubt when a full-scale biography of Lugar is eventually written, these matters will be dealt with extensively.

RICHARD G. LUGAR,

STATESMAN OF THE SENATE

1

✣

Snapshots of a Statesman

I

One of the last places in the world one might expect to find a senior American senator during the waning days of summer is on the western fringe of Siberia gazing at a half-finished bridge. But for Senator Richard Lugar, the two-time chairman of the Senate Foreign Relations Committee and now its top Republican, the bridge he was looking at on that spectacular late August day in 2007 was a symbol of cooperation between the United States and Russia—and a harbinger of hope that the world will be able to secure, and then dispose of, weapons of mass destruction.

Lugar was joined on the trip by former Democratic senator Sam Nunn, his long-time partner in the effort to help the nations of the former Soviet Union secure their weapons of mass destruction. Nunn, now the chief executive officer of the Nuclear Threat Initiative, was traveling with Lugar on a weeklong trip to Russia, Ukraine, and Albania to get a first-hand assessment of how their signature program, the Nunn-Lugar Cooperative Threat Reduction Program, was working on the ground. Lugar is one of the most knowledgeable lawmakers on foreign policy issues and is highly respected in diplomatic and military circles. He is seen as one of those rare American politicians who understands the nuances of foreign policy, is willing to work hard at non-glamorous issues, and is effective in using the tools at his disposal to influence foreign policy.

He is willing to do those time-consuming and tedious tasks of legislating that capture few headlines and confer few political benefits, such as studying a half-finished bridge on the edge of Siberia.

On that pleasant August day, Lugar, in a blue sport jacket and white running shoes, earnestly spoke with Russian officials, American diplomats, and a team of construction workers about the bridge over the Miass River. He asked quietly stated but well-informed questions about construction schedules, engineering complications, and the river's flood patterns. When completed, the bridge will be used to transport almost two million artillery rounds and warheads filled with sarin, soman, and VX agents from poorly secured, half-dilapidated barn-like buildings to the state-of-the-art Shchuchye Chemical Weapons Destruction Facility, then under construction a few miles away.[1]

After a 30-minute visit to the bridge site, Lugar, Nunn, and their traveling party of congressional staffers, executive branch officials, and reporters boarded a modern bus and drove through several Russian villages seemingly unchanged since the time of Tolstoy. Upon arriving at Shchuchye, the bus circled the heavily secured facility and passed an administration building, fire station, and water treatment plant before stopping at Building 101a. Here, the United States and Russia, six other countries, and the European Union were working to build a facility to eliminate a large number of Russia's cold war era chemical weapons.

Wearing white construction hardhats, Lugar and Nunn walked through Building 101a, which will become one of the world's most important chemical weapons destruction facilities but at the time resembled a half-completed parking garage. Lugar peppered the guides with practical questions about the construction of the facility, seeking clarity on when it will be fully operational. Shchuchye had been dogged by delays, cost overruns, and bureaucratic disputes between American and Russian officials and provoked deep skepticism from the U.S. Congress. For this project, Lugar had to summon his considerable patience and tenacity as he pleaded with skeptical lawmakers and an indifferent administration to free up the funds to allow for the completion of the facility. The senator personally lobbied Secretary of State Condoleezza Rice and President George W. Bush to allow funds for the project to go forward.

After this tour, Nunn and Lugar were driven to an outdoor ceremony on the outer fringe of the campus. Standing behind a dozen flags of countries and groups that supported the project, they were the featured speakers at a haphazard celebratory event. Both spoke clearly about the urgent need for global cooperation and the moral imperative of controlling weapons of mass destruction.

"The mission here is to make sure these weapons of mass destruction will not be used by anyone, to make sure that they will not get in the hands of terrorist groups who would not hesitate to use them," Nunn said. Then referring to the bridge they viewed earlier in the day, Nunn became more poetic. "Bridges are not individual accomplishments. Bridges are built by many people as a way of uniting people. This bridge is a key symbol of global partnership."

Lugar, introduced by a Russian military official as "the famous Senator Lugar," spoke next. Standing in the soft Siberian breeze, he said the challenges posed by weapons of mass destruction are daunting but solvable. A man of prose and pragmatism rather than poetry and abstraction, Lugar spoke plainly and hopefully. "Mankind," he said, "can rise to the occasion."

II

On an early April evening in 2008, Richard Lugar received the Paul H. Douglas Ethics in Government Award at a ceremony in the Senate's elegant Mansfield Room, across the hall from the Senate chamber. Like many senators, Lugar is a frequent recipient of awards, most of which don't mean very much. But he took this award seriously. He admired Paul Douglas, a former senator from Illinois, as a serious, consequential, and honest legislator. Lugar's brief but revealing remarks went to the core of how he sees his work as a senator.

He spoke on the topic of bipartisanship, which he said is the only workable strategy for a successful congressional career. Too often, he argued, it is misrepresented as the product of moderate political views or the willingness to strike deals. But bipartisanship is not centrism and it is more than just compromise. Rather, he declared, it is a way of approaching one's duties as a public servant that requires self-reflection, discipline, and faith in the goodwill of others.

Constructive public service, Lugar said, demands that members of Congress and other public officials avoid succumbing to a partisan mindset. In carefully chosen but searing words, he challenged the essence of the Republican governing strategy during the years of George W. Bush's presidency. "Particularly destructive is the misperception in some quarters that governing with one vote more than 50 percent is just as good or better than governing with 60 percent or 70 percent support. . . . The problem with this thinking is that whatever is won today through division is usually lost tomorrow. The relationships that are destroyed and the ill will that is created make subsequent achievements that much more difficult. A 51 percent mentality deepens cynicism, sharpens political vendettas, and depletes the national reserve of goodwill that is critical to our survival in hard times."

Then, in a series of rhetorical statements, he outlined what it takes to be a successful lawmaker:

- It requires, he said, that you accept that members of the other party love their country and are people of goodwill and should be respected.
- It requires that you accept that members of the other party can make important contributions to policy and that you make an effort to include them in early deliberations and even seek opportunities to work with their leaders.
- It requires that even as you participate in partisan debates, your first impulse is a sober reflection on what is good for the country.
- It requires that you study an issue in depth with an open mind and avoid an over-reliance on your party's orthodox positions and arguments. In other words, you should allow your thinking to evolve as circumstances and evidence evolve.
- It requires that while recognizing the essential imperative to represent your constituents and listen to their ideas, you should be willing on occasion to disagree with them and explain your reasoning.

· It requires that you maintain your civility, even when others around you do not, and that you measure your words. A bipartisan lawmaker avoids unnecessary inflammatory rhetoric and an over-reliance on simplistic partisan sound bites.

Lugar said that he was fully aware that politics is a competitive business, recalling his own difficult campaigns for the Indianapolis school board during an era of desegregation, two mayoral races, seven Senate elections, and one run for the GOP nomination for president. "I know that politics is and always has been a tough business that cannot be reduced to purely idealistic tenets. But it cannot be devoid of idealism, either," he declared.[2]

III

A senator with national and even global interests and aspirations can accomplish little without a secure political base at home. With grim clarity, Richard Lugar can recite the recent leaders of the Senate Foreign Relations Committee who were defeated for re-election because they appeared to lose touch with their roots. Lugar has avoided this fate, but not by accident. He is highly respected and admired in Indiana. His small-government conservatism resonates in his Republican-leaning state. He has been an elected official in Indiana for more than 40 years and has earned a reputation as a solid, hard-working lawmaker who keeps in touch with his constituents. As many in Indiana know, the senator continues to manage a 604-acre corn, soybean, and walnut tree farm outside of Indianapolis and delights in his heritage as a fifth-generation Hoosier. Lugar has also created a formidable political operation that carefully tends to the home front. It manages and expands his network of supporters, keeps an eye out for potential rivals, raises money, and communicates regularly with the people of Indiana. Nothing important about Indiana politics escapes the notice of the Lugar machine.

Since 1977, his first year in the Senate, Lugar has held an end-of-the-year symposium in Indianapolis to give his assessment of world affairs. Every December, he invites each Indiana high school to select two of its top juniors to participate in a daylong event called the Lugar Symposium for Tomorrow's Leaders. More than fifteen thousand students have attended these events held at the University of Indianapolis. The senator sometimes meets Hoosiers in airports and coffee shops who tell him they attended a symposium when they were students. It has become such an institution that the university created the Richard G. Lugar Center for Tomorrow's Leaders as a permanent home for the symposium. Lugar regards the talk he gives at the symposium as one of his most important each year and he spends a considerable amount of time organizing his thoughts.

In December 2008, the senator returned to the Lugar Center to give more than four hundred students a tour of the complicated world that President-elect Barack Obama was about to inherit. Lugar had been thinking about this talk throughout the fall, setting aside newspaper and magazine articles to review as he prepared his notes. Standing behind a lectern engulfed in flowers, Lugar spoke in his formal style for 45 minutes. There were no humorous stories or wisecracks from the senator, just a polite greeting to the serious and clean-scrubbed students sitting before him.[3]

The senator discussed developments in places that seem far removed from the lives of high school students in the heart of the Midwest: China, India, Iraq, Afghanistan, Pakistan, North Korea, Iran, Israel, Latin America, and Somalia. He gave a preview of a trip he was about to take to Russia in an effort to ease the transition from the Bush to the Obama administration. He briefly described the need for the two countries to get back to work on arms control negotiations. But most of his remarks focused on the faltering U.S. economy, an issue that had his constituents in Indiana perplexed and worried. This economic crisis, Lugar said, also constrained America's conduct of its foreign policy. His description of the crisis was striking; he avoided buzzwords and jargon as he talked about the economic crisis in a concrete way. In words both somber and calm, Lugar acknowledged the U.S. economy was in deep trouble and nobody knew how bad it might get.

"Suddenly we have a world economic crisis of huge significance. It is too early to see if it will be of the same magnitude of the Great Depression of 1929 and the early 1930s." World trade had broken down, he said, global tensions were rising, and American economic policy had fallen seriously off track. Lugar did not profess to have answers to all the problems but made it clear that he was trying to fully understand the crisis and figure out the best way ahead.

He described the emergence of the housing bubble and how troubles in the housing sector infected the American and world economies. He said the new economic landscape was unfamiliar and puzzling, even to a senior American senator, and observed that the United States had recently issued $30 billion of bonds at an interest rate of nearly 0 percent. "I'm still trying to wrap my thoughts around this. That is really unparalleled." Lugar emphasized his concern that America's soaring budget deficits are largely financed by savings coming from China. "We are dependent upon the Chinese to buy our bonds to pay for deficit," he said, giving a stark summary of the nation's predicament.

There was no happy talk here, but Lugar ended his remarks by summoning his midwestern stoicism and optimism, urging the students to study the crisis, examine the mistakes that had been made, and retain hope for the future. He responded to questions for 30 minutes and then remained at the symposium for several hours, chatting with students and the adults who were with them. The senator posed for pictures with pairs of students from each of Indiana's 92 counties. A few days later, his office sent a letter and a photo to all the students, thanking them for their participation and wishing them success in the future. His office also e-mailed photographs to dozens of small-town newspapers, many of which would publish them with a story about Senator Lugar, his symposium, and the comments of the local students who attended.

IV

One of the keys to Lugar's success has been his ability to connect the three worlds of Indiana, Washington, and international politics. His political strength in Indiana has allowed him to focus on national issues and this national prominence has given him a platform to operate in the international arena. Lugar has developed a working style during his years in the Senate that allows him to stay on top of his heavy workload and sustain his mastery of foreign policy.

An early riser, Lugar gets up most weekday mornings around 5:30 A.M. and is on his way to work an hour later. For many years, he drove himself from his home in McLean, Virginia, to the Capitol, a trip that takes about 30 minutes. Now he is usually picked up by a staffer around 6:30 A.M. and arrives in his office a little after 7 A.M., before most Senate staff. On his morning commute he listens to a Virginia NPR station that plays classical music and gives news updates.

Once he arrives at his office in the Senate Hart Building, Lugar turns on his computer and goes online to read the *Indianapolis Star,* the newspaper from his hometown. His pile of morning newspapers includes the *Washington Post, Washington Times, New York Times, Wall Street Journal, Investor's Business Daily, Financial Times,* and *USA Today.* He also goes through several Capitol Hill publications: *Politico,* the *Hill, Roll Call, Congress Daily,* and *CQ Daily.* He clips articles to save for his files and reviews Indiana-focused news clips that have been assembled the previous night. The senator also goes through magazines such as *Business Week, Indianapolis Business Journal, Congressional Quarterly, National Journal, Time, Newsweek, U.S. News & World Report, Forbes, Fortune, National Review, Weekly Standard, Washington Diplomat,* and the *New Republic.* He also reviews two Indiana-based political newsletters: *The Howey Political Report* and *Indiana Legislative Insight.*[4] Lugar reads voraciously. He says that he does not typically read books from cover to cover but might read a chapter or two of a book to study a topic that is of interest.

Lugar likes to have an hour or 2 before scheduled meetings and hearings to prepare for the day. He checks in with his staff about projects that are pending and gives out additional assignments. He jots ideas in a notebook, keeps lists, and sends notes to staff, friends, and colleagues. "One of the things I've always admired about Senator Lugar is that he makes it a point to work into his schedule time to think and read. Unfortunately not many senators do that any more," says Bill Hoagland, a former Senate staffer. "You'd be surprised how rare that is."[5]

On most Thursday mornings, Lugar attends a breakfast meeting in the Capitol sponsored by the Aspen Institute with a policy expert and other lawmakers. He sometimes hosts a breakfast meeting with visitors from home in the Senate Dining Room. He meets with his staff as necessary but does not hold weekly staff meetings. "He doesn't want to have meetings just to have meetings. When he needs information or wants to discuss something we bring in the people who are needed," says Marty Morris, his chief of staff.

The Senate Foreign Relations Committee typically holds its hearings at 10 A.M. on Tuesdays, Wednesdays, and Thursdays, with some afternoon sessions as well. As the ranking member of the committee, Lugar almost always arrives before the hearing begins and doesn't leave until it concludes several hours later. He attends as many Agriculture Committee hearings as he can, but if the two panels are holding hearings simultaneously, Lugar will usually attend the Foreign Relations hearing because of his responsibility as the top Republican on the committee. He tries to avoid the common congressional practice of stopping by meetings or hearings for a few minutes and then leaving. "He thinks that's disrespectful. When he is there, he is there. He doesn't like to be distracted," says one former staffer.[6] Lugar does not use a Blackberry or carry a cell phone but is usually accompanied by aides who do so the senator can be reached by his office throughout the day. Lugar likes to know when his staff is holding meetings with important political or business visitors from Indiana so he can drop by the meeting to say hello if he has a few minutes or so he can say a few words to visitors if he sees them in his office suite.

Twice a week, on Tuesdays and Thursdays, Lugar attends a lunch with fellow Senate Republicans. The Tuesday meeting is with the entire Senate Republican caucus. The Thursday meeting—called the Thursday club—is with between 25 and 30 Republicans. Lugar speaks rarely at the Tuesday lunches but usually prepares brief comments for the smaller Thursday lunch, viewing this as an opportunity to offer his ideas on current topics to his colleagues and hear what they are thinking.

In the afternoons, the senator may have several meetings or go to the Senate floor for votes. Lugar spends very little time on the Senate floor—much less than most senators. During roll call votes, he usually walks in, casts his vote, offers polite greetings to senators he encounters, and then leaves the chamber. "Dick has never been a backslapper. He's never been one to hang around on the floor to chat," says former senator Chuck Hagel.[7]

Lugar moves between his office in the Senate Hart Building and a hideaway office in the Capitol, one floor above the Senate chamber. If there are votes on the Senate floor, he may spend much of the afternoon at the hideaway. His hideaway was previously occupied by Democratic senator Daniel Moynihan until he retired in 2001 and is considered one of the nicest offices in the Capitol. The best hideaways are given to senators with the most seniority.

When he works out of his suite of offices in the Hart Building, Lugar often holds meetings in a conference room dominated by a board that tallies the number of weapons destroyed by the Nunn-Lugar Cooperative Threat Reduction Program. His personal office is often cluttered with files and books stacked on a round table that once was in Senator Sam Nunn's personal office and was used by the two senators when they developed the Nunn-Lugar program. When Nunn retired from the Senate in 1997, Lugar arranged to have the table brought to his office.

Lugar meets frequently with diplomats, both those posted in Washington and visitors from overseas. Lugar's day is full and his staff says he never wastes a minute. But he does not like to be frantically busy and have his day carved into 15-minute blocks of time with hurried meetings and little flexibility. "He gets his batteries charged by the more things he is doing," says his wife, Charlene. "But he's never in a hurry to get to the next thing. He pays full attention to what he is doing at the time."[8]

Current and former staffers say that Lugar is consistently polite and appreciative. "He is always grateful. He always says thank you. He always makes you feel appreciated," said one staffer.[9] Morris, his chief of staff, says Lugar believes in civility and shows it by example. "I've worked for him for 30 years and he has never raised his voice to me. But he is very, very firm. When he says 'Oh my,' you know he is angry."[10]

Mark Lubbers, a former Lugar staffer and now a consultant in Indianapolis, said Lugar motivates people by his hard work. "He is one of the most gentle souls you'll ever meet. I don't think I've ever heard him raise his voice. That's not how he motivates people. As a Lugar staff person, you'd be crushed if you ever disappointed him. Without ever saying a cross word or having to invoke authority, he has the capacity to motivate people to do their absolute best work. That's a very remarkable, 'leading by example,' approach. He treats people so well you didn't want to let him down," Lubbers said. "He is working way harder than anyone else. He's usually the first one to arrive in the morning and frequently among the last to leave at night and you know when he goes home he is going to be working more."[11]

Unlike most senators, Lugar takes a real interest in the interns that work in his office. In a typical year, more than 50 interns spend time in his office and he makes it a point to take them to lunch, either individually or in small groups, during their time in his office. He also meets with them as a group to discuss policy issues and describe his work as a senator. The office posts the pictures and names of interns on a wall so the full-time staff knows their names. Charlene Lugar says her husband loves to teach and his work with interns provides him an opportunity to pass on what he has learned to young people who might enter politics or government.

Lugar's regular staff is highly regarded on Capitol Hill. Most have worked for him for over a decade and many have worked for him for more than 20 years. About a dozen have left his office and then returned to work for him. He expects his staff to be prepared and to be on top of their jobs and provide him with accurate information. There is a story that former and current staffers have heard Lugar tell frequently about when he and several other naval officers served as intelligence briefers to Admiral Arleigh Burke. Burke asked one of Lugar's colleagues for some information. The briefer wasn't certain and made an educated guess that turned out to be wrong. He was reassigned to the Philippines a short time later. The message conveyed by this story is that it's better to say, "I don't know," and quickly track down information than to guess and turn out to be wrong and get dispatched to the Philippines.

If there are no evening votes, the senator usually leaves his office by 7 P.M. Lugar takes home a binder that has the next day's schedule and briefing papers. The schedule outlines events and meetings that he has committed to and those that he has been invited to but has not yet made a commitment to attend. The senator often listens to the PBS *NewsHour* in the car as he makes his way home or to an evening reception.

Lugar enjoys quiet evenings at home with his wife. After dinner and talk about the day's activities, he often goes to the sunroom, where he does his evening reading. The Lugars go to occasional movies, plays, and concerts. One staffer remembers the senator raving about the film *Shakespeare in Love*. Almost everyone who has worked for him has heard Lugar mention one of his favorite movies, *Animal House,* which he says reminds him of his fraternity experience at Denison University. "I think everyone I've seen in world politics I saw in the Beta house during those years. *Animal House* is not precisely what happened in my college experience, but it's pretty close," he said.[12]

Both the Lugars enjoy music; Charlene plays the violin and the senator plays the piano and cello. Three of their four sons and their families live in the Washington area and on weekends they often drop by. The senator enjoys weekend runs at the track at McLean High School.

V

By all accounts, Lugar has a calm, steady, and placid temperament. Courtly and polite, he is well liked and respected in the Senate. He is not, to be sure, one of the chamber's most colorful figures. One writer has described him as the embodiment of a "Washington Gray Man."

"Among the many kinds of political animals found in Washington, few are as widely admired as the Gray Man. Quietly competent, somewhat bland, respected by Democrats and Republicans alike, and most comfortable working tactfully behind the scenes, the Gray Man is a dying breed in today's American politics," writes journalist Brian Winters. He says that modern examples include Lugar, former Defense Secretary Robert Gates, and former Senate Majority Leader George Mitchell.[13]

When the senator works on speeches or opening statements for committee hearings, he confers with aides who are responsible for the subject in question and with Dan Diller, a senior staffer who is also his de facto "editor in chief." Diller, who is considered an expert in writing in Lugar's voice, usually develops a draft, which Lugar then edits. Often, Lugar's statements for committee meetings are completed several days before the hearing—a rare occurrence in the Senate.

On critical issues, Lugar often sends out "Dear Colleague" letters to other senators outlining his views. He also instructs his staff on the Foreign Relations Committee to research an issue and write a detailed report. In recent years, he has commissioned staff reports on changing the country's Cuba policy, U.S. financial assistance to Syria and Yemen, reforming international financial institutions, confronting global food challenges, overhauling foreign aid programs, assessing the consequences of the expanding role of the Pentagon in overseas embassies, improving U.S. bilateral relations with Saudi Arabia, the merits of U.S. trade agreements with Panama and Colombia, and American policy regarding Moldova. He views these reports as a way to present facts and shape the debate. But some congressional analysts are skeptical about the persuasive value of "Dear Colleague" letters or detailed reports from the Foreign Relations staff. They say that more Senate business is conducted by brief personal exchanges on the Senate floor and in informal conversations—forms of communication in which Lugar does not excel.

Senator Bob Corker of Tennessee, the second ranking Republican on the Senate Foreign Relations Committee, said Lugar never personally tried to persuade him to support the New START treaty even though he was considered a critical swing vote. Corker said he received "Dear Colleague" letters from Lugar addressing specific points of the treaty, but Lugar never made the case to him personally. "He has never lobbied on the treaty, never tried to sway me. He just laid out his views, put them down on paper, and left it up to others to decide," Corker said.[14]

During committee hearings, Lugar reads his opening statement and pursues a careful line of questions. "He asks the practical, even boring questions that are so important. What happens next? Where does this take us? Where are we going?" says Hagel. "When you analyze where he is going on his questions there is always a very clear purpose. He knows where he wants to end up. Because he is very self-effacing and very quiet and doesn't elbow his colleagues out of the way to get in front of TV cameras, he sometimes gets lost in the cacophony of retorts and posturing and showtime entertainment."[15]

But Lugar does less well in the give-and-take that sometimes occurs in congressional committees or on the Senate floor. During the battle over the nomination of John Bolton to be U.S. ambassador to the United Nations in 2005, Lugar presided over his nomination hearing as chairman of the committee. He seemed uncomfortable when the hearing went off script and even appeared confused. In a memorable moment, his then colleague Senator Joe Biden, who opposed Bolton's nomination, even tried to warn Lugar that he was about to call for a roll vote on Bolton that he was poised to lose. In the fall of 2010, Lugar largely stayed out of the sharp back-and-forth during the Senate Foreign Relations Committee debate over the New START treaty, even as several conservative Republicans leveled serious charges related to the treaty that Lugar had the stature and knowledge to rebuff.

Lugar is a wooden public speaker who is not always adept at gauging his audience and ascertaining the level of detail they are able or willing to absorb. He is far more impressive when speaking to small groups and in informal settings. He rarely speaks on the Senate floor, saving floor speeches for occasions he deems important. But when he does speak, senators from both parties tend to take notice.

VI

In *Friends and Foes: How Congress and the President Really Make Foreign Policy*, Rebecca Hersman argues that most of American foreign policy is developed and implemented in a low-key professional way between leaders in the legislative and executive branches. She describes the occasional dramatic clashes as "waves" and the steady day-to-day accommodations as the "ocean." She argues that it is in the regular interactions regarding often highly technical issues where most foreign policy is made. Lugar pays attention to both the "waves" and the "ocean" of American foreign policy, tackling major issues and smaller matters that are still important.[16] On these smaller issues, Lugar is willing to take the time to understand them and assign his staff to handle them. For example, for more than 7 years, Lugar worked on technical defense trade cooperation treaties with Australia and the United Kingdom. He and his staff worked with officials from the two governments and with the State, Justice, and Defense Departments in the United States to develop a system that controlled the export of weapons technologies and ensure the Senate's oversight prerogatives on matters related to export control. He pressed the Bush and Obama administrations to come up with practical solutions, and when a sound agreement was reached in the fall of 2010, Lugar helped push it through the Senate on a voice vote.

Lugar takes the long view on projects and believes that patient, dogged work can solve most problems. He is willing on occasion to wait and simply outlast his opposition. "One of the most important aspects of a Senate seat is that it's a 6-year term, so there's a different potential timeline for getting things done. If you have ideas or ambitions then, while 6 years is not an eternity, it's a long time in public life. You can outlast a number of people. And if you have six terms, then you have an even more significant timeline. There may be some periods of time and it may last for a year or 2, that are dormant and the tide goes out. But cycles change," he told me.[17]

Senate Historian Don Ritchie says Lugar has seen remarkable changes in his career and serves as a stabilizing force in the current Senate. "The Senate as an institution has not changed as much as the two political parties have. The Democratic and Republican Parties of the 1970s were very different than they are today. Back then there was not a party line vote on anything. Both parties had liberal and conservative wings and everyone took it for granted that the liberals in one party would vote with the liberals in the other party and the conservatives of one party would vote with the conservatives of the other party."[18] Ross Baker, a congressional expert at Rutgers University, said the Senate that Lugar came to in the late 1970s was a "gentler place and seemingly a more thoughtful place. Compared to what we have today, it almost looks like the Age of Pericles."[19]

VII

As we sharpen our focus on Richard Lugar, it is important to briefly note that American politics and government have undergone major changes in the course of Lugar's career. Two institutions that have been central to Lugar's professional life are the U.S. Senate and the Republican Party. The transformations of each provide an important backdrop to, and offer critical context for, understanding Lugar's career.

The Senate has not changed in structure since Lugar entered in 1977. There are still 100 senators chosen from 50 states and the upper chamber continues to operate under the same essential rules. But there is much about the Senate that is different. When Lugar entered the Senate, Gerald Ford was completing his final days as president and Jimmy Carter was preparing for his inauguration. There were no women senators, very few party line votes, frequent bipartisan coalitions, and only the occasional filibuster. Senate deliberations were not broadcast on television; C-SPAN did not begin covering Senate floor debates until 1986. The three TV networks and a handful of national newspapers and regional papers chronicled the work of senators. There were very few computers on Capitol Hill and senators didn't have websites nor did they use the Internet to communicate with their constituents. Most senators lived in Washington with their families and traveled back to their states only during congressional recesses. They did the bulk of their fund-raising during the last 2 years of their Senate terms as they geared up for re-election. The basic rhythm of Senate life was captured by Senator Richard Russell when he famously said that senators spent the first 2 years of their term acting as statesmen, the second 2 years as politicians, and the final 2 years as demagogues.[20]

The Senate that Lugar entered in 1977 was in the midst of a profound change in how senators approached their jobs. Barbara Sinclair, the author of *The Transformation of the U.S. Senate* and *Party Wars,* argues that the Senate of the mid-1970s was transforming dramatically. It was no longer the clubby, inward-looking body that was dominated by its various committees and their crusty chairmen. Under the older model, senators specialized on the issues that were within the jurisdiction of the two committees they typically served on. Senators endeavored to become policy specialists and were reluctant to get involved in matters outside their areas of expertise. They were very reluctant to offer amendments to legislation that was developed by other committees. Sinclair argues that as a consequence of an influx of new members in the late 1950s and 1960s and growing demands in American society for congressional action to address mounting problems, the Senate changed in the 1970s. Senators became generalists who were more active in a range of issues and more attuned to the media. They became more willing to use the considerable powers given to individual senators to try to impose their agenda on the body and offer amendments to virtually any bill. By the mid-1970s, when Lugar arrived in the Senate, the new ethos of the individualist senator was taking hold. Senators were more active and aggressive across a range of topics, were members of four committees, actively engaged the media, and were more public in their work.[21]

Sinclair says that during the 1980s and the 1990s, the rise of the individualist senator continued and the Senate also became polarized along partisan and ideological lines. Party polarization made it more important for senators to be active and loyal to their parties than when the parties were more heterogeneous and the ideological difference between them was smaller. She adds that the 1990s saw an influx of ideologically committed conservatives into the Senate, many of them veterans of the highly partisan House.[22]

When Lugar entered the Senate, both the Democratic and Republican Parties were broad-based parties with liberal, moderate, and conservative factions. Analysts agree that the Republican Party has moved sharply to the right during the past three decades. While there is some disagreement on the cause and timing of this rightward shift, few dispute that it has occurred and has been deeply consequential for American politics and government. Sinclair, in her book *Party Wars,* observes that the policy agendas of Barry Goldwater in 1964 and Ronald Reagan in 1980 were similar, but Goldwater was seen by many as a dangerous radical while Reagan was heralded as being well within the mainstream of the Republican Party. Between Goldwater and Reagan, conservatism of a hard-edged and uncompromising variety became ascendant in the Republican Party. According to Sinclair, the GOP was propelled in a more conservative direction by the religious right, which became a core GOP constituency, and the intellectual right, which was comprised of intellectuals who wrote books and journal articles and spoke on public policy from positions at the American Enterprise Institute, the Heritage Foundation, the CATO Institute, and the Manhattan Institute. She adds that the religious and intellectual right converged with other conservative forces such as the western-based property rights movement, the gun rights lobby, and small business advocates. This rightward tilt was solidified and expanded by the rise of talk radio in the 1980s and cable television in the 1990s, especially the rise of Fox News, which was launched in 1996.[23]

"It is thus the Republican Party's move to the right that accounts for much of the ideological polarization of the parties since the 1970s," Sinclair writes. She said the Democratic Party has moved to the left in some areas, but not on economic and social welfare issues. The Republican Party, however, has moved to the right on the entire spectrum of issues that drive political activists and ordinary voters, especially social and cultural issues.[24]

Many analysts believe the Republican Party's move to the right was advanced by the Senate debate on the Panama Canal treaties in 1977. Partly as the result of this debate and the intensity it created among Republican activists, a number of conservative GOP candidates were elected in the 1978 and 1980 Senate elections. Journalist Adam Clymer, in a book about the Panama Canal debate, describes this debate as an "overlooked turning point in American political history" that energized the New Right and "transformed the Republican party." He argues that the political balance within the GOP shifted due to the 1978 and 1980 elections, propelling the Republican Party in a sharply more conservative direction.[25]

Another journalist, Ronald Brownstein, argues that both parties have become more ideologically cohesive and are no longer the broad coalitions they once were. He says that for much of twentieth century, the two parties operated as broad, ramshackle coalitions that allowed for diverse and even antithetical views. However, since the early 1980s, the differences within each party have narrowed and the differences between the parties have widened. Brownstein says the 1970s were the high mark of cross-party coalitions in the Senate, but the last three decades have been a time of polarization and party estrangement.[26] Former Senate Majority Leader Trent Lott has said "there is no question that the middle in the Senate has shrunk considerably," while his former colleague former senator John Danforth has said there is "more of a demand in each party for a degree of purity or inflexibility that was not there before." Brownstein believes this intense partisanship is causing a more cautious ethos in which senators are increasingly reluctant to stray from the party line. "Rather than heralded as iconoclasts, those legislators who deviate too often from that centrally directed consensus now face pressure from their colleagues; a cold shoulder from leadership; blistering criticism from the overtly partisan media aligned with each side; and with growing frequency, primary challenges bankrolled by powerful party interest groups."[27]

Regarding the Republican Party's foreign policy posture, a leading analyst says the GOP has shifted to the right on foreign policy over the last several decades. Colin Dueck, in a definitive history of Republican foreign policy, argues that the realist school, which was once dominant, has seen its influence decline. Dueck describes the rise of what he calls a hawk-nationalist faction within the Republican Party. This group tends to be skeptical about arms control agreements, the efficacy of the UN, or the possibility of fruitful talks with North Korea, Cuba, and Iran. It offers strong support for Israel, Taiwan, NATO expansion, and missile defense. It supports tough measures against terrorists; sees China and Russia as strategic competitors, not partners; and believes in a global mission for the United States. "They offer clear, bold arguments that resonate with popular feeling regarding American exceptionalism and strong national defense. They believe in what they are doing. Finally, they operate within a party that is basically hawkish and nationalistic, as they are, on foreign policy matters, and has been for several decades. This gives them a natural influence and a natural audience, regardless of temporary setbacks," Dueck writes. He argues that "a hawkish American nationalism forms the center of gravity of the Republican Party, especially in its conservative base, when it comes to foreign policy issues."[28]

How have these changes in the Senate and the Republican Party affected Lugar and his career? Lugar has generally adapted well to the prevailing norms of the Senate and has become a respected, admired, and effective senator. His working style blends the approach of the "New Senate" with its focus on individual rights and aggressiveness with the "Old Senate" norms of policy specialization and committee focus. Lugar occasionally gets involved in issues outside the jurisdiction of his two committees, Senate Agriculture and Foreign Relations, but he does so carefully and judiciously. He rarely speaks on the Senate floor, unless a foreign policy or agricultural issue is under consideration. He would rather have a substantial impact on a handful of issues than a superficial impact on a number of policies.

Lugar's relationship to the Republican Party is complex. He is a loyal, lifelong Republican who has carried the party's standard in elections going back to the 1960s. When he entered the Senate in 1977, he was viewed as a conservative Republican and he remains so today. But as the GOP has shifted sharply to the right over the past 30 years and party leaders have come to emphasize conservative social and cultural issues, Lugar is sometimes called a moderate Republican. "Sometimes when you stand still, the ground still shifts from under you. I think that has happened to Senator Lugar in many ways. His party has changed markedly over the past several decades," Ritchie says.[29] Lugar has a very conservative record on economic issues but has never been comfortable emphasizing contentious social and cultural issues. He believes the Republican Party should be the champion of robust economic growth, strong national defense, and confident global leadership. He also believes that the GOP should be less focused on tactical political skirmishing with Democrats and more committed to presenting a clear policy agenda—and win elections on the basis of this agenda. In the fall of 2010, as congressional Republicans were poised to make considerable gains in the mid-term elections, Lugar chided party leaders for stoking dissatisfaction with Democrats rather than offering a positive Republican agenda based on economic growth, fiscal discipline, free trade, and confident international engagement.[30]

While a loyal Republican, Lugar also believes that it is essential that a successful senator work with members of the other party to accomplish anything important, especially in the current environment in which 60 votes are needed in the Senate to pass almost all consequential legislation. Throughout his career Lugar has developed strong working relationships with both Democrats and Republicans. He displays independence in areas that some Republicans object to such as gun control measures, immigration reform, and arms control negotiations with Russia. There is little doubt that many younger Republican leaders do not really know what to make of Lugar. His inclination to work for consensus and to join bipartisan coalitions seems to belong to a different era.

2

❦

The Senator from Indiana

On March 18, 2009, near the end of a series of Senate votes on a controversial public lands management bill, Senate Majority Leader Harry Reid and Senate Minority Leader Mitch McConnell stopped the Senate's proceedings to pay tribute to Richard Lugar, "the senator from Indiana." Lugar had just cast his 12,000th vote as a U.S. senator. Only 12 other senators in American history had cast more votes. The mere act of showing up to vote is, of course, not necessarily a great accomplishment. But Reid and McConnell used the occasion to honor Lugar and review the highlights of his career.

"It is a special pleasure to recognize someone who has always been so reluctant to speak about himself. Few Americans have more to brag about than Senator Richard Lugar. Yet I know of no one who is less likely to do so," McConnell began. He briefly discussed Lugar's achievements, describing his days as a high school valedictorian and Eagle Scout and his later successes as a Rhodes Scholar, big city mayor, and United States senator. "He has been a counselor to presidents and one of the most widely respected voices on foreign relations within the Senate for decades. Before he finishes out his current term, he will have served almost twice as long as any Indiana senator before him—a milestone he has approached with characteristic humility," McConnell said.[1]

The Senate Republican leader described the respect that Lugar has garnered throughout Washington, from members of both political parties, and by the current occupant of the White House. "As a measure of Senator Lugar's reputation for bipartisanship, historians will note that when our current president launched his presidential campaign at the Illinois statehouse 2 years ago, he mentioned just one politician by name: Richard Lugar. No one in the Senate commands more bipartisan respect." McConnell went on to note that Lugar remains a formidable figure in Indiana politics, so much so that the Democrats did not even run a candidate against him in 2006.

Reid spoke next, offering praise and citing Lugar's personal and political accomplishments, calling him one of the most intellectually sound members of the Senate. "In the Senate, Richard Lugar has been a national leader on the environment, foreign policy, and let's not forget agriculture," Reid said. "This milestone is the latest in a career filled with remarkable accomplishments."

Lugar sat quietly at his desk in the back of the Senate chamber during the remarks by McConnell and Reid. When they finished, Lugar, wearing his trademark blue suit and red tie, stood and was recognized by the presiding officer. He seemed embarrassed at the attention paid to him by his colleagues, yet touched by the praise. His remarks lasted only about 30 seconds. Lugar thanked the two leaders for their "overly generous comments that give me great encouragement and inspiration," and thanked his wife and their four children and thirteen grandchildren for their support. He then sat down and received a standing ovation from his fellow senators before casting his 12,001st vote.

I

Richard Green Lugar was born on April 4, 1932, the oldest of three children. Lugar grew up in Indianapolis and later lived part of the year on the farm his parents purchased when he was a young boy. His parents, Bertha and Marvin Lugar, were industrious, conservative people and lifelong Hoosiers.

Marvin Lugar studied agriculture at Purdue University, was an excellent student, joined a fraternity, and played on the college basketball team. He was a hardworking and frugal man and an ardent Republican. He loathed President Franklin D. Roosevelt and even made a point of returning Roosevelt dimes when he received them as change. He disliked FDR's big government activism, praised free markets, and loved his farm. "It was his pride and joy," the senator says.[2]

Bertha Lugar was an organized and energetic woman who was a leader at both Tech High School and at Butler University. Lugar remembers her as kindly and purposeful. She had lists of projects scattered about the house and checked off each item after having completed each task. As a young girl she traveled extensively and her interest in the larger world beyond Indiana may have had an influence on at least one of her sons.

Marvin and Bertha raised their three children—Richard, Tom, and Anne—on the north side of Indianapolis. In 1931, they also bought 604 acres of land in Marion County, outside of Indianapolis, that the senator still owns and works. "My soul is on that farm," he says.[3] Lugar's earliest memories of his parents were of their activity and energy. His father was up at 5 A.M. every day except Sunday to do chores on the farm. His mother often stayed up until 2 A.M. working on projects around the house. Lugar and his brother, Tom, earned small allowances by sweeping walks, cutting the lawn, and doing household chores. His parents, Lugar recalls, had a "calm expectation that the work had been done thoroughly and competently."[4]

Young Dick Lugar was an eager, earnest midwestern boy involved in Boys Scouts and the Methodist Youth Fellowship. He sold war bonds as a teen and also made time for piano and cello lessons. He and his brother were encouraged by their father to learn about the day-to-day challenges of running the farm, and also to appreciate its delicate relationship to nature and the fragility of its finances. One year, they invested $17 in an acre of wheat but saw their investment washed away when the White River flooded the farm and destroyed the crop on their acre. "We had taken a risk, and we had lost everything," Lugar recalls. "We lost the whole thing. That's the risk you take."

Lugar's parents encouraged education, and the children were raised in a house full of books. This ignited a passion for learning and study for Richard that continues nearly three-quarters of a century later. "I started to read biographies of generals, politicians, scientists, and educators. With my vivid imagination, I could see myself in all those roles," he says.[5] Though only 8 years old when fellow Hoosier Wendell Willkie secured the Republican presidential nomination in 1940, Dick began to dream about a career in politics, imagining himself at a political convention in a leading, and winning, role.

While Lugar's recollections of his youth emphasize health and vigor and his love of basketball, he also notes that he was often sick with sore throats and earaches due to serious allergies. "Endless sneezing, loss of voice, throat X-rays, braces, corrective shoes—all of these meant a seemingly endless stream of doctor appointments, tests, shots, and treatments," Lugar says. "My mother never stopped pursuing remedies and solutions. She praised me for being so patient and long-suffering. With her encouragement to stay the course, I did," he adds.

He praises his parents for giving him self-confidence, diligence, and discipline. "They worked hard to make certain that my ego was not inflated and equally hard to make certain that I had boundless self-confidence. Every day they were loving, caring advocates, and I wanted to please them."[6]

Lugar's promising political future was not evident at Shortridge High School in Indianapolis, where he lost the election for class president. However, he did graduate first in his class and went on to Denison University in Granville, Ohio. His political career was more successful in college; he became co-president of his senior class. His partnership with Charlene Smeltzer, his co-president, was so successful that they eventually married. Dick Lugar was a stellar student, again graduating first in his class as well as Phi Beta Kappa. He was a committed member of the Beta Theta Thi fraternity and the first Denison student to win a Rhodes Scholarship.

II

Lugar traveled by ship to England in 1954 with other Rhodes Scholars. He attended Pembroke College at Oxford University and received an honors degree in politics, philosophy, and economics. He also used his time in this academic environment to indulge his intellect by plunging into the works of Edmund Burke, Joseph Schumpeter, Fyodor Dostoyevski, and C.S. Lewis. His time at Oxford was one of the pivotal experiences in his life, deepening his love of learning and fueling his interest in international affairs.[7]

As his second year at Pembroke was ending, Lugar went to the U.S. embassy in London and enlisted in the navy. After completing his studies he returned to the United States, married Charlene in Detroit, and attended Officer Candidate School in Rhode Island and Intelligence School in Florida. Lugar was assigned to the Pentagon and became an intelligence briefer for Admiral Arleigh Burke, chief of Naval Operations. Burke was a near legendary military man who later co-founded a powerful Washington think tank, the Center for Strategic and International Studies. Lugar says Burke was one of the most influential mentors in his life, and the experience of working for the demanding admiral gave him a glimpse of the American government at the highest level. One of Lugar's jobs was to give intelligence briefings by closed circuit TV to President Eisenhower. Working for the admiral was an invaluable experience. "I watched power being exercised by a master. Arleigh Burke was a mentor for me on how America as a world power makes a difference," he says.[8]

When his navy service ended in 1960, Lugar returned to Indianapolis and joined the family business. He became the treasurer and secretary of the Thomas L. Green Manufacturing Company, a food product machinery company, and the Lugar Stock Farms. His brother, Tom, who earned an engineering degree at Purdue University, dealt with the firm's machinery and plant while Dick focused on financial and legal matters. The experience gave him an understanding of running a company and managing people. "Tom and I opened the plant gates in the morning and closed them at night. We turned the lights on and off. We did everything. There wasn't anybody else. You do things yourself or it doesn't happen," he says.[9]

After settling in as a local businessman living with his wife on the west side of Indianapolis, Lugar decided to run for the city's school board at the suggestion of a delegation of fellow Westside citizens. He had not given much thought to the work of the school board but was interested in education, had children in public schools, and decided to enter the race. He won and became a member of the school board on July 1, 1965.

The 1960s were a difficult and contentious time for the Indianapolis school board. Lugar cast the deciding votes to enroll the city in a school lunch program and to accept federal aid under the Education Act. He supported voluntary school desegregation and promoted the Shortridge Plan, which was an early version of a magnet school. These actions generated some discontent on the board. When he made a bid to become president of the school board in 1966, Lugar was defeated on a 4 to 3 vote. At that point, he assumed his political career had been both brief and unsuccessful. "I was devastated by it. I can't remember a political defeat that was ever more memorable," he recalls.[10]

But his work on the school board caught the attention of political leaders in Indianapolis, including Keith Bulen, an aggressive new power broker in the Republican Party of Marion County who was looking for fresh faces. Bulen saw Lugar as a possible Republican mayoral candidate for Indianapolis—a city not inclined toward Republican mayors. In fact, from 1925 until 1967, Indianapolis had elected 12 Democratic mayors and only 4 Republicans.[11]

Lugar's possible candidacy for mayor was first publicly suggested by Irving Leibowitz, managing editor of the Indianapolis Times, who wrote a column arguing that Lugar would be an intriguing candidate given his contributions to the school board. Lugar was inclined to defer to Paul Oakes to run for the GOP nomination. Oakes had just run a competitive, but losing, race for Congress in the 11th District and Lugar had served as his campaign manager. When Oakes relocated to Hartford, Connecticut, Lugar decided to present his credentials to a GOP screening board chaired by Bulen. He faced stiff competition for the Republican nomination for mayor. Judge William Sharp and former mayor Alex Clark were also interested in the nomination and were the more obvious choices. But the screening committee, dominated by Bulen, selected Lugar as their nominee, a decision that shocked many local Republicans and enraged Clark, who decided to challenge Lugar in the Republican primary. Lugar won over the selection committee by vowing to push aggressive reforms to revitalize Indianapolis. In May 1967, Lugar prevailed over Clark in a hard fought primary, receiving about 22,000 votes to Clark's 17,000.[12]

Lugar still faced an uphill struggle in the November election to defeat the incumbent Democratic mayor John Barton, who was well liked and controlled thousands of patronage jobs and numerous city contracts. But Barton faced divisions within the Democratic Party and had to beat back a challenge from a more liberal candidate, James Beatty, in the Democratic primary. Despite starting with considerable disadvantages, Lugar campaigned energetically. Bulen ran the campaign and had volunteers scouring the city to identify problems that needed to be addressed. They reported back with lists of curbs and sidewalks needing repair and poorly lit streets. Lugar's campaign later drafted individualized letters from the candidate to residents of different neighborhoods citing specific problems he pledged to fix if elected. The letters attracted attention and solidified Lugar's narrative that he was a hardworking problem solver.

As they geared up for the general election in November, Lugar and Bulen created 20 volunteer task forces to examine problems facing the city. The findings of each task force were used both to sharpen the candidate's campaign message and build his governance agenda. The task forces examined such issues as police morale and recruitment, parking, traffic safety, snow removal, garbage and refuse disposal, citizen involvement, and city governance.[13]

The central theme of Lugar's mayoral campaign was the promise to revitalize Indianapolis and make it a model city. "The promise of the campaign had been to create a new Indianapolis, a city of excellence in aspiration and greatness in achievement," Lugar said later.[14] He also credited the tough, detail-oriented campaign that Bulen organized. One Sunday morning before the election Lugar walked back and forth across a downtown Indianapolis intersection more than 70 times while a photographer tried for a perfect "walking man shot." Bulen finally found the shot he liked and reproduced the photo on a billboard 50 feet wide overlooking the old West Washington Street Bridge.[15]

In the campaign's final weeks, Lugar ran half-hour TV specials introducing himself and his agenda to the people of Indianapolis. The campaign also produced a 12-page color brochure about Lugar and his plans called *Forward Indianapolis,* which was inserted into newspapers. The campaign had its own jingle with soothing, if not profound, lyrics: "Dick Lugar, he's first rate. Dick Lugar for a town that's great."[16]

Bulen created a strong political operation with representatives in nearly every block of the city to make sure all potential Lugar voters were registered. In November, Lugar won with 53 percent of the vote, securing 72,278 votes to Barton's 63,284 votes.[17] Lugar was the first Republican mayor elected in Indianapolis in 16 years and the only Republican to win a mayoral election that year in a major city. He was sworn in as mayor in January of 1968 at the age of 35.

III

Just months into his tenure as mayor, Lugar helped calm the city's tense racial situation when Dr. Martin Luther King was killed in Memphis at the same time that Robert Kennedy was campaigning in Indianapolis for Indiana's presidential primary. Lugar was visible during the crisis, appearing often on local television, urging calm and pleading for racial reconciliation. On April 9, 1968, he went on television and vowed to work for a fairer Indianapolis. "It is extremely important that in this community we deliver ourselves from the hypocrisy that every man may live wherever he wishes. Presently this is just not so," he said. "We are committed to change. It can and will occur within the system and the fabric of democracy we enjoy here," Lugar said. We are committed to an integrated society in which color does not make a difference in terms of the enjoyment of life."[18]

During his campaign, Lugar offered few specifics about how he would reform city government. He had set up a task force on reform and was aware of a study under way by the Greater Indianapolis Progress Committee. He was frustrated by the diffusion of responsibility and power among various government agencies in the city and Marion County. "Why are eight different authorities responsible for drainage, five for transportation and so many for the development of the 4,000-acre Eagle Creek Park that the whole lake is becoming a quagmire of frustration and not a park?" he asked in a speech delivered in Portland, Oregon.[19]

In early 1968, leading Republicans in Marion County and Indianapolis held informal discussions about possible government reforms, including a consolidation between the city government of Indianapolis and that of Marion County. Participants at these meetings, which Lugar often attended, began to sketch out a plan for a new structure of government. Lugar studied city-county government consolidation in Nashville and Jacksonville and believed that consolidation of city and county would lead to greater government efficiency and provide the foundation for revitalization of Indianapolis. In the late spring of 1968, Lugar asked Lewis C. Bose, an Indianapolis attorney, to prepare a memo on how government reform in Indianapolis might work. He later asked Bose to head up a legal research team to prepare draft legislation that would have to be approved by Indiana's General Assembly.

As Lugar worked on the government mechanics of what became known as Unigov, he moved aggressively on the political front, supporting Republican candidates for county and state offices in the 1968 elections. When Republicans swept these races, he felt the political and policy foundation was in place to go forward with the Unigov plan. Almost immediately after the 1968 elections, Lugar created a task force for transforming the governmental structure of Indianapolis and Marion County. The task force had 52 members with 29 business and civic leaders; the remaining 23 were members of the Republican Marion County delegation to the Indiana General Assembly, which would have to approve the reorganization. In his letter to the task force members, Lugar gave them three assignments: to prepare legislation for the General Assembly; to explain to members of the General Assembly and the public the Unigov concept; and to give him guidance in establishing the precise government structure after legislation allowing a consolidation was approved. The main elements of the proposed reorganization were consolidation of the executive and legislative functions of the city and county, election of a single strong chief executive, election of a single city-county council, a substantial degree of administration integration, and the exemption of school districts and some other government units from the new arrangement. Marion County and the city of Indianapolis were to continue as separate legal entities and the 11 independent school systems were untouched, as were the 9 affected townships.[20]

The Indiana General Assembly considered the Unigov bill in the spring of 1969, and it was passed with relatively minor changes. Governor Edgar Whitcomb signed it into law on March 13, 1969. Most Republicans supported the plan as representing improved government efficiency. Democrats suspected the program had less to do with government efficiency than a power grab by Republicans to win political control of Indianapolis by making the Republican stronghold of Marion County part of the city's pool of voters. Lugar later acknowledged that political considerations were part of the calculus. "I'll be candid. I know this is good for Republicans. That's how I sold it to the state legislature," he said.[21]

But Lugar describes Unigov in loftier terms. Writing in 2005, Lugar said the chief purpose of the reorganization was to "bring all the citizens of the 'real Indianapolis' together with one mayor and one City-County Council, with all the money and the necessary authority for action around the same table. This would make possible an honest and open discussion of racial issues, of social justice and of how we could employ all of our creative and financial talents to build a city that could provide public safety, better job opportunities, stronger cultural institutions, and a potential tax base to pay for these ambitions."[22]

Lugar has long argued that creating Unigov was the pivotal act that led to the revitalization of Indianapolis that took hold in the early 1970s. His success in pushing through the consolidation won him a national reputation. At the end of 1969, he defeated New York City mayor John Lindsey to become vice president of the National League of Cities. The following year, Lugar was elected president of the group. In 1970, President Richard Nixon held a cabinet meeting in Indianapolis to show his support for Lugar's creative work in urban development. In 1971, Lugar was easily re-elected to a second term as mayor of Indianapolis by a 60 percent to 40 percent margin over his challenger, John Neff. Lugar was convinced that his 1971 re-election was a referendum on Unigov and years later could recall the almost exact results of the race: 151,000 votes for him and 100,000 for Neff. "It was a very decisive triumph and that meant that we had 4 more years to consolidate whatever had not been pinned down in the period that followed the 1969 enactment of Unigov legislation," he said. "By the time we came through that election campaign there was a proven record that the system worked—the city was being well-governed and people were rather enthusiastic about the trend of affairs."[23]

In 5 of his 8 years as mayor of Indianapolis, Lugar was able to reduce property taxes that were the central revenue source for funding government. Lugar was active in downtown redevelopment, supporting the construction of Market Square Arena by providing a $12 million capital grant to the arena. As mayor, he worked with the neighborhoods to improve their physical appearance. He was fascinated by the mechanics of running a city—of paving streets, fixing sidewalks, chopping down trees, and cleaning up houses and lots. He loved his work as mayor, relishing both the practical challenges and the tangible results. "It was very tough for me to leave that," he said, but added that in life there is often "a graceful time to get involved in another agenda. But I loved every moment of it."[24]

IV

Having enjoyed success as mayor of Indianapolis, Lugar began to consider opportunities to move to the national stage. In 1974, he agreed to challenge incumbent Democratic senator Birch Bayh, fully aware that the race would be very difficult, especially given the political backlash against Republicans due to the Watergate scandal. For much of the campaign year, polls showed that Lugar was within striking distance of Bayh, but his support dropped sharply in the summer of 1974 when President Richard Nixon resigned and Ford later pardoned Nixon. In November, Lugar was defeated by Bayh, 51 percent to 47 percent. Lugar bided his time as a visiting professor before launching his 1976 campaign against Indiana's other Democratic incumbent senator, Vance Hartke. Lugar won the Republican primary against former Indiana governor Edgar Whitcomb and then went on to easily defeat Hartke, 59 percent to 40 percent.

Senator Lugar has been re-elected five times. After a challenging race in 1982, he won re-election by steadily rising majorities in 1988, 1994, 2000, and 2006. In these races, Lugar ran for re-election as a businessman, farmer, and fifth-generation Hoosier. He pointed out that he was one of the few senators in Washington who had served as both a mayor and school board member.

In 1977, Lugar arrived in Washington as a conservative Republican who believed in small government, low taxes, and minimal regulation. He did not rail against government, arguing rather that it should be efficient and modestly sized. He supported loan packages to Chrysler and New York City and crafted an economic stimulus plan that was ultimately vetoed by President Reagan. Lugar began his career, as did most senators in that era, by keeping a relatively low profile, speaking carefully, and working diligently in his committees: Agriculture, Banking, and Intelligence. During the campaign he had pledged that getting on the Senate Agriculture Committee would be his primary goal when he arrived in Washington.

Two years later, in a move that foreshadowed the future of his congressional career, Lugar joined the Senate Foreign Relations Committee. He earned a reputation as a serious and hardworking member who followed the lead of the Reagan administration. Ronald Reagan seriously considered Lugar for his running mate in 1980 but decided instead on George H. W. Bush. And 8 years later, Bush reportedly contemplated asking Lugar to be his vice president, before stunning the political world by choosing Lugar's fellow Hoosier Dan Quayle.

Eager to enter the Senate Republican leadership ranks, Lugar defeated his colleague Robert Packwood to chair the Senate Republican campaign committee for the 1984 campaign cycle. Packwood had chaired the committee twice before and was widely praised for running a successful campaign organization. But he was frequently at odds with the Reagan White House on high-profile issues, and the president's political team made it clear that they preferred Lugar for the Senate leadership post. Working closely with his top aide, Mitch Daniels, Lugar raised more than $9 million for Senate GOP races in the first half of 1983, then a record amount, helping the party eventually retain its majority in 1984.[25]

Hoping to move to the top of the Senate GOP leadership ladder in 1984, Lugar made a bid to succeed the retiring Senate Republican leader Howard Baker. Lugar plunged into a five-way race with Robert Dole of Kansas, Ted Stevens of Alaska, Pete Domenici of New Mexico, and James McClure of Idaho. Lugar ran third in the five-senator race, which was eventually won by Dole.[26] But Lugar was given a golden consolation prize: the chairmanship of the Senate Foreign Relations Committee.

Lugar's loss of the Senate Republican leadership race and his elevation to the chairmanship of the Foreign Relations Committee in 1985 fundamentally changed Lugar's Senate career. Initially aspiring to build influence in the Senate through party leadership posts, Lugar now shifted his attention to building influence as head of the Senate's most storied committee and developing policy expertise in foreign policy.

V

Richard Lugar's ascension to the chairmanship of the Senate Foreign Relations Committee caught many by surprise, including the senator. He had been a quiet and capable member of the committee since 1979 but was not generally thought ready to take on the prestigious chairmanship. However, the electoral defeat of incumbent chairman Charles Percy opened the door for Lugar. Another Republican senator, Jesse Helms of North Carolina, had more seniority than Lugar and was in line for the chairmanship of the Foreign Relations Committee. But Helms had made a campaign pledge to take the chairmanship of the Senate Agriculture Committee, so Lugar assumed the leadership of the Foreign Relations Committee.

He plunged into his chairmanship in typical dogged Lugar fashion. He installed a new staff and scheduled 2 months of hearings to review the main challenges and goals of American foreign policy. Lugar said that for members these sessions would be "like going to school" on international affairs, adding they would serve as an "educational experience for us, for our colleagues and maybe for the American public." Lugar later said that these introductory hearings were also designed to show that the committee was under new, energetic leadership.[27]

During this time, Lugar developed a close relationship with Secretary of State George Shultz. Lugar was able to work with the Democratic chairman of the House Foreign Affairs Committee, Dante Fascell, to pass the first foreign affairs authorization bill in several years. This bill identifies and updates the various American foreign assistance programs that receive funding. It is the committee's best opportunity to outline its vision of American foreign policy.

Lugar's 2-year chairmanship was dominated by his critical role in two international events: the defeat and removal from power of Ferdinand Marcos in the Philippines and American support for economic and political sanctions against the apartheid government in South Africa.

Lugar served as an election observer in the Philippines presidential race between President Marcos and challenger Corazon Aquino. During the crisis, Lugar was a fixture in the American and international press, declaring that Marcos had attempted to steal the election and proclaiming the real winner was Aquino, an interpretation of events that differed from President Reagan's. Lugar's calm but persistent delineation of the evidence of Marcos's electoral fraud finally persuaded Reagan to drop his support of Marcos.

Lugar had a longer, tougher fight with the Reagan administration over U.S. policy toward South Africa. The president clung to the approach of constructive engagement with the apartheid government and opposed sanctions. Lugar initially worked with the administration to defeat a congressional effort to impose sanctions but began to doubt that the administration would insist on fundamental reforms from the South African government. In a sharp deviation from his preferred approach, Lugar publicly broke with the administration and worked to override Reagan's veto of a sanctions bill in the Senate. In a passionate, even fiery, speech on the Senate floor, Lugar said the time for a new American policy for South Africa was at hand. Lugar's show of independence won him widespread praise among America's foreign policy leaders but also provoked some grumbling by Senate Republicans who thought he was too willing to get ahead of the GOP leadership and his party on key foreign policy issues.

Democrats won back control of the Senate in November 1986, ending Lugar's chairmanship of Foreign Relations. Later, Republican senator Jesse Helms used GOP seniority rules to assume the position of ranking Republican on the panel, effectively pushing Lugar into the periphery of the committee's work. Lugar did not accept this demotion passively. He formally challenged Helms for the Republican leadership role in the Foreign Relations Committee. Lugar easily defeated Helms when the issue was voted on by Republicans within the committee, but when the matter was considered by all Senate Republicans, Helms was elected on a 24 to 17 vote. Helms framed the issue as just a question of seniority, but Lugar said the vote was about which man Senate Republicans wanted to be their spokesman on foreign policy. One account of the leadership battle between Helms and Lugar said it was a "struggle for the ideological soul of the Republican party."[28] Lugar has called this time "very close" to the lowest point in his political career, as he fell from the chairmanship to the second ranking minority member of the Senate Foreign Relations Committee.[29] Joe Biden said he believes the defeat was a "searing experience" for Lugar.[30]

The period from 1987 to 2003 was a difficult time for Lugar. His relationship with Helms ranged from cool to acid, and Helms went out of his way to exclude Lugar from the deliberations of the committee Lugar loved. They agreed on little and battled each other, often quietly, sometimes publicly, on matters, including support of the Chemical Weapons Treaty, pushing for the payment of American dues to the United Nations, and backing President Clinton's nomination of Massachusetts governor William Weld to be the American ambassador to Mexico. The decision by George Bush to choose Dan Quayle as his vice presidential running mate in 1988 appeared to close the door on Lugar's chance to become president or vice president in the near future. But Lugar pressed ahead. He became the ranking Republican on the Senate Agriculture Committee and then served as chairman of that panel for 6 years from 1995 to 2001. With some success, he pushed his vision of market-based agriculture in the United States. He helped write the historic, but later reversed, Freedom to Farm bill that cut back agricultural subsidies. From his post on the Agriculture Committee, he also worked on soil conservation, food stamp reform, renewable energy expansion, and trade promotion.

He remained active in foreign policy, but mostly as a kind of free agent. He strongly supported the First Gulf War in 1991 and even urged George H. W. Bush to remove Saddam Hussein from power. Having mastered the nuances of arms control, Lugar served as an observer to arms control talks in Geneva, developing good working relationships with Soviet arms control officials. He was active in Senate debates and ratification of the START I, START II, and Intermediate Range Nuclear Forces treaties, as well as the Chemical Weapons Convention. Lugar was also an early and influential supporter of NATO expansion and helped win support for the first wave of expansion that brought Poland, Hungary, and the Czech Republic into NATO in 1998.

When the Soviet Union collapsed in 1991, Lugar joined Democratic senator Sam Nunn to create a program to secure and destroy chemical, biological, and nuclear weapons in the former Soviet Union. This program, discussed in chapter 4, became a centerpiece of Lugar's congressional work and legacy.

Lugar decided to run for the Republican presidential nomination in 1996. It is difficult to know when he first thought about running for the presidency, but several of his close aides believe he began considering it during his time as mayor of Indianapolis when he became a national figure. He was mentioned as a possible vice president as early as 1973, when Nixon was searching to replace Spiro Agnew after Agnew was forced to resign. Lugar was considered as a vice presidential candidate in both 1980 and 1988 but was not selected.

Lugar announced his presidential bid in April 1995 in Indianapolis. He acknowledged that it was an uphill fight. "The conventional wisdom of generous columnists seems to be that Dick Lugar would be a good president. They contend that he is intelligent, has broad experience, exercises courage and prudence appropriately. But they add that such a person is rarely nominated or elected," he said.[31] His campaign focused on the dangers of terrorism and nuclear weapons, which, though prescient, were not politically compelling issues in peacetime. He also called for scrapping the federal income tax and replacing it with a national sales tax and endorsed fiscal austerity, cutting back federal spending in some areas such as agricultural subsidies.

Columnist George Will wrote of Lugar's campaign that Lugar's "conspicuous normality and undeniable gravitas certainly improve the Republican field."[32] But Lugar struggled to raise money and failed to capture the interest of Republican primary voters in a crowded field. He was frequently described as a wooden public speaker who had trouble connecting with large audiences. He seemed to relish his campaign's aversion to simple messages and compelling themes. "I want to be elected on the right terms," he said at one point. "I've still got the high ground," he said later.[33]

Lugar performed poorly in the Iowa caucus, finishing in seventh place with only 4 percent of the vote. In the New Hampshire primary he finished in fifth place with 5 percent of the vote. He left the race. "Unlike some of his competitors, Lugar survived the experience with both his integrity and dignity intact," one observer wrote.[34]

He returned to life in the Senate, seemingly without bitterness or regret. Indeed, he came to terms with the idea that he was never going to be elected president and redoubled his efforts to be a consequential senator. He continued to work closely with Democrats, building productive working relationships with Nunn and Biden, who became the top Democrat on the Foreign Relations Committee. Jesse Helms's decision to retire from the Senate in 2002 was welcome news for Lugar, as was the Republican victory that November that won back control of the Senate. Those two events catapulted Lugar back into the chairmanship of the Foreign Relations Committee in 2003, 16 years after he first held the gavel. The Iraq War dominated Lugar's second chairmanship. Lugar had worked with Biden in 2002 on an alternative war resolution, which was brushed aside by Republican leaders in Congress and the Bush White House. With the war in Iraq about to begin when he assumed the chairmanship in January of 2003, Lugar vowed to hold "pointed hearings" about Iraq, pledging to press the administration hard on its plans for a postwar Iraq.[35]

Lugar held more than 30 Iraq-related hearings during his 4-year chairmanship. While the senator frequently expressed concern that the administration had not prepared sufficiently for the war's aftermath, his hearings were muted and restrained sessions. They were a far cry from the politically charged and powerful 1966 hearings that then committee chairman J. William Fulbright held, which many believe helped eventually end the war in Vietnam.

Lugar used his second chairmanship to aggressively and creatively challenge American policymakers to rethink the nation's haphazard energy policy. He held a comprehensive series of hearings on energy policy and offered sweeping legislation to expand the production of alternative fuels and increase conservation. He also continued his bipartisan practices working with Biden and a freshman senator from Illinois, Barack Obama. Lugar helped persuade Obama to join the Foreign Relations Committee when he entered the Senate in 2005. That summer, Lugar invited Obama to join him on an oversight trip to evaluate the workings of the Nunn-Lugar program in Russia and Ukraine. Lugar was impressed by the young senator and Obama was intrigued by the work of the veteran from Indiana. "I couldn't have had a better guide than Dick, a remarkably fit 73-year-old with a gentle, imperturbable manner and an inscrutable smile that served him well during the often interminable meetings we held with foreign officials," Obama writes in *The Audacity of Hope*.[36]

The two senators visited key weapons sites in Russia and Ukraine, including visits to Saratov, Perm, and Kiev. At the airport in Perm, a young Russian border officer detained the senators for 3 hours because they wouldn't let him search the plane. Lugar and Obama sat calmly on the plane as their staffs worked with officials in the U.S. embassy in Moscow and Russia's foreign affairs ministry to resolve the situation.

Lugar and Obama continued to work together throughout the Illinois senator's brief tenure. They teamed up on energy-related legislation as well as a bill to expand the reach of the Nunn-Lugar program to control the proliferation of conventional weapons.

VI

During his career in the Senate and on the Foreign Relations Committee, Lugar developed a comprehensive worldview, which he detailed in his 1988 book, *Letters to the Next President*. Lugar has continued to refine his foreign policy views in recent years, and in an updated 2004 edition, Lugar emphasizes the importance of the presidency in leading American foreign policy. It is in the foreign policy realm, he argues, "that the president has the most authority to exercise power." But he insists that the president should work with Congress to craft a bipartisan American foreign policy. He acknowledges that this isn't easy but is very important. "The consensus on foreign policy that once was prevalent in U.S. political discourse has badly eroded. Too often the motivation for important national security positions of both parties is driven by politics that are disconnected from any credible analysis," he writes. "A consensus on foreign policy cannot be wished back into being, nor can it be manufactured overnight in response to an immediate crisis. It can only be restored gradually over time through presidential attention and the development of mutual trust between Congress and the Executive branch."[37]

He urges lawmakers to find areas of bipartisan agreement, display competence, develop good relations with the press, and build strong contacts with the president and secretary of state. Good foreign policy must be worked on day by day, in a careful and meticulous way. American leaders must also work closely with allies to address international challenges. The senator believes that multilateral cooperation is needed to successfully solve most problems.

Lugar's foreign policy statements over 30 years are low on abstractions, sweeping assertions, and epigrams and high on solving specific problems, be they arms control, proliferation, energy, or global hunger. After September 11, 2001, Lugar outlined what he called the Lugar Doctrine. In this policy statement, he argued that the proliferation of weapons of mass destruction is not just the security problem of our time. It is also the economic dilemma and the moral challenge of the coming age. He noted that on 9/11, the world witnessed the destructive potential of international terrorism. But these attacks did not come close to approximating the destruction that would be unleashed by a nuclear weapon. The consequences of a nuclear attack would be very large, he said, especially since there would be a fear that additional weapons might be coming, creating deep uncertainty and possibly panic.

"I believe that the campaign to control weapons of mass destruction stands out as the most urgent. Terrorists armed with high explosives or firearms represent tremendous risk to society, but they do not constitute an existential threat. Therefore, if we can positively control weapons of mass destruction—particularly nuclear weapons—we can greatly reduce the risks of catastrophe."[38]

3

✿

The Tools of the Trade

I

In September 2005, Richard Lugar gave a lecture at the Library of Congress sponsored by the John Brademas Center for the Study of Congress, a research center based at New York University. The center was beginning a lecture series to consider how Congress shapes American public policy, and Lugar and Democratic senator Paul Sarbanes were asked to give the inaugural lectures to a group of invited guests that included current and former members of Congress and congressional scholars.

Sarbanes, a former chairman of the Senate Banking Committee, focused his remarks on domestic policy, discussing the history of the Sarbanes-Oxley law that he helped write to strengthen corporate accounting standards in response to a raft of business accounting scandals. Lugar, then the chairman of the Senate Foreign Relations Committee, described the various tools and techniques that individual lawmakers and Congress use to influence American foreign policy. He observed that in the foreign policy realm Congress has a mixed record, with notable failures as well as striking successes. The successes, he said, prove that Congress can be a serious player on foreign policy even though the president's power to initiate foreign and military policies is enormous. The president can dispatch hundreds of thousands of troops around the world and negotiate agreements with foreign governments, with no need for congressional consent, at least at the outset. Congress alone can declare war, though in the contemporary world this essentially means approving the use of force at the request of the president. And Congress's formidable budget and taxing power is usually a response to the president's fiscal agenda. Congress's reactive approach to foreign policy is reinforced by the modest resources allocated for staffing and research compared to the executive branch. This makes it more difficult for lawmakers to develop policies that are relevant to a complex, fast-changing world.

But even with these limitations, Lugar pointed to examples of how Congress has shaped American foreign policy. It developed anti-apartheid sanctions against South Africa in the mid-1980s, pushed for the expansion of NATO in the 1990s, and created the Nunn-Lugar program in 1991. "In each of these cases, the initiative for the policy, its basic outline and its main political support at its inception and over time came from the Congress. In each case, representatives of the executive branch voiced either outright opposition to the policy or discomfort with it. However, Congress was able to build strong majorities in favor of the policy and to solidify public opinion in favor of it," he said.[1]

Lugar offered a detailed account of how the Nunn-Lugar program emerged in the face of an indifferent White House and an often hostile House of Representatives. From his perspective, the doggedness and determination of several committed lawmakers prevailed over inertia in the executive branch and outright resistance in the lower chamber. He observed that Congress has several unique strengths that allow it to create successful foreign policies. The first is sheer staying power. Presidents serve for only 4 or at most 8 years, while some on Capitol Hill write laws for decades. Veterans in the House and Senate can develop policy expertise, institutional memory, and the political understanding of an issue that carries over from administration to administration.

Congress can also reflect public opinion and demonstrate broad support for an idea among the American people. Lawmakers can advance policies and programs by arranging votes in the House and Senate, holding public hearings, gathering large numbers of co-sponsors, or taking other steps to show the executive branch evidence of public sentiment. In this way, Congress can provide shortcuts to the establishment of foreign policies that otherwise might be delayed by months of debate or turf battles within the executive branch. Finally, Congress can confer a bipartisan framework on a policy that might otherwise be viewed with suspicion by one or both parties. A bipartisan group of co-sponsors for a bill or policy can disarm potential opposition and establish a more unified and sustained basis for congressional support.

Lugar acknowledged that Congress makes mistakes on foreign policy, such as its tendency to impose economic sanctions when it lacks other means to express displeasure with a given country. While congressional overreach and blunders are part of the historical record, Lugar argued that the nation has suffered more from Congress's inattention to foreign policy than its overinvolvement. "Members of Congress know too little about the world and are too hesitant to speak about it with their constituents," he said.[2] He concluded by encouraging his colleagues to develop foreign policy expertise and create bipartisan coalitions to transform good ideas into constructive law. He predicted their constituents would usually support and respect this work. The senator's message was clear: lawmakers who are informed, strategic, and determined can make a real difference in crafting American foreign policy. But first they must learn the tools of the trade.

II

The American Constitution has been described by political scientist Edwin Corwin as "an invitation to struggle for the privilege of directing American foreign policy" by the executive and legislative branches.[3] It gives both the president and Congress substantial foreign policy powers but does not establish a procedure for resolving overlapping authorities. Nor does it clearly assign a preeminent role for either branch. One scholar observes that the references to foreign policy powers in the Constitution are "very brief and sufficiently vague to provoke widely varying interpretations about the Framers' intent. References to foreign policy powers are not contained in separate sections of either article, but are interspersed among references to powers in domestic policy."[4]

The Constitution confers upon the president substantial, but limited, foreign policy powers. Article 2, section 2 says the president "shall be the Commander in Chief of the Army and Navy of the United States."

It adds that the president shall have the authority with the advice and consent of the Senate to make treaties, provided that two-thirds of the Senate present and voting agree. The President is empowered to nominate "and by and with the Advice and Consent of the Senate, appoint Ambassadors, other public Ministers and Consuls."[5]

The Constitution confers more numerous and specific foreign policy powers on Congress. Article 1, section 1 gives Congress the general legislative power. Article 1, section 7 and Article 1, section 8 confer on Congress the power of the purse. Article 1, section 8 also grants a wide array of foreign policy authorities to Congress. These include the power to "provide for the common Defence and general welfare of the United States," to "regulate Commerce with foreign Nations," to "define and punish Piracies and Felonies committed on the high Seas, and Offenses against the Law of Nations," and to "declare War, grant Letters of Marque and Reprisal, and make Rules concerning the Captures on Land and Water." It also charges Congress to "raise and support Armies," "to provide and maintain a Navy," and to regulate naval forces.[6]

Two analysts have declared that the constitutional delegation of foreign policy powers for Congress is "both wider in scope and more specific in nature than its delegation of powers for the presidency."[7] This is true even though the president is the principal foreign policy actor. As commander in chief and head of the executive branch, he manages the nation's day-to-day dealings with other governments.

Based on these constitutional provisions, scholars have placed Congress's central foreign policy authorities into several categories. First, Congress has war powers. The Constitution divides this power between Congress and the president. Scholars have noted that the Constitutional Congress changed Congress's authority from the power to "make war," which was in an early draft, to the power to "declare war" so as to leave the president the authority to repel sudden attacks, but not initiate war.[8] The evolution of the balance in war powers between Congress and the president has been driven more by precedents and circumstances than the intentions of the founders. Congress has declared war only five times in American history: the War of 1812, the Mexican-American War, the Spanish-American War, World War I, and World War II. It should be noted that formal declarations of war are no longer standard practice in diplomacy. Since 1941, the United States has not declared on war on any nation but has been involved in dozens of armed interventions including in Korea, Vietnam, the former Yugoslavia, the Persian Gulf, Afghanistan, and Iraq.[9]

Second, Congress has treaty powers. Ratification of treaties, which is the formal acceptance of a treaty by the U.S. government, is the power of the president. But the Constitution mandates the president can ratify a treaty only after the consent of two-thirds of the senators present and voting. The Senate does not vote on the text of the treaty but on a resolution of ratification that begins, "The Senate advises and consents to the ratification of the Treaty." If the Senate consents, the president then exchanges the documents with the other parties and the treaty is ratified. The president could decide not to put the treaty in force by withholding the ratification documents.[10]

For many decades the treaty clause was regarded as one of Congress's major foreign policy authorities. From 1789 to 2011, only 18 treaties have been rejected outright by the Senate. The Senate's defeat of the Versailles Treaty, for example, was one of the signal events in American history. However, to avoid a possible confrontation with the Senate, the executive branch has increasingly relied on executive agreements as a vehicle to advance international agreements. Kay King, a former congressional staffer now an analyst at the Council on Foreign Relations, calculates that the executive branch now only conveys on average 32 treaties in each Congress, which is only 16 a year. She adds that over the past 20 years, treaties have accounted for less that 10 percent of all international agreements entered into by the United States.[11]

Third, Congress has the power to "regulate Commerce with foreign nations." This gives Congress critical powers in the area of trade and economic affairs. Fourth, there is the power of the purse, the requirement that Congress approve both of raising revenues and authorizing and appropriating of expenditures. This gives Congress substantial authority to fund military and international assistance programs as well as the overall operations of the executive branch. Finally, Congress has the general legislative power that allows it to write laws that shape the nation's military and diplomatic apparatus and articulate specific aspects of foreign policy. For example, through this power Congress mandated the establishment of the Arms Control and Disarmament Agency and then later voted for its abolition. It has instructed the president to develop a missile defense system, mandated the State Department to create a bureau of human rights, and in the 1980s prohibited agencies of the U.S. government from providing training, equipment, or other forms of support to overthrow the government of Nicaragua.

The power balance between Congress and the executive branch regarding foreign policy has shifted over the nation's history, with periods of presidential dominance and times of congressional ascendancy. For example, Congress was the leading institution in crafting American foreign policy in 1837–1861, 1869–1897, 1918–1936, and 1973–1980. These were all periods in which the country was not involved in a major war. (The Vietnam War was winding down in 1973 and American involvement ended in 1975.) There have also been periods of presidential dominance over foreign policy. Presidents have taken decisive actions that have set a clear policy course, such as Thomas Jefferson's purchase of the Louisiana Territory, Theodore Roosevelt's decision to build the Panama Canal, Franklin Roosevelt's actions to provide assistance to allies in the run-up to World War II, and Lyndon Johnson's expansion of the Vietnam War.[12]

Many argue that the president has dominated American foreign policy since World War II, except for the latter part of the Vietnam period. Steven Hook argues that the president's formal and informal powers have allowed him to direct U.S. foreign policy. The president is able to set the agenda, respond directly to the flow of day-to-day events, and manage the country's foreign policy bureaucracy. Hook also says that one way to measure the president's ability to set the agenda is to note the tendency over the past 60 years for presidential goals and stances regarding foreign affairs to be articulated as "doctrines," giving us the Truman Doctrine, the Eisenhower Doctrine, the Nixon Doctrine, the Reagan Doctrine, the Clinton Doctrine, and the [George W.] Bush Doctrine.[13]

Most American presidents have had little doubt about which branch dominates foreign policy. President Harry Truman, when asked who set American foreign policy, had a succinct answer: "I do."[14] Speaking several decades later, Rep. Lee Hamilton, then chairman of the House Foreign Affairs Committee, didn't dispute Truman's assessment. "The fact of the matter is the President of the United States makes foreign policy," Hamilton said.[15]

Scholars have long debated the issue of congressional power over American foreign policy and have generated a substantial and contentious literature on the topic. The literature is so vast and complex that it defies easy summary, but there are several schools of thought that bear discussion.

First, there are those who believe that Congress has not used, in a rigorous or reliable way, the ample powers it has been provided to shape American foreign policy. For example, Stephen Weissman, in *A Culture of Deference: Congress's Failure of Leadership in Foreign Policy*, argues that Congress has largely abandoned its responsibility to co-determine U.S. foreign policy. In his view, Congress has essentially ceded its fundamental constitutional role in foreign policy. As he sees it, congressional deference is due to a powerful set of internal norms, attitudes, customs, and institutions that constitute a culture of deference. This culture of deference has several elements. Congress gives the president wide latitude to unilaterally undertake ambitious initiatives that imply a future commitment of legislative support. It fails to use its resources to ensure that it develops an independent perspective from the executive branch. Congress displays an uneven commitment to make and uphold clear and binding laws. It is sometimes driven by narrow special interests with access to a few key legislators to develop policies that do not have broad support. And Congress reviews some foreign policies in almost total secrecy, narrowing its access to critical information and limiting its choices. This is especially true in intelligence. Weissman believes that Congress was an active player on foreign policy until World War II, especially during the century from the War of 1812 until the Versailles Treaty of 1919. But during and after World War II, Congress has been passive and often yielded the decision to use force to the president, Weissman concludes.[16]

Barbara Hinckley's *Less than Meets the Eye: Foreign Policy Making and the Myth of an Assertive Congress* questions Congress's role in foreign policy. Hinckley argues that Congress is keener to display the appearance of foreign policy influence than to ensure the reality of that influence, and symbolism often takes precedence over substance in congressional foreign policymaking. The appearance of frequent clashes between the legislative and executive branches of government over foreign policy is just that—"in large part an illusion, perhaps at times deliberately encouraged." The two branches, she argues, support each other in this symbolic display, staging dramatic last-minute compromises or complaining about each other's usurpation or meddling. Executive branch officials fiercely protest the restrictions that Congress writes into law, but then routinely invoke the escape clauses that allow them to avoid the strictures of the law. Moreover, when Congress speaks on foreign policy, it often does so to support the president. "It may be that neither the President nor Congress makes much of the nation's foreign policy. They are not natural antagonists in a fight for increased influence, but collaborators in a routine policy process whose origins are the bureaucratic agencies and the policies of the past. Claims of an adversarial relationship therefore obscure the real problem that no one is minding the store," she writes.[17]

An intriguing component of the literature on Congress and foreign policy features current or former practitioners who argue that Congress is relevant in fashioning foreign policy but is less effective and constructive than it should be. For example, former House Foreign Affairs Committee Chairman Lee Hamilton has written extensively about the relationship between Congress and the executive branch on foreign policy issues. Hamilton characterizes Congress as a significant underachiever in the realm of foreign policy. In *A Creative Tension: The Foreign Policy Roles of the President and the Congress,* Hamilton argues that Congress has substantial foreign policy authorities but does not discharge them effectively. Too often, Congress defers to the president or develops foreign policy in an ad hoc way. Too often, it fails to serve as either an informed critic or a constructive partner with the executive branch.[18]

Hamilton contends that the foreign policy capacity of Congress has grown both more sophisticated and more fractured in recent decades. Congress challenges the president more frequently, but often in incoherent or poorly coordinated ways. Part of the confusion, he writes, is due to the splintering of power in Congress. Congressional foreign policy work is now spread out among dozens of committees rather than concentrated in the two main foreign policy committees that have traditionally contained the greatest foreign policy expertise. To the extent that foreign policy power is concentrated, it resides in the appropriations committees in which international concerns are usually secondary to domestic political and fiscal concerns. He notes that the House and Senate foreign affairs committees have not passed comprehensive legislation authorizing U.S. foreign assistance programs since 1985. He believes this is because committee members often want to avoid making decisions on controversial foreign policy matters and administrations aren't eager to encourage Congress to use these bills to offer restrictive riders to authorizing legislation. Consequently, important foreign policy issues are now frequently decided as part of enormous omnibus spending bills that are drafted near the end of congressional sessions by a small number of congressional leaders and staff and the White House.

Congressional foreign policy power is further dissipated by the growing tendency of Congress to form ad hoc caucuses on issues such as trade, terrorism, and the environment. This fragmentation of power has made it all the more difficult for Congress to develop a foreign policy consensus. Hamilton concludes that all of these changes have made Congress more representative, assertive, fractured, and inconsistent on foreign policy. Congress challenges the president's authority far more often today than it did four decades ago, but it often acts rashly and speaks in "a cacophony of conflicting voices."[19]

King also believes Congress punches below its weight on foreign policy. In the report *Congress and National Security*, she argues that in the critical areas of development, diplomacy, and intelligence, Congress is inconsistent and often counterproductive. Like Hamilton, she laments Congress's inability to pass a foreign assistance authorization bill, saying this has weakened its ability to examine aid programs in a comprehensive and careful way. She observes that in its current committee and jurisdictional structure, Congress is not well equipped to deal with the growing number of complex and interconnected issues. Committee jurisdictions reinforce artificial divisions and diminish opportunities to work systematically to integrate challenges such as immigration, energy, and trade into the larger foreign policy debate.[20]

King believes Congress can function as the co-equal branch in national security matters, but to become more relevant it must go back to fundamentals. Congress should fulfill its basic responsibilities such as holding carefully organized hearings, considering legislation in a timely way, debating bills on the floor of the House and Senate, and promptly considering appointments of ambassadors and senior diplomats. Committees should review the reporting requirements they impose on the agencies they oversee, eliminate the outdated ones, and set a reasonable limit on the number of reports they require from the executive branch. Congress should also devote more effort to oversight, international affairs funding, and its advice and consent responsibilities, she argues.[21]

Other observers argue that Congress has had more impact in foreign policy than many realize. For example, Robert David Johnson, in *Congress and the Cold War,* argues that Congress played a critical role in crafting U.S. policies after World War II that eventually won the cold war. In Johnson's view, Congress has been at the forefront of developing American foreign policy and then later challenging its central features. Congress was pivotal, he asserts, in developing, funding, and sustaining the strategy of containment, and it was at the forefront of challenging the Vietnam War, shattering the foreign policy consensus that had been built up after World War II.[22]

Rebecca Hersman's observations about "waves" of clashes and the "ocean" of daily interaction in foreign policy also reflect the idea that Congress's role in the development of foreign policy is greater than is sometimes acknowledged. She points to the informal universe in which lawmakers and congressional staff work with the executive branch as the key to understanding the operations of the foreign policy machinery, because much of the interaction between Congress and the executive branch occurs outside the formal legislative process and official communications. While institutional fragmentation and ideological polarization limit Congress's institutional leadership over foreign policy, the expansion of informal and procedural powers has increased the power of individuals to shape foreign policy. Fewer members of Congress are focusing on foreign policy, but those that do are playing a disproportionately important role, she argues.[23]

Choosing to Lead: Understanding Congressional Foreign Policy Entrepreneurs, by Ralph Carter and James Scott, is one of the most forceful arguments about Congress's important role in foreign policy. They assemble historical evidence that shows that members of Congress have been influential participants in the creation of foreign policy. Focusing primarily on the post–cold war era, they see the fingerprints of Congress on dozens of foreign policy innovations and decisions. For example, in the 1940s, Congress helped frame the debate for the United Nations and encouraged the development of the European Common Market. In the 1950s, Congress helped develop the ideas for the Peace Corps and NASA. In the 1960s, Congress framed the debate for detente with the Soviet Union and rapprochement with China, created rules for high technology trade with communist states, raised the issue of returning the Panama Canal to Panama, and outlawed political contributions by foreign agents. In the 1970s, Congress worked to improve relations with Mexico, pressured U.S. citizens to stop funding the Irish Republican Army, began funding the Afghan mujahideen and provided relief for refugees in Afghanistan. In the 1980s, Congress publicized Soviet violations of the Anti-Ballistic Missile Treaty, developed a peace plan for Central America, and championed human rights. In the 1990s, Congress ended U.S. intervention in Somalia by cutting off funding, forced the administration to intervene in Haiti, pressured the Swiss to return looted Jewish art, promoted debt relief for the poorest nations, pressed the administration to recognize Vietnam, and framed the debate for enlarging NATO. In the 2000s, Congress banned the trade in conflict diamonds, created a Russian-American exchange program, and pressed the administration for greater commitment toward reconstruction in both Afghanistan and Iraq.[24]

III

Most experts agree that the Senate plays a more important role in shaping foreign policy than does the House. Less than a quarter the size of the House, the Senate has a higher profile and its members have more opportunities to participate in policy debates, including those involving treaties and the executive branch's nominees for diplomatic appointments.

When the Senate considers treaties, one of its main roles under the advice and consent powers granted by the Constitution, it can attach amendments, reservations, understandings, and policy declarations to the ratification resolutions. This sometimes allows the Senate to shape foreign policy without having to negotiate extensively with the House or even the president. For example, during the 1998 Senate debate on NATO expansion, the Senate approved three policy initiatives as part of the treaty debate. They limit U.S. financial contribution to the alliance, prevented NATO from altering its defensive mission, and prohibited American security commitments beyond the current NATO membership.[25]

James Lindsay, an expert on Congress and foreign policy, argues that the Founding Fathers were wary of allowing the House to consider "the grave matters of state that treaties were presumed to entail." He adds that in excluding the House from treaty making, the framers elevated the Senate and sowed the seeds for an institutional rivalry that continues today.[26] While less influential than the Senate in foreign policy, the House is a full partner on general legislative matters, especially in matters of funding and debates over spending for defense and international programs. The House's oversight responsibilities also contribute to its being a key player on foreign policy.

In a paper on the Senate and foreign policy, Lindsay identifies several phases in the Senate's involvement in foreign policy over the last 60 years. He refers to the period extending from the 1950s through the 1960s as "Consent Without Advice." During this time the Senate was usually willing to follow the lead of the president; there was considerable bipartisan deference to the executive branch. Both parties were persuaded of the need for strong presidential leadership in foreign policy and encouraged the president to be assertive. "This is not to say that the Senate slavishly followed the White House's lead. Senators could be counted on to quibble with the details of the annual foreign aid budget and from time to time they demanded that more be spent on defense. But much of the Senate's activity on foreign policy addressed marginal issues," Lindsay writes.[27]

The next period, which Lindsay labels "Reclaiming Advice," extended from the 1970s through the 1980s. During this time, the Senate sought to assert itself on foreign policy with mixed results. Lindsay argues that Senate activism did not translate into commensurate influence over foreign policy. "Senators discovered that powers easily surrendered are not easily recaptured," he writes.[28] But the Senate did try to assert itself on foreign policy. It played a leading role in passing the War Powers Resolution in 1973, which tried to reassert the central role of Congress when it comes to taking the nation into war. The Church Committee, led by Senator Frank Church, conducted an aggressive probe of the U.S. intelligence community, and the Senate was at the forefront of efforts to cut off funding for the Vietnam War.

Lindsay describes a third period, extending from the 1990s until now, as "Advice, But Not Necessarily Consent." Senators frequently battle the White House over foreign policy. With the collapse of the Soviet Union, the country's much-feared cold war rival, U.S. lawmakers feel less constrained about challenging the administration on virtually all aspects of foreign policy. As an example, senators battled the Clinton administration over relations with China, involvement in the Balkans, assistance to Mexico, combat operations in Somalia, trade policy, and missile defense. An embattled Clinton described congressional asser-tiveness, much of it emanating from the Senate, as "nothing less than a frontal assault on the authority of the president to conduct the foreign policy of the United States." Lindsay argues this tendency toward unre-lenting confrontation was illustrated in the 1999 defeat of the Compre-hensive Test Ban Treaty. It was only the 21st time in American history that the Senate rejected a treaty, and it occurred after Clinton and 62 senators, including 24 Republicans, tried to delay the vote. But a group of conservative senators, sensing they were poised to defeat a key Clin-ton initiative, rejected pleas to delay it and forced the final vote.[29]

IV

Throughout American history the Senate Foreign Relations Com-mittee has been the institutional stronghold through which the Senate, and indeed the Congress, has sought to shape American foreign policy. Established in 1816 as one of the original ten standing committees of the Senate, it has been involved in the crafting of American foreign policy from the early years of the Republic through the purchase of Alaska in the nineteenth century, the debate on the Treaty of Versailles, creating the United Nations, and the passage of the Marshall Plan and the Gulf of

Tonkin Resolution. It has been one of Congress's most prestigious committees, with senators often vying for seats on the panel. Seven American presidents were members of the Foreign Relations Committee during their tenures in the Senate: Andrew Jackson, James Buchanan, Andrew Johnson, Benjamin Harrison, Warren Harding, John Kennedy, and Barack Obama. Nine U.S. vice presidents were members of the panel when they were in the Senate, as were 19 secretaries of state.[30]

The Foreign Relations Committee has been a powerful platform to debate and shape American foreign policy. Members can learn about the world, meet global leaders, travel internationally, and shape American foreign policy. With a broad mandate to oversee U.S. foreign policy, the Senate Foreign Relations Committee was regarded as the most important congressional committee for more than a century.[31] It has jurisdiction over diplomatic nominations, treaties, relations with the United Nations and affiliated organizations, arms control, legislation pertaining to U.S. foreign policy, the State Department, and foreign assistance programs. The panel oversees foreign economic, military, technical, and humanitarian assistance. It also has jurisdiction over international law as it relates to foreign policy, declarations of war, commercial relationships with foreign nations, and relations between the United States and foreign nations generally. The Foreign Relations Committee is the only committee of the Senate with jurisdiction to review and report to the Senate on treaties submitted by the president for advice and consent to ratification.[32]

Donald Matthews, author of the 1960 classic on the Senate, *U.S. Senators and Their World,* said the Foreign Relations Committee was for senators with large ambitions. "Service on Foreign Relations, for example, does not help many senators back home in their states—indeed, in most cases, it is a distinct liability—but it provides the best committee position from which to build a national reputation and launch an assault on the presidency."[33]

Two of Congress's foreign policy giants of the post–World War II era spent much of their careers on the committee and used it as a platform to shape American foreign policy in profound ways. Senator Arthur Vandenberg, a Republican from Michigan, served on the panel for several decades and had a decisive influence on American foreign relations. A former newspaper reporter, editor, and publisher from Grand Rapids, Vandenberg was elected to the Senate in 1928 and served on the panel from 1929 until his death in 1951.

At first an isolationist who defended neutrality legislation and op- posed U.S. entry into World War II, Vandenberg's worldview changed dramatically after Pearl Harbor. As the Republican chairman of the Foreign Relations panel from 1947 to 1949, he supported robust Ameri- can engagement with the world and played a critical role in helping the Truman administration secure bipartisan backing for the Truman Doctrine, the Marshall Plan, and the creation of NATO. He was a strong proponent of a bipartisan foreign policy and felt it was imperative to develop consensus policies through cooperation among the president, the State Department, and congressional leaders. Bipartisanship, in for- eign affairs, was essential, he believed. "In the face of any foreign policy problem, our unity is as important as our atom bombs," he said.[34]

Senator J. William Fulbright, a former university president and Democratic congressman from Arkansas, was first elected to the Senate in 1944. He joined the Foreign Relation Committee in 1949 and served as chairman from 1959 to 1974. He is the longest-serving chairman of the panel and, in the eyes of one analyst, "transformed the committee into a kind of miniature State Department."[35] A strong internationalist, Fulbright was the chief author of an international educational exchange program that is one of his main legacies: the Fulbright Scholars pro- gram. A frequent critic of American military interventions, Fulbright broke sharply with fellow Democrat President Lyndon Johnson, first over the U.S. invasion of the Dominican Republican and especially over Vietnam. In a case study of how a determined lawmaker can influence American policy, he held high-profile hearings in 1966 in the Senate Foreign Relations Committee on the Vietnam War that both reflected and intensified public skepticism about the war. He viewed these hear- ings as an important exercise in public education. Many historians be- lieve these hearings were important in causing the American public and opinion leaders to fundamentally reassess the wisdom of continuing American involvement in the war.

Fulbright was a prolific writer who published several popular books about America's role in the world. He frequently lamented that Congress had become too reticent to assert itself as a full partner with the executive in international affairs. "Out of a well-intentioned but misconceived notion of what patriotism and responsibility require in a time of world crisis, Congress has permitted the President to take over the two vital foreign policy powers which the Constitution vested in Congress: the power to initiate war and the Senate power to consent or withhold consent from significant foreign commitments," he said in an important speech. Congress, he argued, should use its foreign policy powers to pass or reject legislation, including military funding bills, to consent or withhold consent from proposed foreign commitments, and to authorize or refuse to authorize the initiation of war. "Congress has not only to start using these powers again: it has to reestablish its right to use them," he declared. Fulbright also argued that the most important service a legislator could perform is to challenge the executive branch and educate the public. He said Congress should let nothing of consequence go unquestioned or unexamined. The legislator's job, he argued, is to analyze, scrutinize, and criticize, responsibly and lawfully, but vigorously, candidly, and publicly. Congress, he believed, should help formulate American foreign policy.[36]

After Fulbright's defeat for re-election in 1974, the committee lost some of its luster. Experts say the decline of the Foreign Relations Committee has been due to a complex mix of personal and institutional factors. For one thing, the leadership of the Senate Foreign Relations panel passed on to chairmen who often came and went quietly. Fulbright's successors were far less forceful than he was and less insistent that the committee be at the center of critical foreign policy debates. Several of Fulbright's successors, such as Democrat Frank Church and Republican Chuck Percy, were defeated in their re-election campaigns. Senators came to view membership on the panel, and certainly leadership on it, as politically dangerous in a country that focuses on domestic issues.

Second, the committee has been unable to pass a foreign aid authorization bill since 1985, arguably its most tangible and important responsibility. This bill allows the committee to outline its views about U.S. foreign policy and to authorize specific programs to implement its vision. Committees that are unable or unwilling to pass legislation are usually seen as backwaters by lawmakers. Senator Chris Dodd, a long-time member of the Foreign Relations Committee, said that its consistent failure to pass a foreign assistance authorization bill has been central to its decline. "By frittering away its authorizing function, the Foreign Relations Committee became a largely irrelevant debating society," he said.[37]

In the last several decades, the Foreign Operations subcommittee of the Senate Appropriations Committee has become more important in setting American foreign policy than the Foreign Relations Committee. This appropriations subcommittee develops and passes the annual spending bill that allocates about $50 billion in annual funds for foreign policy programs. This bill is often the vehicle by which changes in foreign policy programs are moved through Congress. Policy measures that were once contained in the foreign aid authorization bill are now often placed in the annual spending bill.

Vice President Joe Biden, a member of the Foreign Relations Committee for more than 30 years, recalls that when he first entered the Senate in 1973 and sought out Fulbright's advice on how to become involved in foreign policy, the chairman of the Foreign Relations Committee told him that he could best do this by securing a seat on the Appropriations Committee.[38]

Johnson, author of the definitive account of Congress and the cold war, argues that the decline of the Foreign Relations Committee was fully evident by the late 1970s when Church took over its chairmanship. During the debate over the SALT II treaty in 1979, the committee's preeminence over an arms control treaty was indirectly challenged by the Senate Armed Services Committee even though it did not have jurisdiction over the treaty. The Foreign Relations Committee narrowly approved the treaty, but then the Senate Armed Services Committee voted to disapprove the same treaty, even though it had no formal jurisdiction over the matter. The vote by the Armed Services Committee was seen as a signal that it did not accept the Foreign Relations Committee's judgment in this matter.[39] When Republicans took control of the Senate in 1981, leadership of the committee went to Senator Charles Percy of Illinois. Percy's control of the committee was tenuous, as he was frequently challenged by some Democrats and, more seriously, from within his own party by Senator Jesse Helms. Percy was defeated for re-election in Illinois in 1984, with his opponent charging that Percy was more interested in global affairs than the developments in Illinois.

Two scholars, Linda Fowler and Brian Law, have written extensively about the Senate Foreign Relations Committee. They argue that it was a very consequential committee in crafting and sustaining the successful strategy of containment during the long years of the cold war. They say the committee also played a major role during the debate over the Vietnam War, forcefully challenging the wisdom of the war policy. Fowler and Law conclude the Foreign Relations Committee was the most prestigious committee in Congress until the mid-1970s, but since then its reputation and desirability have dropped sharply. They cite a committee ranking system called the Grosewart Index, which calculates the level of seniority on committees; they see this as a useful way to measure of the desirability of a committee. According to the Grosewart Index, the Foreign Relations Committee was the most prestigious Senate committee from the early twentieth century to the end of World War II. It remained a very important and respected committee for several decades but then fell in stature to below the Finance, Rules, Appropriations, and Armed Services Committees.[40]

Fowler and Law believe the decline of the Foreign Relations Committee can be partly traced to Senate changes in its committee system so that all senators are guaranteed a spot on one of the four so-called Super A Committees: Foreign Relations, Armed Services, Appropriations, and Finance. According to Fowler and Law, the Foreign Relations Committee has suffered from its Super A designation because junior senators are often placed on the committee to satisfy the requirement that everyone gets a top committee slot, but then they transfer off of the panel as soon as they can. The committee is well known as being the home to junior senators, many of whom leave it after a short period of time.[41] For example, in 2010, 13 of its 18 members were first-term senators.

They also note that the Foreign Relations Committee oversees the State Department and has jurisdiction over far fewer programs than does the Armed Services Committee, which oversees the Pentagon and the $550 billion annual defense budget. Additionally, some of the main programs the committee oversees, the foreign assistance programs, are typically unpopular with the public. As we have noted, the Foreign Relations Committee has not passed a foreign aid authorization bill since 1985, so any adjustments to foreign aid programs are now often passed in either an appropriations bill or the defense authorization bill that is written by the Armed Services Committee. In either case, the reputation of the Foreign Relations Committee is damaged.

Finally, many have observed that in the current era of costly political campaigns, the Foreign Relations Committee is a less useful committee to raise campaign funds from than are the Finance, Appropriations, Commerce, and Banking Committees. Former senator Chuck Hagel, who served on the Foreign Relations Committee throughout his 12-year Senate career, put the matter succinctly: "Foreign Relations has been a kind of wasteland. It is not a particularly strong committee to fundraise from."[42]

V

Even those who are skeptical about the institutional impact of Congress on foreign policy often acknowledge that individual lawmakers can shape foreign policy significantly. From Henry Clay to Henry Cabot Lodge to Charlie Wilson, American lawmakers have deeply influenced American foreign policy. A helpful way to examine the role of lawmakers in U.S. foreign policy is outlined by Carter and Scott in *Choosing to Lead*. They argue that when studying Congress's impact on foreign policy, it is instructive to examine individual lawmakers rather than Congress as a whole. They use the concept of "foreign policy entrepreneurs," whom they describe as members of Congress seeking to initiate action on certain foreign policy issues rather than wait for policy from the administration. Carter and Scott argue that foreign policy entrepreneurs try to shape foreign policy by either initiating a new policy or by changing a current policy.[43]

They divide the actions of foreign policy entrepreneurs into four categories. First, there is direct action in the legislative realm such as introducing legislation, sponsoring funding bills, or advocating for or against treaties. Second, there is direct action in the non-legislative realm such as holding congressional hearings or participating in oversight activities. Third, there is indirect action in the legislative realm.

This pertains to work on non-binding or procedural legislation. Finally, there is indirect action in the non-legislative realm such as helping frame the policy agenda through speeches, articles, or interviews.[44]

With this template in place, Carter and Scott examine foreign policy activity in Congress over the past 6 decades and identify foreign policy entrepreneurs playing a critical role. For example, they describe Senator Lyndon Johnson's work to create NASA, Congressman Henry Reuss's development of the idea of the Peace Corps, and Senator Church's legislation to end funding for the Vietnam War and to create House and Senate Intelligence Committees. They also outline House Speaker Jim Wright's advocacy of a Central American peace plan, Congressman Charlie Wilson's efforts to secure funds for Afghan rebels battling the Soviet army, and Congressman Chris Smith's work to curtail funds for abortion and population control programs.[45]

Carter and Scott describe Republican senator Jesse Helms as the most active and influential foreign policy entrepreneur of the post–World War II era. During his 30-year Senate career, Helms worked relentlessly to influence American foreign policy. He opposed many foreign assistance programs and tried to fundamentally overhaul the country's foreign affairs bureaucracy. He worked to limit American contributions to the UN and other international organizations. He opposed American arms control agreements with the Soviet Union. To advance his goals, Helms used virtually every tool available to a senator. He halted business meetings of the Foreign Relations Committee, held up hundreds of diplomatic nominations, and blocked scores of treaties and other international agreements, including START II and the Chemical Weapons Convention.[46]

Carter and Scott argue that congressional foreign policy entrepreneurs have been a significant feature of American foreign policy formulation and implementation. They have shaped the broad goals of foreign policy and they have the means to achieve those goals. As they see it, foreign policy entrepreneurs can work as "insider-incrementalists" as they try to achieve their goals quietly with an administration. They can also go the "legislative" route and try to create new laws, or they can embrace a "direct action" strategy in which they deal directly with international leaders. The particular strategy foreign policy entrepreneurs use often depends on whether they are in the same party as the president, whether their party is in the majority in their chamber in Congress, and what the particular policy context is. For example, policy vacuums often stimulate legislation, while policy corrections often call for either an "insider-incrementalist" or "direct action" strategy.[47]

Carter and Scott see Richard Lugar as a leading foreign policy entrepreneur of the post–World War II era. They say he has shaped American foreign policy by developing legislation, framing policy debates, and influencing colleagues.[48]

VI

As this review has demonstrated, Congress has considerable powers and authorities regarding foreign policy. Throughout American history, Congress has been a major force in formulating and implementing foreign policy. While there is a history of deference to the president, the Congress was clearly created to be a co-equal branch in this realm.

The Senate has historically been the more consequential of the two houses of Congress in the foreign policy realm given its higher profile and its special powers of advice and consent. The Senate Foreign Relations Committee has been the preeminent congressional panel involved in foreign policy. While its stature has faded in recent decades, it is still a formidable and powerful platform to shape foreign policy. Skilled and purposeful lawmakers, working in committees, informal partnerships, or alone, can shape foreign policy profoundly.

All of this context is important to consider as we examine Senator Richard Lugar's more than 35-year quest to shape American foreign policy from Capitol Hill.

4

A World Awash in Weapons

I

In May 2009, Richard Lugar attended a conference on Islam hosted by the Aspen Institute in Dubrovnik, Croatia. After the initial session concluded, Lugar left and headed for the airport, where he boarded a U.S. military plane for a 5-hour flight to Chelyabinsk, Russia, on the western edge of Siberia. The senator interrupted the comfort of the Aspen conference to attend the opening ceremonies of the Chemical Weapons Destruction Facility in Shchuchye. Lugar arrived at Chelyabinsk a little before midnight, checked into a Holiday Inn, and was on the road by 7 the next morning for the 2.5-hour drive to Shchuchye. This trip, Lugar's fourth visit to Shchuchye, represented the culmination of a long struggle to help build this chemical weapons destruction facility in Russia.

Lugar's more than decade-long battle to support Russia's construction of this facility included tense congressional tussles with those who opposed helping Russia until it behaved better in the world and fully adhered to its obligations under treaties it signed regarding the elimination of biological and chemical weapons. The Shchuchye project ran into serious cost overruns, disputes with contractors, misunderstandings with Russian officials, and bewildering certification requirements in American law. On at least a dozen occasions over the past decade, Lugar interceded to keep the project on track. He made calls to Secretary of State Condoleezza Rice and personal pleas to President George W. Bush, sent letters to congressional colleagues, and maneuvered to push America's funding commitments through Congress and the complex Pentagon bureaucracy.[1] Lugar viewed the building of a state-of-the-art chemical weapons destruction facility in Russia as hugely important for practical and symbolic reasons. To help get it built, he took on multiple roles: senior statesman, legislative dealmaker, international diplomat, and bureaucratic operative.

The nearly two million chemical weapons that will eventually be destroyed in this facility were housed for years in 14 dilapidated wood buildings. Sam Nunn was shocked when he first saw the ramshackle buildings and quipped that he wouldn't keep a good horse in them—let alone a huge arsenal of deadly weapons.[2] After intense collaboration among the United States, Russia, Canada, the European Union, the Czech Republic, Italy, Norway, Switzerland, and the United Kingdom, the facility was about to open. A temporary bandstand-like structure had been constructed for the opening ceremony on a parade field outside the facility. Lugar was given 5 minutes to explain why a chemical destruction plant on the edge of Siberia was important to Russia, America, and the world. "The path to peace and prosperity for both Russia and the United States depends on how we resolve the threats posed by arsenals built to fight World War III. Thankfully, that confrontation never came. But today we must ensure that the weapons are never used, and never fall into the hands of those who would do harm to us or others." Lugar recalled that in 1991 he and Nunn understood that a unilateral American effort to address the threats posed by weapons of mass destruction would not succeed. Working within the Congress, they created a new program to provide American funds and technical expertise to help safeguard and then dismantle stockpiles of nuclear, chemical, and biological weapons in the former Soviet Union. "We challenged the United States and our former enemies to work together," he said, referring to the creation of the Nunn-Lugar program. This program helped persuade Kazakhstan, Ukraine, and Belarus to give up their nuclear arsenals and led to years of collaboration between the United States and Russia to secure and then destroy Russia's weapons and nuclear materials.[3]

The Nunn-Lugar program, the senator said, is the primary tool through which the United States still works with Russia to safely destroy nuclear, chemical, and biological arsenals. He noted that the United States and Russia, working cooperatively, had eliminated more nuclear weapons than the combined arsenals of the United Kingdom, France, and China. "Even during moments of tension between our two countries, the Nunn-Lugar program has remained a constant," he said proudly. Lugar acknowledged that the journey to complete Shchuchye had been complicated, arduous, and sometimes acrimonious. "The road to this day has not been smooth. There have been delays caused by the apprehension of the U.S. Congress, bureaucratic obstruction, problems with Russian funding, and contractor disputes. Through it all, Americans and Russians worked together to resolve difficult challenges. The product of their efforts stands behind me today," he said.

The experience of the Nunn-Lugar program in Russia, the senator said, demonstrated that the threat of weapons of mass destruction could lead to extraordinary outcomes based on mutual interests. As dangers emerge in other countries he urged the United States and Russia to use their partnership to aggressively pursue non-proliferation opportunities that might appear around the world. That joint work has already produced impressive results beyond the borders of Russia. A new generation of leaders in Albania used personnel trained, and expertise developed, in Shchuchye to destroy a stash of chemical weapons found in their country. The success in Albania, Lugar declared, owed much to the important lessons learned from cooperating at Shchuchye.

Lugar concluded on a hopeful note. "Our policies toward one another have frequently been characterized by ambiguities and difficult choices. But this facility is testament to the fact that we can make progress on areas of collaboration that are essential to our common interests. I remain optimistic that we will summon the courage and perseverance required to move our nations toward mutual successes."[4]

II

During the protracted cold war struggle between the United States and the Soviet Union, the issue of weapons of mass destruction rarely came up in political discussions as a discrete problem. The two super-powers were armed with nuclear, biological, and chemical weapons and these arsenals were seen as manifestations of a geopolitical rivalry be-tween the two great powers. In other words, the rivalry was the prob-lem; the arsenal of weapons was just a symptom. In the last 20 years of the cold war, the United States and Soviet Union participated in wide-ranging arms control negotiations to limit and ultimately reduce their nuclear arsenals. And both nations signed global treaties to eliminate chemical and biological weapons.

When the Soviet Union came apart in 1991, American policymakers had to confront the profound and unexpected challenge of dealing with the sudden collapse of a global superpower with a massive arsenal of nuclear, chemical, and biological weapons. Lugar had serious apprehen-sions about the security of the estimated 25,000 to 30,000 operational nuclear warheads that were deployed in four of the Soviet Republics and on Soviet submarines. He joined with the conservative Democratic senator Sam Nunn to confront this problem. Nunn was elected to the Senate from Georgia in 1972. In 1991, he was the chairman of the Senate Armed Services Committee and happened to be in Moscow during that summer. While meeting with then Soviet leader Mikhail Gorbachev, Nunn was deeply shaken by the strong suspicion that Gorbachev had not been in full control of the Soviet nuclear arsenal during a coup at-tempt just weeks earlier.[5]

Trying to find a way to help the Soviet Union secure its weapons, Nunn worked with House Armed Services Committee Chairman Les Aspin to craft a $1 billion assistance package for the USSR. The two dif-fered on what the focus of the funding should be but ultimately reached a compromise that was later rejected by Congress. Lawmakers from both parties argued that the first installment of the country's so-called peace dividend, a reduction in defense spending, should be directed to American domestic needs. Nunn then approached Lugar and suggested a collaboration. He showed Lugar a report by security expert Ashton Carter, from Harvard University, on how the United States could help safeguard and then help dismantle nuclear weapons in the collapsing Soviet state. The thrust of Carter's paper was that aggressive, out-of-the-box thinking and bilateral cooperation between the United States and the crumbling Soviet Union was needed to protect the latter's nuclear arsenal.

Lugar and Nunn convened a bipartisan meeting of Democratic and Republican senators to discuss Carter's paper and consider a legislative response. They crafted the Soviet Nuclear Threat Reduction Act of 1991 that would provide up to $500 million in assistance to the states of the former Soviet Union for safeguarding and dismantling their weapons of mass destruction. The funds were to come from the Pentagon's budget. The group worked with virtually no participation by the first Bush administration—and few signs of interest. The two senators initially met with skepticism and even resistance from other members of Congress. But they each met with small groups of colleagues to explain why the assistance program to the Soviet Union was in America's national interest. They were persuasive and the slightly revised Nunn-Lugar amendment with $400 million in funds for the program was approved by the Senate 4 days later on a vote of 86 to 8. The House followed suit the next day by an overwhelming vote. Lugar believes the wide margin of the vote was indispensable to establishing the credibility of the program. Since the program lacked an executive branch advocate, Lugar was convinced that it required close oversight and strong political support from Congress if it was to succeed.[6]

The two authors of the Nunn-Lugar program are quick to acknowledge that their program began as an emergency, even ad hoc, response to an unforeseen problem. From the beginning there was resistance to the Nunn-Lugar concept in both the United States and Russia. In the United States, opposition often has been fueled by the view that Nunn-Lugar money is foreign assistance or by the belief that Pentagon funds should only be spent on troops, weapons, or other war fighting capabilities. Lugar says that latent and persistent cold war attitudes toward Russia have led some critics of the program to be suspicious of the very concept of cooperation with Moscow. Some Russian officials have long suspected that the United States had an ulterior motive in developing this program: to get an extensive inside look at the military infrastructure built by the Soviet Union during the cold war and to use this to find military vulnerabilities in its successor states, including Russia.[7]

Once the program was launched, the two senators pushed for a gradual expansion of Nunn-Lugar from a narrow focus on safeguarding strategic nuclear weaponry in the former Soviet Union to more broadly preventing the theft of weapons of mass destruction, including chemical and biological weapons. The original program has evolved from an emergency effort in the Defense Department into a broader, multidepartment attempt to keep WMD, the materials to build them, and the talent behind them out of the hands of hostile states and terrorist organizations. With the help of others, including Republican senator Pete Domenici of New Mexico, the Nunn-Lugar concept expanded into a family of related programs run by the Defense, State, and Energy Departments. Lugar helped push through Congress the Nunn-Lugar Expansion Act that President George W. Bush signed in 2003. This allowed $50 million in Nunn-Lugar funding to be used outside the former Soviet Union. The authority was first used in Albania in 2004 to begin construction of a facility that eventually destroyed all 16 tons of Albania's previously secret chemical weapons.

The focus on terrorism was further reinforced by a high-level White House task force report in early 2001 chaired by former Senate Majority Leader Howard Baker and former White House counsel Lloyd Cutler. The report argued that the theft of WMD-related materials from Russia and their use in the United States was the "most urgent unmet national security threat" facing the United States. The terrorist attacks of September 11, 2001, deepened concern across the country about what would happen if terrorists got their hands on weapons of mass destruction.[8]

After nearly 20 years of sometimes purposeful, often improvisational, evolution, the Nunn-Lugar program is a complex of programs that are spread over three executive branch agencies, Defense, Energy, and State, at a cost of about $1 billion a year. Since their inception, the U.S. government has spent about $20 billion on what are now called cooperative threat reduction programs. By the fall of 2011, the Nunn-Lugar program had deactivated or destroyed 7,600 strategic nuclear warheads, nearly 800 intercontinental ballistic missiles, 500 ICBM silos, 155 bombers, 194 nuclear test tunnels, and 33 nuclear submarines capable of launching ballistic missiles. It had also built and equipped

34 biological monitoring stations.[9] Lugar argues the program's most important accomplishment is that Ukraine, Belarus, and Kazakhstan are no longer home to nuclear weapons. In 1991, they were the third, fourth, and eighth largest nuclear weapons powers in the world. Beyond nuclear, chemical, and biological elimination, the Nunn-Lugar program has worked to redeploy scientists and facilities related to w m d to peaceful research initiatives. Moscow's International Science and Technology Centers, of which the United States is the leading sponsor, hired 58,000 former weapons scientists in peaceful work. The International Proliferation Prevention Program has funded 750 projects involving 14,000 former weapons scientists and created some 580 peaceful high-tech jobs.

Nunn retired from the Senate in 1996; he continues to aggressively support the program as a private citizen and as the president of the Nuclear Threat Initiative, a non-governmental organization devoted to reducing the global threats from chemical, biological, and nuclear weapons. Lugar continues to support the program vigorously in Congress. He travels regularly to examine how the Nunn-Lugar program is working on the ground, usually accompanied by several staffers and by senior officials from the executive branch who run the program in the United States. They meet with leaders and technicians from the various countries in which the program is in place to understand what practical issues need to be resolved.

III

Most experts agree that the initial Nunn-Lugar program and its progeny have been effective, even inspired, government programs. But many say they have been too modest given the challenge the world is confronting. The United States has spent only $20 billion over nearly 20 years for these programs to address what Lugar calls an existential threat. By way of contrast, the United States spent $10 billion a month during various phases of the war in Iraq.

Joseph Cirincione, president of the Ploughshares Fund and a noted nuclear expert, said the Nunn-Lugar program has been successful but far too limited. He argues that the program has safeguarded or eliminated about half of the nuclear material in the former Soviet states, but the other half remains, under varying degrees of security. He adds that after 9/11 and the Iraq War, the danger of nuclear terrorism greatly increased, but the programs that can prevent it have languished.[10]

In a comprehensive review of cooperative non-proliferation programs several years ago, the Henry L. Stimson Center, a Washington-based think tank, concluded the programs have been very successful. But, the Stimson Center report argued, despite their broad success in containing the spread of nuclear, biological, and chemical weapons, materials, and expertise, the potential of these programs had not been fully realized due to bureaucratic obstacles, a sustained lack of White House and congressional support, and lingering vestiges of cold war suspicion. The Stimson study said that America's partners in the former Soviet Union have not been fully reliable. But it also identified several important areas in which the U.S. government has not distinguished itself.

First, while these programs were created during a time of great uncertainty in the early 1990s, there has been little effort to systematically align and prioritize existing programs with current threats. This has resulted in a raft of underperforming programs, some of which are directed at dated threats and others that fail to maximize return on national security investment. The Stimson study also said U.S. non-proliferation programs are hampered by unrealistic expectations. The Russians tend to think the United States has overpromised and under-delivered. And American officials, especially lawmakers, question why a now-prosperous Russia isn't doing more to pay its own way. These programs also confront an ongoing dilemma: lawmakers in general have little interest in them yet demand detailed reports on the programs' progress.[11]

Elizabeth Turpen, a non-proliferation expert at Stimson and one of the co-authors of the report, says one of the main weaknesses of U.S. programs is that they have not successfully tackled the challenge of finding meaningful employment for the thousands of scientists from the former Soviet Union who were involved in WMD work. The Soviet Union's ten closed nuclear cities employed more than 150,000 nuclear scientists, and its WMD complex also employed 65,000 biological weapons specialists and more than 6,000 chemical weapons experts. "None of the advances that have been made under these programs are sustainable unless these Russian scientists have been given long-term employment in other places. This is the key to irreversibility, of shoring up the gains we've made," Turpen says. She also argues that non-proliferation programs have not been funded at appropriate levels, in part because lawmakers and congressional staff do not understand them and there is little political payoff for supporting them. "These programs have never been organized to be commensurate with the threat we face. It's a classic illustration about how hard it is to get funds for prevention. The problem is funding prevention. Peace is a non-event. You can never prove how many dirty bombs have been prevented. The numbers are hard to understand. The metrics are fuzzy," she says.[12]

IV

Richard Lugar says that he is proud of what has been accomplished under the Nunn-Lugar program and determined to keep pushing for its expansion. The proliferation of weapons of mass destruction is the number one national security threat facing the United States and the international community. He says that creativity and constant vigilance are required to ensure the Nunn-Lugar program is not encumbered by bureaucratic obstacles, starved by inadequate funding, or undercut by political disagreements. The United States should not complicate its own efforts to destroy WMD with self-imposed bureaucratic red tape. He also argues that more resources are needed to capitalize on opportunities to advance the threat reduction process.

The senator pushed for a $100 million funding increase in 2007 so that critical biological projects would be supported and dangerous pathogens such as anthrax, plague, smallpox, hemorrhagic fever, and avian influenza would not be left unprotected and vulnerable to theft or diversion. Lugar ultimately secured $80 million and with these funds the United States began projects in seven additional countries. He also inserted language in a defense spending bill that directed $5 million of the Nunn-Lugar budget be appropriated for chemical weapons destruction in Libya. Lugar says that while the program continues its important work in addressing threats in the former Soviet Union, new challenges are emerging. He supports the extension of the Nunn-Lugar program into North Korea, Pakistan, and Iran if those countries reach agreements with the United States. And he envisions a day when U.S. and Russian non-proliferation teams work together to secure WMD around the world.[13]

Many members of Congress believe their job is simply to write good laws and then rely on the executive branch to implement them. That is not Lugar's inclination, especially given that the Nunn-Lugar program has usually had only modest support from the executive branch. So the senator has been very active in making sure his most important legislative legacy continues to solve the problems it was designed to solve. Lugar gives regular speeches about the status of Nunn-Lugar, touting its successes, acknowledging its limitations, pleading for additional support, and outlining new areas in which it can be used to advance the national interest. He issues a monthly press release describing how many weapons were destroyed the previous month as well as an end-of-the-year summary to highlight the year's accomplishments. In his office conference room in the Senate Hart Building, he displays a large Nunn-Lugar scoreboard on a wall that tracks the program's accomplishments, as well as photos and artifacts from visits to sites.

Lugar and his staff keep in regular contact with officials in the Pentagon and State and Energy Departments who run the various Nunn-Lugar programs to learn what their practical concerns are and how they can ease them. One of the senator's top assistants for more than a decade, Kenneth A. Myers III, was appointed by President Obama in 2009 to head the Defense Threat Reduction Agency, the agency responsible for implementing Nunn-Lugar.

Lugar is also looking for ways to expand and modernize the program; he is convinced the proliferation problem is far more serious than the response by U.S. government—and other governments—would suggest. The senator seized on a report that was released in the spring of 2009 by the National Academy of Sciences that said the Nunn-Lugar program has been a major success but should be updated, restructured, and expanded. A restructuring could provide the security and destruction of chemical weapons stockpiles in the Middle East, biological safety, security and disease surveillance programs in Africa and Asia, and border security and counterproliferation assistance in Asia and the Middle East.[14]

The findings were music to Lugar's ears. He praised the report and said it argued persuasively that the Nunn-Lugar program should be expanded geographically, updated in form and function, and supported as an active tool of foreign policy. The senator noted a number of the recommendations did not require legislation and could be implemented by the administration immediately. Then he introduced legislation that would give the Nunn-Lugar program more flexibility for future work in unforeseen locations around the world. It would allow the Pentagon to shift up to 10 percent of Nunn-Lugar funds for bilateral and multilateral activities relating to non-proliferation or disarmament and would expand the scope of the program to allow it to secure biological pathogens. And within a few weeks of introducing his legislation, Lugar managed to get most of it tucked into a defense authorization bill moving through the Senate. It did not make the day's news cycle, but Lugar managed to quietly give his signature program a nudge into the future.[15]

In the late fall of 2010, even as the Senate was gearing up for an important debate on an arms control treaty, Lugar led a team of Pentagon arms control experts on a trip to Africa to inspect labs in Kenya and Uganda that are designed to study infectious diseases and facilitate treatment to prevent outbreaks. Lugar was concerned there is insufficient security at these labs and that terrorists might target them in an effort to obtain biological weapons. "Deadly diseases like Ebola, Marburg, and Anthrax are prevalent naturally in Africa," Lugar said during the nearly weeklong trip, which emphasized his program's new name, Nunn-Lugar Global. "These pathogens can be made into horrible weapons more simply than any dealing with chemical or nuclear devices. Just one of the deadly viruses I witnessed could, if in the wrong hands, cause death and economic chaos."[16] Lugar said the stakes could not be higher: "We cannot wait for terrorists to get their hands on these terrible diseases. We cannot wait for local outbreaks to spread as worldwide pandemics."

Lugar and his team concluded their Africa trip by stopping in Burundi to examine the workings of a program that is an offshoot of the Nunn-Lugar program. The program, which he developed with then senator Barack Obama, seeks to secure conventional weapons that could be used in civil wars, regional conflicts, or attacks by terrorists.

5

✦

Ending the American Addiction
to Foreign Oil

I

On a cold, windy late October day in 2006, Richard Lugar sat in a small storefront office in Fowler, Indiana, sipping coffee from a Styrofoam cup and listening to a discussion about the power of wind. Seated next to two state legislators, Lugar paid close attention as Wayne Hoffman, the president of Orion Energy, walked through a detailed PowerPoint presentation about the potential of a wind farm, then under construction in Benton County, a farming community in central Indiana. Hoffman made the case that wind energy could be critical to the future of the state while also producing profits for his company. Wind energy, he said, is a free, inexhaustible, and widely available domestic resource. It generates electricity in a way that does not pollute the air or water, nor does it emit greenhouse gases. Hoffman argued that wind energy is a hedge against continuing increases in the cost of fossil fuels and increasing restrictions on pollution from fossil fueled power plants. Moving from the big picture to the specific, Hoffman pointed out that Orion's project in Benton County could be a significant energy and economic asset for the town of Fowler and the surrounding area. He walked through the details of the project and said that if all went well, Orion might be interested in building up to eight hundred towers with wind generators, making the Benton County wind farm the largest in the United States, and might build additional farms in Indiana if this project was successful.

Lugar nodded his head politely throughout the presentation and asked probing, politely stated questions. The senator observed that based on his study of the numbers it would initially cost Orion more to produce electricity than the firm would get for selling it. How long was this sustainable from Orion's perspective? When did it expect to turn a profit on the Benton project? "You have a great eye for detail," Hoffman said and then launched into a lengthy discourse on how Orion would recover its expenses over time and eventually make money.

Lugar had more questions about the company, the project, and its financial implications for central Indiana. He knew, for example, that the firm was anticipating the renewal of a federal tax credit and the implementation of a state or federal rule mandating the use of renewable energy to generate a certain amount of electricity. Such actions were possible but not certain. Nonetheless, Lugar remained upbeat and encouraging and said the project that Hoffman was describing would propel Indiana in a positive direction. He emphasized his "fascination and now enthusiasm and almost evangelical attitude" toward renewable energy alternatives. Developing these renewables, he said, would be critical to the country's and Indiana's future prosperity. "In Indiana we have a lot of catching up to do. That's why I'm so passionate about it, trying to push everyone to the nth degree."

Broadening the discussion and connecting the resources in Indiana with the global politics of energy and his work on the Senate Foreign Relations Committee, Lugar recalled a meeting he had with Col. Muammar Qaddafi in a tent in the Libyan desert to talk about oil and global politics. The local government officials, farmers, business leaders, and local press sat up in their chairs as Lugar described his encounter with Qaddafi. The details of the conversation were less interesting than the image of the senator from Indiana huddled in a tent in Libya with Qaddafi. But Lugar made his main point clearly and forcefully. "We are living in a world in which we are not going to have these oil reserves forever. Rather than having a big crisis in Indiana or the United States, the wind is blowing here; they can't take that away from us. This is ours. So is the corn in our fields and the soybeans. It's here and now. We should begin to forge our own energy independence. Some of us will have to push and shove very hard," he said. Lugar thanked Hoffman and those at the meeting for providing him with an education on wind energy. "I'm hoping to hear about other windmills soon. We're on the threshold of some very promising things."[1] The Benton County Wind Farm began commercial operation in April 2008 with 87 wind turbines, and in early 2009, the nearby Fowler Ridge Wind Farm became the second wind farm in Indiana. Two others opened later that year, and by 2010, Indiana ranked tenth among all states in wind power capacity.[2]

But on that fall day in 2006, Lugar was on the first day of a weeklong, thousand-mile trip across Indiana. Traveling just 2 weeks before the November 2006 mid-term elections, he had good reason to be relaxed. He was running unopposed for his sixth term as a senator and was the only senator up for re-election who did not have a major party opponent. With his re-election certain, Lugar decided to use the several million dollars in his campaign war chest to conduct a public education campaign about the imperative for the United States to develop new energy technologies and embrace new policies. In his speeches, ads, and on his campaign website, he argued that energy is the albatross of U.S. national security. Unless the nation adopted a more visionary energy policy, it faced a real long-term risk of economic and political decline.

Lugar predicted that oil could become an even stronger magnet for conflict and threats of military action than it already was at the time. So the United States must start down a new path of energy independence. He urged the people of Indiana to join with him to promote domestic alternatives to oil, including ethanol and wind energy, and to embrace the ethic of conservation and stewardship. To emphasize his beliefs, Lugar set up this energy tour of Indiana, in which he crisscrossed the state in a flexible fuel car using a special E85 fuel of 15 percent regular gasoline and 85 percent ethanol. With his native Indiana in full October splendor and with campaign signs dotting the stunning autumn countryside, Lugar took to the road as a kind of traveling energy evangelist. He visited innovators in electricity generation, including Hoffman from Orion, and with executives of I-Power in Anderson, producers of advanced portable generators. He traveled to Wabash River Energy, a clean coal power generating facility in Terre Haute, and to Midwest ISO, the

Carmel-based nerve center of the electrical grid for 15 states. He toured Altair Nanotechnologies, the Anderson company that is developing batteries for the next generation of hybrid cars; Evergreen Renewables, a soy-diesel processing plant in Hammond; and the construction site of a new ethanol plant in Marion. He spent an afternoon touring Fair Oaks Dairy, a massive farm that used tons of cow manure to produce a million gallons of ethanol each year. Along the way, Lugar refueled at gas stations with E85 pumps, stopping in small towns like Lebanon, Reynolds, and Noblesville. At each carefully scheduled and staged stop he would meet with farmers, business leaders, government officials, students, entrepreneurs, and the local press, eager to preach his energy doctrine. Lugar told the gathered crowds that Indiana should lead the nation into a vibrant and prosperous energy future. Shifting from the lofty to the practical and mixing the big picture with the nitty-gritty, he said that ethanol and bio-diesel plants could be a major part of a rural economic revolution in Indiana that would create thousands of jobs and ensure strong economic growth. At every stop, he declared that there was no more important issue that confronted the United States from a foreign policy standpoint, and he vowed to spend his next term in Washington working passionately on energy. "This is what my life is going to be like for the next 6 years. These things don't happen overnight. We still have a long way to go. Senate terms are long enough and if you are re-elected sufficiently you can outlast your opponents. I think in many of these issues we'll prevail."[3]

As he traveled across Indiana, Lugar's trademark style was on display. Dogged and disciplined, he listened carefully, absorbed information, and asked practical questions. Connecting one briefing to the next, he integrated insights from each stop into his narrative about the energy challenges and opportunities for Indiana and the United States. At each stop he talked with experts, posed for photographs with local officials, and chatted with the press before moving on to the next event.

At the end of that weeklong tour, Lugar said he wanted to be an "agent provocateur" on energy policy in the Senate, a leader "who keeps pushing the envelope relentlessly and even gets people to leap outside the envelope." "For me," he said, "this is not fooling around with interesting new projects, but a fundamental feeling that our national security depends on our working on this. The American people have not been that excited about alternative fuels. It will take a while. That's why I'll keep talking about it. This is very important. Our future depends on it."[4]

II

While interested in a wide range of international issues, Lugar is especially focused on what he calls the main existential challenges facing the United States: controlling the spread of weapons of mass destruction and energy independence. Lugar's interest in energy brings together many strands of his public passions: international affairs, global economics, climate change, generational stewardship, agriculture, and ethanol-propelled prosperity for Indiana. A man who is not given to hyperbole, he often uses the word "revolutionary" when talking about the kind of changes that are needed in American energy policy, and he argues that the country's future depends on the nation transforming its approach to energy. As mayor of Indianapolis, he observed the energy crisis of the 1970s from the vantage point of the leader of a major midwestern city that grew very unhappy with long lines and soaring gas prices. He brought his interest in energy to his work in the Senate when he arrived in 1977. Through his work on the Senate Foreign Relations and Agriculture Committees he developed a view of energy as a state, national, and global issue with economic and national security implications.

When he assumed the chairmanship of the Agriculture Committee in 1995, Lugar launched a series of hearings on energy policy and began pushing a national ethanol research program. Ethanol is a fuel converted from biomass materials, including Indiana corn, and used in combination with gasoline to form gasohol. During these Agriculture Committee hearings, Lugar listened to dozens of experts and deepened his conviction that ethanol would be good for the energy and economic future of his state and the country. One of the witnesses who caught Lugar's attention was former Central Intelligence Agency director James Woolsey, who testified on the virtues of cellulosic ethanol, which is made from many kinds of urban, agricultural, and forestry sources. Woolsey and Lugar began to collaborate, and in 1999 they co-authored

"The New Petroleum" in the journal *Foreign Affairs*. The essay linked American foreign policy and the high cost of securing the foreign oil flowing to the United States with the development of homegrown ethanol derived from any form of cellulose.[5] Lugar and Woolsey argued that a new American energy policy is needed because the struggle to control oil is a major source of conflict around the world. Well over two-thirds of the world's remaining oil reserves are in the Middle East and the Caspian Basin, leaving the rest of the world dependent on that region's collection of unsavory regimes and unappealing autocrats. This heavy reliance on Middle Eastern oil not only adds to that region's disproportionate leverage but also provides the resources with which rogue nations support international terrorism, and it allows them to develop weapons of mass destruction and the ballistic missiles to deliver them. Lugar and Woolsey also noted that the possibility that greenhouse gases will lead to catastrophic climate change is substantially increased by what was then 40 million barrels of oil burned every day by motor vehicles.

Lugar and Woolsey said that recent and prospective breakthroughs in genetic engineering and processing are radically changing the viability of cellulosic ethanol as a transportation fuel. Cellulosic ethanol would radically improve the outlook for rural areas throughout the world. Farmers could produce a cash crop simply by collecting agricultural wastes or harvesting grasses or crops natural to their region. Agricultural nations with little or no petroleum reserves would begin to see economic stability and prosperity as they steadily reduced massive payments for oil imports. Cellulosic ethanol, they declared, is the only alternative fuel that requires, at most, modest changes to vehicles and the transportation infrastructure. It is a first-class transportation fuel, able to power today's cars as well as tomorrow's, use the vast infrastructure already built for gasoline, and become a part of the transportation system quickly and easily. It can be shipped in standard rail cars and tank trucks and is easily mixed with gasoline.

"Our growing independence on increasingly scarce Middle Eastern oil is a fool's game—there is no way for the rest of the world to win. Our losses may come suddenly through war, steadily through price increases, agonizingly through developing-nation poverty, relentlessly through climate change—or all of the above," they wrote. "It would be extremely short-sighted not to take advantage of the scientific breakthroughs that have occurred and that are in the offing, accelerate them, and move smartly toward ameliorating all of these risks by beginning to substitute carbohydrates for hydrocarbons. If we do, we will make life far less dangerous and far more prosperous for future generations. If we do not, those generations will look back in angry wonder at the remarkable opportunity we missed."[6]

III

Among the hearings that Lugar scheduled in the Senate Foreign Relations Committee on the nation's energy challenge, the one that sparked the most interest featured former Federal Reserve Board Chairman Alan Greenspan, who was back on Capitol Hill in June of 2006 for his first congressional testimony since retiring a few months earlier. Anticipating a large crowd and plenty of reporters, Lugar's staff moved the hearing from the Foreign Relations Committee's regular hearing room to one of the largest hearing rooms in the Senate.

Lugar said his panel was interested in a getting a clearer picture of how high energy prices affected the U.S. economy, how the American economy could react to supply disruptions, and what steps the United States should take to reduce the economic risks of its energy vulnerability. Speaking with his trademark complexity, Greenspan described how the balance of the world's oil supply and demand had become so precarious that even small acts of sabotage or local insurrection have a significant impact on oil prices. He noted that even before the devastating hurricanes of the previous summer, world oil markets had been subject to a degree of strain not experienced for a generation.[7] World oil production stood at about 85 million barrels a day and little excess capacity remained. The buffer between supply and demand was much too small to absorb shutdowns of even a small part of the world's oil production. The former Fed chairman also pointed out that the country's voracious appetite for oil is helping create the fragility in global markets. Greenspan noted that one out of every seven barrels of oil produced in the world is consumed on American highways.

But Greenspan saw a silver lining; the current period of pain might cause Americans to make better long-term decisions about energy production and consumption. "Current oil prices over time should lower to some extent our worrisome dependence on petroleum. Still higher oil prices will inevitably move vehicle transportation to hybrids, and despite the inconvenience, plug-in hybrids. Corn ethanol, though variable, can play only a limited role, because its ability to displace gasoline is modest at best. But cellulosic ethanol, should it fulfill its promise, would help to wean the United States of its petroleum dependence, as could clean coal and nuclear power. With those developments, oil in the years ahead will remain an important element of our energy future, but it need no longer be the dominant player."[8]

This hearing was part of a series of hearings Lugar's Foreign Relations panel organized to link the issue of energy with foreign policy and elevate the topic in the public mind. It garnered solid coverage by several Capitol Hill publications and gave Lugar a platform from which to continue outlining the energy challenges the United States faced to the public and other policymakers. Under Lugar's chairmanship, his panel held sessions on the high costs of crude, the hidden costs of oil, energy security and oil independence, oil dependence and economic risk, and energy in the context of U.S. relationships with India, China, the Persian Gulf states, Latin America, and Russia. The public hearings were not designed to produce a specific bill but to frame the debate on energy policy. Lugar believes that senators are often most effective when they use their mini bully pulpits to describe problems, identify possible solutions, and educate other lawmakers, the executive branch, and the wider public.

Lugar was determined to use his chairmanship of the Senate Foreign Relations Committee to teach the nation and the world about the perils of oil dependence. In 2006, he launched a long-term global public education campaign on energy. In February of that year he traveled to New York to give a wide-ranging foreign policy speech to the United Nations Security Council. It is very rare for a member of Congress to address the UN Security Council, and Lugar used the opportunity to tell the council that the potential scarcity of energy supplies and imbalances that exist among nations represent grave threats to global security and prosperity. He noted that up to this point in history, the main concerns surrounding oil and natural gas have been how much is paid for them and whether supply disruptions occur. But in decades to come, the issue may be whether the world's supply of fossil fuels is abundant and accessible enough to support continued economic growth, both in the industrialized West and in large, rapidly growing economies such as China and India. He explained that when the world reaches the point that oil-hungry economies are competing for insufficient supplies of energy, fossil fuels would become an even stronger magnet for conflict than they already are.

Lugar said that in the short run, dependence on fossil fuels has created a drag on economic performance around the world, as higher oil prices have driven up heating and transportation costs. In the long run, this dependence is pushing the world toward an economic disaster that could mean diminished living standards, increased risks of war, and accelerated environmental degradation. Increasingly, he said, energy supplies are the currency through which energy-rich countries leverage their interests against energy-poor nations. "The bottom line is that critical international security goals, including countering nuclear weapons proliferation, supporting new democracies, and promoting sustainable development, are at risk because of overdependence on fossil fuels."[9]

The following month Lugar accepted an invitation from the Brookings Institution to deliver a major energy speech. He asserted that the exploding demand for energy, the vulnerability of energy supplies to terrorism and warfare, the increasing concentration of energy assets in the hands of unfriendly governments, the growing willingness of these governments to use energy as geopolitical weapons, and the evidence that climate change has accelerated have all fundamentally altered the energy debate. Therefore, "the balance of realism" in U.S. energy policy had shifted from the proponents of a fossil fuel–based, laissez-faire approach relying on market evolution to advocates of energy alternatives who recognize the imperative of a reorientation of the way the United States uses and obtains energy. In the absence of a revolutionary change in U.S. energy policy, the nation was risking a future that would constrain living standards, undermine foreign policy goals, and leave the United States vulnerable to "economic and political disasters with an almost existential impact." The new energy realist, Lugar said, must ask, "how can we shape our energy future before it shapes us in calamitous ways?"[10]

A few months later, Lugar appeared at a forum on energy issues sponsored by Foreign Policy magazine. Moderated by the magazine's editor, Moises Naim, Lugar joined New York Times columnist Tom Friedman at a session that was televised live by C-SPAN and replayed several times that week. Lugar repeated his main themes about the need for the United States to take big steps to become independent of oil. He urged his fellow lawmakers and the White House to think in larger and more creative ways about energy. Lugar said America's energy dependence had become a limiting force in U.S. foreign policy. He pointed to Russia's threat a few months earlier to shut off shipments of natural gas to Ukraine. He said the incident showed that nations that can control the flow of oil could wield substantial power on global politics and economics. "As more than three-quarters of all oil and natural gas and reserves are now controlled by governments, not private firms, it's dawning on people in this country that we are strategically vulnerable."[11]

At the event, Lugar implored the State Department to pay more attention to energy and to initiate "big conversations" with China, India, and other nations on the need for energy efficiency and the importance of greater use of renewables. Intriguingly, Lugar suggested that major American reforms on energy policy might be linked to the overhaul of key domestic programs such as Social Security. He was hinting at a sweeping compromise in which very different issues are linked in an economic reform plan. "It just occurs to me that while we're thinking through one problem, we might be very thoughtful about another," he said.[12]

Several months later, Lugar attended an energy conference at Purdue University and outlined a detailed program to address the U.S. energy problem. The Lugar Energy Security Initiative, as he called it, was built on the premise that dependence on imported oil has put the United States in a position that no great power should tolerate. "Our economic health is subject to forces far beyond our control, including the decisions of hostile countries. The hundreds of billions of dollars we spend on oil imports each year weakens our economy, enriches hostile regimes, and is used by some to support terrorism."[13] The essence of America's geostrategic problem, he said, is reliance on imported oil in a marketplace that is dominated by volatile and hostile governments. The United States can start to break petroleum's grip by making ethanol as important as gasoline in its transportation fuel mix. He said his plan would dramatically improve the country's energy posture by replacing 6.5 million barrels of oil per day, which is the rough equivalent of one-third of the oil used in America, and one-half of its current oil imports. His plan called for expanding ethanol production by 100 billion gallons a year by 2025, requiring all new cars sold in America to be flexible fuel vehicles that run on E85, requiring the installation of E85 pumps in at least 25 percent of U.S. gas stations within 10 years, establishing a variable ethanol tax credit in order to set an effective floor price for crude oil at $45 a barrel, and approving new mileage standards for American cars that set a target of steadily improving fuel economy every year.

A year later, in 2007, Lugar delivered another major energy speech at Brookings in which he argued that the next American president should make energy policy an urgent priority. "Today I would state unequivocally that energy security and the economic and environmental issues closely associated with it should be the most important topics of the 2008 presidential election." Energy, Lugar argued, is the issue with the widest gulf between what is required to make the nation secure and what is likely to be achieved through the inertia of existing proposals and the normal policymaking process. Substantial progress, he said, requires "dramatic, visionary and sustained presidential leadership."[14]

He argued that Congress and the private sector can make incremental advances, but "revolutionary national progress in the energy field probably is dependent on presidential action." Lugar said the new president should elevate energy security to the status of a core national goal and directly engage the American people. "The president must be relentless. He or she must be willing to stake the reputation of the administration on politically difficult breakthroughs that meaningfully contribute to U.S. energy security. The president must be willing to have his or her administration judged according to its success or failure on this issue." Presidential candidates, he argued, should explain how they will personally tackle energy issues, how they would organize their administration's energy policies, and how they would build public pride in achieving energy goals.[15]

IV

Lugar is convinced that while it is important to frame the policy debate, it is also critical to accomplish concrete things and demonstrate leadership on energy issues. In 2005, he purchased a Toyota Prius, and he makes frequent references to it during his speeches on energy. His message is clear: I don't just talk about conservation, I practice it. On St. Patrick's Day 2008, Lugar playfully but pointedly extolled the virtues of green driving. In a press statement, he noted that from March 12, 2005, to March 12, 2008, he had driven his Prius 24,203 miles, averaging 45.8 miles per gallon. According to his calculations, if he had purchased a conventional mid-size car in 2005, he could have expected about 23.8 miles per gallon. By choosing to drive a Prius, he saved 488 gallons of gasoline, amounting to savings of $1,337 in gas, almost as much as the total amount he spent on gas over those 3 years. As for the environment, he calculated that by saving those 488 gallons of gas, he reduced his carbon dioxide emissions by 4.8 tons. And Lugar estimated that he would recoup the higher cost of buying a hybrid in 4.91 years.[16]

Lugar's farm was the first in Indiana to enroll in the Chicago Climate Exchange. About 20 years ago, he began converting about 200 of the 604 acres on his farm to hardwood trees. As these trees grow, they absorb and store carbon from the air around Indianapolis, and Lugar announced that his trees sequestered an estimated 400 tons of CO_2 in 2007. He says that the ability of farmers and others to remove carbon from the atmosphere and store it through methods such as tree farming and no-till planting are an important environmental contribution.[17]

Determined to stay on top of developments in energy technology, Lugar hired a staffer in his personal office, Neil Brown, who is charged to carefully follow the international energy portfolio. He monitors daily developments, drafts letters of congratulation and encouragement to innovators for Lugar's signature, and has helped Lugar create an international network of kindred spirits on energy issues. Lugar sends letters to "almost everyone in America who is doing something significant on energy issues. We're building day-by-day a pretty good network of people who know of our intense interest in energy issues." The senator also sends a stream of "Dear Colleague" letters to fellow senators to discuss energy challenges and opportunities. He created an Energy Patriot award given monthly to a student, researcher, or business leader who is taking concrete action to reduce U.S. dependence on foreign oil. The recipient's profile is posted on Lugar's website and the individual receives a letter from Lugar and a certificate that designates him or her as an Energy Patriot.[18]

Though he does not sit on either of the Senate's two energy committees, Lugar has introduced dozens of energy-related bills and is constantly working to attach his ideas to legislation moving through Congress. Lugar wrote and passed the Biomass Research and Development Act of 2000, which remains the country's premier legislation guiding renewable fuels research. It requires the Department of Agriculture and the Department of Energy to coordinate research efforts to develop energy from biomass production. He was able to insert important provisions in the 2005 energy bill, including a requirement that oil companies blend a total of 7.5 billion gallons of renewable fuels into the nation's fuel supply by 2012.

The senator was also able to insert key items in the 2007 energy bill, which President Bush signed into law. The bill included a renewable fuel standard that would guarantee a market for investment in new bio-fuels production, with special preference to bio-fuels such as cellulosic ethanol. The 2007 energy law also raised vehicle fuel efficiency standards that Lugar had strongly supported for years. The bill included a Lugar provision that urges the secretary of state to integrate energy security and priorities into core State Department activities. It also creates a new coordinator for international energy affairs.

Several provisions of the energy efficiency section of the bill came from legislation that Lugar co-sponsored. This section reduces U.S. use of fossil fuels by improving the efficiency of vehicles, buildings, home appliances, and industrial equipment. Lugar's long-standing desire to promote flexible fuel vehicles in order to reduce the usage gap between E85 and regular gas was partially addressed by initiating a study to examine the issue. Lugar's Ethanol Infrastructure Expansion Act was also reflected in the 2007 energy law that called for a feasibility study of shipping bio-fuels via pipeline. This would connect current production in the Midwest with markets throughout the country.

V

By the summer of 2010, Lugar had grown very concerned about the state of the energy debate in the U.S. Congress. The House had passed the previous year a controversial "cap and trade" bill in an attempt to slow the growth of greenhouse gas emissions. A months-long effort in the Senate to craft a less ambitious "cap and trade" alternative, led by Democrat senator John Kerry, independent senator Joe Lieberman, and Republican senator Lindsey Graham, faltered. Lugar believed that it was important to try to assemble a compromise bill to lessen the nation's dependence on foreign oil that would attract bipartisan support. Drawing on a presentation he heard at an Aspen Institute seminar by the ClimateWorks Foundation, Lugar crafted an alternative plan that prompted considerable congressional interest.

Lugar told his congressional colleagues that "without aggressive action to decrease our long-term energy dependence on foreign sources, we are risking economic and security disasters, as well as even more severe trade imbalances and costs for consumers." He said that as the Congress battled to a stalemate on climate change legislation, he decided to focus on policies that would be clear, practical, and help Americans save money while cutting U.S. foreign oil consumption and boosting energy security. His plan focused on policies that reduced foreign oil, targeted achievable energy efficiency, and increased diversity in domestic clean power generation. His package, Lugar argued, would by 2030 reduce by two-thirds American dependence on foreign oil, cut national energy consumption by 14 percent, reduce average household electric bills by about 10 percent, and reduce greenhouse gas emissions by 25 percent. It would achieve these result by mandating steady improvements in vehicle efficiency requirements, pushing for substantial energy conservation improvements in federal and commercial buildings, expanding loan guarantees for nuclear power, and encouraging the use of clean coal. "Saving energy is the cheapest and easiest path to energy security—and saving money. Failure to plug the energy leaks in our homes, businesses, and industries is a drag on economic recovery and impinges our global competitiveness," he said in announcing the package. "It is time to recast the debate in Congress and match priorities with a practical alternative."[19]

VI

For much of his 3 decades in the U.S. Senate, Lugar has pushed the United States to adopt more rational domestic energy policies. But he has also been a careful observer of the international energy scene. Probably more than any other current member of Congress, Lugar has studied the geopolitics of energy, mastered its complexities, warned of its risks, and outlined specific policy options.

Lugar's international energy work has included giving speeches to high-level diplomatic audiences, taking overseas trips to meet with key leaders and assess developments on the ground, and even serving as an American emissary at an important international treaty-signing ceremony.

An example of Lugar's decision to address an important international audience about energy issues took place when he traveled to Riga, Latvia, in late November of 2006 to give a speech at a meeting hosted by the German Marshall Fund just before a NATO summit. After praising NATO as the most successful security and defense organization in history, Lugar said that it now faced huge challenges, including the need to address energy realities with force, clarity, and cohesion.[20]

In the coming decades, Lugar argued, the most likely source of war in Europe and the surrounding regions will be energy scarcity and manipulation. The challenge had already arrived with a vengeance. He noted that within the past year and a half, the international flow of oil had been disrupted by hurricanes, turmoil in Nigeria, and continued sabotage in Iraq. Al-Qaeda and other terrorist organizations had openly declared their determination to attack oil facilities to disrupt Western economies. "The use of energy as an overt weapon is not a theoretical threat of the future; it is happening now," he said, referring to Russia's decision earlier in 2006 to shut off natural gas to Ukraine.[21]

The senator argued that a natural gas shutdown in any European nation could cause death and economic loss comparable to a military attack. Given the importance of energy as the lifeblood of modern economies, Lugar said NATO leaders should consider making energy security an Article V commitment, referring to the article in the NATO charter that declares that an attack on one member is an attack on all. It is the bedrock of the alliance and the triggering mechanism for collective action. In the event of an energy shutoff, NATO should have a strategy to resupply a victimized member state, the senator argued. "The energy threat is more difficult to prepare for than a ground war in Europe," he warned.

Lugar said that in addition to creating strong alliance commitments related to energy, NATO should speak forcefully to Russia and other energy-rich nations that had been using energy as a political hammer. NATO needed to tell Russia directly, Lugar said, that its recent actions to temporarily reduce gas supplies to the West, confiscate foreign energy investments, and create further barriers to new investments from the West were unacceptable. "We should speak clearly with Russia about our concerns and our determination to protect our economies and our peoples. We should outline the differences between a future in which Russia tries to leverage for political advantage the energy vulnerabilities of its neighbors and a future in which Russia solidifies consumer-producer trust with the West and respects energy investments that help expand and maintain Russia's production capacity," he said. Lugar argued that NATO and Russia needed a serious discussion about the rule of law, the status of foreign investments, and binational and multinational energy agreements.

The senator acknowledged that bringing NATO into the energy security business was a new role that would be controversial. "But if we fail to reorient the alliance to address energy security, we will be ignoring the dynamic that is most likely to spur conflict and threaten the well-being of alliance members," he said.[22]

Lugar later said he was aware that the Riga audience, which included several NATO foreign ministers as well as respected Americans such as Zbigniew Brzezinski, was divided on the merits of his proposals. Brzezinski told Lugar that he had "hit a home run" with his speech. But others indicated that his remarks, while thoughtful and accurate, were too publicly critical of NATO and Russia. Some argued that the European energy problem was more appropriate for the European Union to tackle than NATO. Lugar's staff later told the senator that Russian news reports of his remarks were very critical, describing the speech as needlessly provocative.[23]

VII

During his career, Lugar has taken a number of international trips to study energy issues. The senator took four high-profile trips in 2008 alone to examine energy-related challenges, traveling through the southern Caucasus, Europe, and Russia.

Early in the year, he traveled to central Asia, making stops in Georgia and Ukraine, which are key energy transit states, and Turkmenistan, Kazakhstan, and Azerbaijan, which are critical energy-producing nations. The senator sought to affirm that the United States was keenly interested in central Asia and the Caspian Sea region and believed it was in the interest of these nations that they have energy export routes that are not entirely dependent on Russia.

While in Ashgabat, the senator met with Turkmenistan's president, Gurbanguly Berdymukhammedov, and other government officials to discuss energy and security matters. During his 90-minute session with Berdymuhammedov, Lugar praised the president for advancing "extraordinary changes" in Turkmenistan. The senator suggested to the president that if Turkmenistan had multiple export options for its natural gas this would enhance the country's strength and independence. Lugar left the meeting in good spirits; he felt the president's views on energy were sound and compatible with American interests. "I felt like he wanted to do business," Lugar said.[24]

Later in the day, Lugar accepted an invitation from the president and the government of Turkmenistan to attend a national day ceremony at a mosque in the outskirts of the capital. Although tired from his long trip, Lugar felt it was important to show American respect to the president and his country. So the senator drove with a senior diplomat from the American embassy in Ashgabat for more than an hour to the mosque where the ceremony was to be held. Lugar, dressed in layers of clothes to keep warm in the bitter cold, joined about two dozen shivering members of the diplomatic corps who were attending the outdoor event. Shortly after Lugar arrived, the presidential limousine arrived and Berdymuk-hammedov walked onto a red carpet toward the ceremony. The president looked over at the huddled group of diplomats to see who was there. He caught Lugar's eye—and may have been surprised that the senior American senator took the time and went to the trouble to attend the ceremony. "It was one of those affairs where they sort of took notes about who was there," Lugar recalls with a smile.[25]

Lugar tried to convey the same respect and curiosity in his earlier visit to Georgia and in his stops in the following days to Kazakhstan, Azerbaijan, and Ukraine. While still traveling through the region, Lugar issued several statements about the importance of Central Asia to the United States. These were attempts to tell the American people and fellow policymakers that important things were occurring far from American shores. "U.S. strategic and economic interests intersect in Central Asia. With Russia to the north and Iran and Afghanistan to the south, energy-rich Central Asia is at the frontline of American national security priorities. We have tremendous opportunities in the region, but it will take time and consistent high-level effort to build construc-tive relationships. This region needs to have a much higher priority on America's foreign policy agenda," he said.[26]

"Kazakhstan and Turkmenistan rely almost exclusively upon Russia to transport their oil and gas to world markets. In turn, Russia has occa-sionally demonstrated willingness to use its control over these supplies for political gain at the expense of our European allies. Opening trans-Caspian export routes will dilute Russia's control over energy supplies. Likewise, having multiple export options will reinforce the political independence of Kazakhstan and Turkmenistan," Lugar said.

When Lugar was in Baku the next day, he issued a separate state-ment, repeating his suggestion that President Bush appoint a special senior American representative for energy in the greater Caspian area. "Appointment of a special representative for energy would be a clear statement of high-level U.S. priority for this strategically critical region. Failure to demonstrate U.S. commitment will jeopardize progress on trans-Caspian energy cooperation, with potentially devastating impacts on long-term U.S. security and economic interests in the region," he said.[27]

For Lugar's August travels that year, the senator and his staff developed a 2-week agenda that was largely focused on energy. The trip would have as one of its focal points a swing through Central Asia and Europe to press for a new pipeline to deliver the natural gas and oil from Central Asia to Europe. For several years, Lugar had supported the proposed Nabucco pipeline that would provide some of this energy flow, but the proposal remained dormant amid divisions within Europe and ambivalence among Turkey's leadership. Lugar traveled first to Paris to meet with officials from the International Energy Agency and then on to Georgia, Azerbaijan, Turkey, Hungary, Ukraine, Germany, and Belgium. At every stop, he spoke of the importance of energy and need for the Nabucco pipeline. To add emphasis, his journey traced where the proposed pipeline would run. Lugar urged European leaders to put aside their differences and support the Nabucco pipeline, which he described as an important project to connect Caspian energy resources to European consumers. Lugar said it was critical to complete an East-West energy corridor to bring oil and gas across the Caspian from Central Asia to European consumers. This would require promoting Caspian sources of energy with independent transportation routes; supporting pro-West governments in Azerbaijan, Georgia, and Turkey that host significant energy transportation routes; and developing strong multilateral support and funding for the Nabucco pipeline.[28]

VIII

While Lugar is an unpretentious man who does not relish diplomatic theatrics, he realizes that sometimes a good ceremony is worth its weight in gold. So in early July of 2009, during a busy summer work period in Congress, Lugar received surprising and much welcomed news: the European Union and the leaders of five nations had reached an agreement to go forward with the Nabucco pipeline. This was what Lugar had spent much of the previous year pleading for. Turkey had decided to host a signing ceremony in Ankara in about a week and its senior leadership wanted the senator to attend. The Turkish president later told Lugar the summit was "due in large part to your unwavering support."[29]

The senator decided to put his Washington work aside, scrap his schedule, and travel to Turkey for the big event. He viewed it as a major breakthrough that had seemed unlikely a year earlier when he met with leaders in the supplying, consuming, and transit countries. "Although the time between receiving the invitation and the summit was very short, I knew that the Nabucco project is so important that I had to drop everything to help represent the U.S. commitment to this strategic priority," he said.[30]

Turkish prime minister Recep Tayyip Erdogan convened the Nabucco Inter-governmental Signing Ceremony and Summit in Ankara on July 13, 2009. Leaders from 12 countries and the EU attended. Russia was invited to the ceremony but declined to send an envoy. Representatives from Iraq, Syria, and Egypt attended, as did the United States, which was represented by Lugar and Ambassador Richard Morningstar, a special envoy to the region.

Under the accord, Turkey and four EU countries—Austria, Hungary, Romania, and Bulgaria—agreed to allow the pipeline to transit their countries. The EU committed about $280 million in seed money for the project, which will ultimately cost about $11 billion. When completed, the Nabucco pipeline will be a natural gas pipeline running from Turkey to Austria and will diversify the current natural gas suppliers and delivery routes for Europe. The Nabucco pipeline will extend for more than 2,000 miles: about 1,200 miles of pipeline will be laid in Turkey, 250 miles in Bulgaria, 290 miles in Romania, 240 miles in Hungary, and 30 miles in Austria. It will be owned by five companies representing the five transit countries, as well as a Germany energy company.[31]

To attend the ceremony, Lugar left Washington early on a Saturday morning. He took a commercial flight to London and spent the evening there. Then he left London early Sunday and flew on a military plane to Ankara. After a brief rest in his hotel, he plunged into a working dinner with American diplomats and senior Turkish government officials, including the minister of defense and the Turkish president's top foreign policy advisor. He began Monday with a breakfast meeting with business executives who will help build the pipeline. Then he attended the elaborate signing ceremony in an Ankara hotel. After the leaders of the nations signing the agreement spoke, Lugar was asked to offer the American perspective. He was introduced by Ambassador Morningstar. "One year ago, I traversed the proposed Nabucco pipeline route on a mission to encourage progress and cooperation. Many people doubted whether the political agreement that is being signed today could ever be achieved. The journey to this point has taken courage and visionary statesmanship by numerous leaders," he began.[32]

The senator said that Nabucco would provide diversification of natural gas that will benefit supply, transit, and consumer countries. Energy security, he said, is at the heart of every nation's security and economic concerns. "We must build relationships with independent states in the Caspian Sea region. We must explore how to improve confidence with Russia on energy. Europe must do more to interconnect its energy infrastructure. The NATO alliance must make energy security a much higher priority. And each nation must explore alternative sources of energy and ways to improve the energy efficiency of its economy," he said in a succinct summary of major challenges ahead.[33]

"The significance of the Nabucco agreement we are celebrating today is far greater than the natural gas it will carry. Agreement on Nabucco is a bold demonstration that governments representing diverse peoples and geographies can overcome division. It is a signal to the rest of the world that partner governments will not acquiesce to manipulation of energy supplies for political ends," he concluded.

The senator then witnessed the formal signing of the agreement, attended a luncheon hosted by Turkey's prime minister, and held private meetings with Iraqi prime minister Nouri al-Malaki, Hungarian prime minister Bajnai Gordon, and Turkish president Abdullah Gul.

He left Ankara Monday evening for the long trip home. After a refueling stop in Hungary and an overnight rest in London, Lugar arrived in Washington late Tuesday morning. Lugar's trip lasted 72 hours, including 33 hours of travel, 14 hours of official meetings, 21 hours for sleep and rest, and 4 hours of waiting for flights.[34] Upon arriving in Washington, Lugar headed immediately to his Senate office and then to a policy luncheon with his fellow Republican senators.

6

✤

The Wars in Iraq and Afghanistan

I

Wars in Iraq and Afghanistan have dominated American foreign policy for a decade, igniting high-decibel exchanges about their importance to the nation's security. Richard Lugar has been an active participant in these debates but has had only marginal influence on the shaping of war policy. Some analysts and even some of his colleagues believe he could—and should—have been more aggressive in challenging the Bush administration's decision to invade Iraq, which diverted attention and resources away from Afghanistan after 2003.

To date, the decision to go to war in Iraq has been far more controversial in the United States than the decision to attack Afghanistan after the September 11 attacks by al-Qaeda. It generated far more passionate debates about the war's rationale, strategy, and tactics. Between 2003 and 2008, policymakers and the American public largely forgot Afghanistan, and it was described as America's "other war." Lugar consistently thought about and commented on America's war in Afghanistan, but much of his attention and focus was directed toward Iraq, given its centrality to U.S. policy debates.[1]

Lugar has a hawkish history on Iraq. After Saddam Hussein invaded Kuwait in 1990, Lugar called for a determined and forceful American response. He was a strong supporter of a congressional resolution in January 1991 that called on President George H. W. Bush to use whatever actions he felt necessary to expel Saddam from Kuwait. But the senator went further in the spring of 1991 as the American-led coalition quickly evicted the Iraqis from Kuwait. Lugar urged the president to send American troops into Baghdad to defeat the regime of Saddam Hussein if Saddam refused to surrender.

In a letter to Bush on April 18, 1991, Lugar said that Desert Storm clearly established the principle that aggression would not be tolerated and he celebrated the liberation of Kuwait. But he warned that it would be dangerous to leave Hussein in power, asserting that he was capable of causing regional havoc by pushing millions of refugees across his borders into neighboring states. In Lugar's view, allowing Saddam to stay in power would result in the "creation of one miserable predicament after another for the UN and U.S.," with the result that the alliance and the United States would grow weary and look for withdrawal options and Saddam would rebuild his military strength. He feared Saddam could—and would—outwait the coalition that removed him from Kuwait. Lugar urged Bush to reach out to world leaders and convince them of the need to depose Saddam. Then the president should call on the UN Security Council to pass a resolution that would give Hussein's regime a deadline for resignation and surrender to the United Nations military command. That command would take physical custody of Saddam and other key Iraqi military leaders and a temporary UN government would be installed pending Iraqi elections. If Saddam declined to surrender, Lugar said, Bush should seek new authority from the U.S. Congress to remove him from power even if this required a U.S.-led march into Baghdad.[2]

Bush sent Lugar a three-paragraph letter a few days later in response, thanking him for "sending me that interesting letter." But Bush quickly said it would be "next to impossible" to get the UN to support Lugar's plan. The international community, he said, would not back the kind of U.S.-led invasion that Lugar envisioned.[3]

As the 1990s unfolded with Saddam regularly making mischief in the region, Lugar never stopped believing, and occasionally saying, that the Bush administration made a grievous error in not removing Saddam from power in the spring of 1991. Lugar supported the George W. Bush administration's request for a congressional authorization to send American forces into Afghanistan to destroy al-Qaeda after the September 11, 2001, terrorist attacks. But Lugar's concern about Iraq also intensified after 9/11. Three months after the attacks, Lugar released a policy paper he called the Lugar Doctrine. In it, he said the United States was in a global war against Muslim religious extremists who wanted to reorder the world by defeating the country and its key allies. "The war proceeds in a world awash with nuclear, chemical and biological weapons and materials of mass destruction stored principally in the United States and Russia but also in India, Pakistan, Iraq, Iran, Libya, North Korea, Syria, Sudan, Israel, Great Britain, France and China—and perhaps other nations," he declared. "Throughout much of the last decade, vulnerability to the use of weapons of mass destruction has been the number one national security dilemma confronting the United States even as it received scant attention."[4]

Lugar said the United States needed to be vigilant in battling terrorists and also in ensuring that all weapons and materials of mass destruction were identified, carefully guarded, and systematically destroyed. He observed that since the UN inspections of Iraq had been suspended for more than 3 years, the status of Iraq's weapons and materials of mass destruction was unknown. This needed to be clarified, Lugar argued, and the facts about Iraq's weapons programs made transparent. This would require intense international diplomacy and "the world must be prepared for military action to destroy weapons and materials of mass destruction if diplomacy fails," he said.[5]

After the decisive U.S. military actions in Afghanistan at the end of 2001, in which the Taliban was ousted from power, the debate in the United States shifted to Iraq. In President Bush's State of the Union address in January 2002, he warned that the country faced serious threats from an "Axis of Evil" that included Iraq, Iran, and North Korea. Several months later, Bush traveled to West Point and outlined the case for preventive war; Iraq was clearly the target. In the summer of 2002 across the United States and especially in Washington, there was an intense debate about a possible American invasion of Iraq. According to the memoir of one administration official, Richard Haass, Bush had decided to go to war by the summer of 2002.[6] Others have argued that the president had not firmly decided to go to war in Iraq but was determined to drive Saddam Hussein from power.

As Lugar contemplated a possible war against Iraq, he read and found compelling a book by foreign policy scholar Ken Pollack, *The Threatening Storm: The Case for Invading Iraq.* The book argued that Saddam's Iraq was a serious and deepening threat and an invasion of Iraq to depose Saddam Hussein was both plausible and necessary.[7] With the possibility of war with Iraq growing, Senate Foreign Relations Committee Chairman Joe Biden and Lugar, the ranking Republican on the panel, prepared a series of hearings to consider America's policy toward Iraq.

On July 31, 2002, the day of the first hearing, Biden and Lugar published a much-noticed opinion article in the *New York Times* in which they outlined their agenda for the hearings. The two senators said that they agreed not to call Bush administration representatives in the first set of hearings because they didn't want to pressure the administration into making decisions prematurely regarding Iraq. Biden and Lugar said that they hoped the hearings would launch a national debate that would focus on critical questions such as what threat Iraq posed to the United States, possible American responses to this threat, and the responsibilities the country would assume if it forced the removal of Saddam Hussein. This question of what Iraq would look like after Saddam was driven from power was critical but had not been adequately explored, they said.

"In Afghanistan, the war was prosecuted successfully, but many of us believe our commitment to security and reconstruction there has fallen short. Given Iraq's strategic location, its large oil reserves and the suffering of the Iraqi people, we cannot afford to replace a despot with chaos," they wrote. "We need to assess what it would take to rebuild Iraq economically and politically. Addressing these questions now would demonstrate to the Iraqi people that we are committed for the long haul. Iraqi neighbors would breathe easier if they know the future had been thought through in detail." Biden and Lugar said the American people also needed assurances that their government had fully examined the consequences of an American invasion of Iraq. It was imperative to know everything possible about the risks of action and inaction. Ignoring these factors could lead the nation into something for which the American people were unprepared.[8]

The Senate Foreign Relations Committee organized 2 days of hearings to examine the threats posed by Iraq. Held on July 31 and August

1, 2002, they captured the attention of Washington as the panel heard from more than a dozen senior members of the American foreign policy establishment as well as some international experts. In his statements and his questioning of witnesses, Lugar raised hard and practical issues. He wanted to know if the current containment regime was working and, if not, how it could be improved to be more effective. He wanted to know if Saddam had a history of cooperating with terrorists and was likely to sell or give them his WMD. Lugar was very curious about the internal politics of Iraq, wondering who would likely succeed the Iraqi leader if he were ousted. And he questioned if this new leadership would be likely to help the United States find and secure Iraq's presumed WMD. He had other questions. How would America's allies contribute to any American-led invasion and then reconstruction of Iraq? What was the likely stance of China and Russia toward an American-sponsored war in Iraq? What would happen in Iraq after Saddam was deposed? What political and security and economic challenges would the American government be inheriting?

During the hearings, Lugar said Congress should be part of the decision-making process regarding Iraq policy, but he also seemed to accept a subordinate role for Congress. "If President Bush determines that large-scale offensive military action is necessary against Iraq, I hope that he will follow the lead established by the previous Bush administration and seek congressional authorization," Lugar said in a formulation some found passive and contrary to the constitutional requirement that Congress be the institution to declare war.[9]

After 2 days of hearings in the Foreign Relations Committee, Congress began its summer recess and Lugar reported to his constituents in Indiana what he had learned through an August essay in the *Indianapolis Star* called "A Road Map to Succeed in Iraq."[10] The senator said that during the recent hearings, witnesses before the committee agreed that the WMD risk from Iraq would be greater with the passage of time and the overall dangers to the United States would grow. But he added that the country "has yet to undertake sufficient diplomatic, economic and political preparations to guarantee the long-term success of a pre-emptive military invasion of Iraq." A more certain road map for the American people, he said, was required.

Lugar argued that the United States needed to be forceful about enforcing the current sanctions regimen on Iraq as well as other UN resolutions. The United States should intensify its intelligence operations so it could identify Iraq's WMD and better understand possible successors to Saddam Hussein. It was also critical to inform the American people of the cost of the war, both in terms of the federal budget and the broader economic impact. He added that the United States needed to build an international coalition based on a compelling case against Hussein's regime and offer a plan to move Iraq back into the community of nations. If the president opted for war, Lugar said Bush should seek congressional authorization so the American people were committed to a potentially lengthy and costly endeavor in Iraq. Successful geopolitical campaigns, he observed, are the result of careful military, economic, diplomatic, and political preparation. If Bush did this kind of careful work, it would be widely seen as a demonstration of American resolve.

The summer debate on Iraq was heated and combative, taking place on opinion pages and on the cable television news shows that drive the discourse in the nation's capital. In one of the most striking developments of the summer, former National Security Advisor Brent Scowcroft, a leading Republican foreign policy expert, wrote a much-noticed essay in the *Wall Street Journal* on August 15, 2002, entitled "Don't Attack Saddam." Scowcroft's views were significant because he was a close advisor and friend of the president's father and was seen as a sober analyst and a loyal Republican. He argued that while Saddam Hussein was a menace, there was little evidence to link him to terrorist organizations and even less to the events of 9/11. An attack on Saddam, Scowcroft argued, would be a diversion from the country's war against terrorism.[11]

"An attack on Iraq at this time would seriously jeopardize, if not destroy, the global counter-terrorist campaign," Scowcroft declared. The United States could defeat Saddam, but the military campaign would have to be followed by a large-scale, long-term military occupation. There was a "virtual consensus in the world against an attack on Iraq at this time." Given this sentiment, the United States would have to pursue a mostly go-it-alone strategy against Iraq, making military operations correspondingly more difficult and expensive.

Scowcroft's plea to the Bush administration to defer a war against Iraq jolted the political debate and threw the administration on the defensive. About 10 days after Scowcroft's article, Vice President Richard Cheney answered with a hard-line and deeply consequential speech to the Veterans of Foreign Wars. Hinting that the administration knew more about Iraq's weapons arsenal than it had said publicly, Cheney signaled the administration had decided to go to war in Iraq. He framed the threat from Iraq in alarming terms. "There is no doubt that Saddam Hussein now has weapons of mass destruction. There is no doubt he is amassing them to use against our friends, against our allies and against us," Cheney said.[12] His comments were widely interpreted as evidence that the administration had decided to attack Saddam and the only question was when.

Upon returning to Capitol Hill after Labor Day, Lugar and Biden tried to re-start the congressional debate on Iraq. They presided over 2 days of hearings on September 25 and 26 called "Next Steps in Iraq." Richard Holbrooke, Robert McFarlane, former secretaries of state Madeleine Albright and Henry Kissinger, and then Secretary of State Colin Powell all testified. But the hearings, even with several star witnesses, had the feeling of a sideshow. Lugar acknowledged that other congressional leaders were already working on a resolution that authorized the president to use force to compel Saddam Hussein to give up his WMD. And he noted that it appeared the Senate Foreign Relations Committee was not going to be a lead player in drafting the war resolution. During the hearing with Powell, Lugar expressed frustration that the war resolution was being drafted without the input of Congress's key foreign affairs panels. Lugar noted that he was following the debate on the emerging war resolution largely through reading newspapers and watching TV reports.[13]

Lugar and Biden joined the debate on a war resolution that Congress would consider by teaming up to offer a proposal. Both were troubled that a draft sent to Capitol Hill in late September by the White House was too broad. The White House sent a war resolution to Congress on September 19 that not only authorized the use of force in Iraq but also implied the president could commit U.S. forces anywhere in the Middle East, wherever the White House deemed it necessary, without restrictions.

In late September, the two senators released their version. It authorized the use of American force in Iraq specifically. It emphasized securing the dismantlement of Iraq's weapons of mass destruction, rather than addressing Saddam's transgressions on human rights, detainees, or failure to return property. The Biden-Lugar war authorization granted less-expansive authority to the president than the administration wanted. It advocated that the United States first seek a UN Security Council resolution calling for an aggressive UN weapons inspection in Iraq, backed by force if necessary. If that resolution didn't make it through the UN, the president would have to certify to Congress that the danger posed by Iraq's WMD could only be addressed by military means.[14]

The Biden-Lugar draft played some role in scaling back the sweep of the final resolution. But the White House largely negotiated the final version with Republican congressional leaders and House Democratic Leader Richard Gephardt. Lugar said his collaboration with Biden was based on a desire to clearly outline the conditions under which the United States would go to war, encourage international cooperation through the UN and with U.S. allies, and provide a bipartisan platform that would achieve a unity of purpose among the American people and the Congress.

According to Lugar, Bush called him on October 2 and affirmed his commitment to enlist allies, push diplomacy to the maximum degree, and achieve compliance with the UN resolutions on Iraq, including those dealing with weapons of mass destruction. Lugar said the final war resolution represented "substantial progress" in the effort to build a consensus in Congress for addressing the situation in Iraq. He cited its explicit support of the involvement of the UN and international community and its call for strengthened consultations between the president and Congress.[15]

But many experts argued, then and since, that the war authorization that Congress approved was both sweeping and dangerous. Douglas Kriner, a political scientist from Boston University, says the language of the resolution was "almost unprecedented in the scope of the power it delegated to the president... It delegated to the president sole authority to determine at an unspecified future time that Iraq posed a threat to the United States and to take military action against it at his discretion."[16]

The war authorization moved quickly through Congress in the fall of 2002. The House International Relations Committee approved the resolution on October 3 on a 31 to 11 vote. The House then held a 3-day debate before passing the resolution on October 10 on a 296 to 133 vote. In the end, 81 House Democrats supported the war resolution and all but 6 House Republicans supported it.

The Senate leadership bypassed the Foreign Relations Committee and brought the war authorization resolution to the full Senate for debate. The debate extended over 5 days on the Senate floor and culminated with a vote early on October 11. It passed 77 to 23. Only one Senate Republican—Lincoln Chafee of Rhode Island—opposed the resolution. Twenty-nine Senate Democrats supported it. Lugar voted for the measure. He said the war resolution had been tightened and improved by congressional deliberation and refinements and deserved support. He hoped a war with Iraq could be avoided but said it might be necessary to eliminate Iraq's WMD. He concluded with a prescient warning. "The United States must have partners if we are to deal successfully with the myriad of complications that will be present in a post-war Iraq. We must have partners if we are to fulfill our important role in building international peace and security."[17]

II

Less than a month after Congress voted to approve the war authorization resolution, Republicans made big gains in the 2002 mid-term congressional elections. The GOP regained control of the House and won back the Senate. For Lugar, the Senate Republican victory catapulted him back into the chairmanship of the Foreign Relations Committee. In interviews after the November election, Lugar pledged to use his regained chairmanship to scrutinize American foreign policy, especially the impending confrontation with Iraq. Describing himself as a "friend of the family" of the Bush administration, Lugar said he would chart an independent course that would demand accountability from the administration. Lugar said he would hold "pointed hearings" regarding Iraq that delved into how long an American deployment to Iraq might last, how much it would cost, and whether a lengthy deployment of U.S. forces in Iraq would leave the United States vulnerable in other theaters such as Afghanistan and the Korean peninsula.[18]

Talking tough, Lugar said that if the administration didn't present plans for postwar Iraq his panel would develop one as well as authorizing legislation to make it American policy. Any U.S.-led invasion of Iraq must be followed up with well-conceived peace and stabilization plans, he said. He warned that postwar Iraq should not be a repeat of the experience in Afghanistan, where U.S. forces had been improvising their efforts to rebuild the nation without coordinated guidance from Washington. "With Iraq, it seems we need to do better. It is a more dangerous situation," he said.[19]

In the first months of his new chairmanship in 2003, Lugar presided over several hearings related to the imminent war with Iraq. Expressing support for the administration's policy that contemplated a U.S. invasion unless Saddam surrendered, he also stressed the importance of clear and plausible American plans for the stabilization and reconstruction of Iraq. He noted archly that if the administration had detailed plans in this regard he had not seen them.

The war began on March 20 and American military forces immediately raced across Iraq, seizing control of the Baghdad airport on April 3 and observing the toppling of Saddam's statue on April 9. President Bush famously landed on the USS *Abraham Lincoln* on May 1, declaring that major combat operations were over. On that same day in Kabul, Defense Secretary Donald Rumsfeld said that the United States had stabilized Afghanistan.

Lugar held more than a dozen hearings in the Senate Foreign Relations Committee in 2003 on Iraq, and the meetings traced the arc of the triumphant invasion followed by confusion and then chaos as the war's aftermath confirmed the worst fears of many. Lugar visited Iraq in the summer of 2003 with a congressional delegation.

In late July, Lugar presided over a hearing with Deputy Secretary of Defense Paul Wolfowitz in which Lugar said he was concerned that "Iraq continues to hang in the balance." He noted that he visited Iraq 4 weeks earlier and saw firsthand that the troops understood the urgency of their work. But he said this urgency did not extend across the American government. Because of "some combination of bureaucratic inertia, political caution, and unrealistic expectations left over from the war, we do not appear to be confident about our course in Iraq," he said. "Our national sense of commitment and confidence must approximate what we demonstrated during the Berlin Airlift—a sense that we could achieve the impossible, despite short time constraints and severe conditions of risk and consequence."[20]

Several months later, Lugar invited Paul Bremer, head of the Coalition Provisional Authority, to testify before his panel, and the senator expressed mounting concerns. Iraqis, he observed to Bremer, could be forgiven for wondering how the United States could conquer their nation so quickly but not be able to get the lights turned on in Baghdad. He asked Bremer what a 5-year plan would look like and how much would it cost. He queried Bremer if he had the right team in Iraq, what worried him about his own plans, and what needed to be fixed within the CPA. He also asked Bremer how the United States could transfer authority to Iraq quickly, how to integrate the Iraqi governmental institutions into the coalition's efforts, and where Iraq fit into the overall global war on terrorism.[21]

At a hearing on April 20, 2004, with senior national security experts James Schlesinger, Sandy Berger, and Richard Perle, Lugar said the stakes in Iraq could not be higher for the United States. "American credibility in the world, progress in the war on terrorism, our relationships with our allies, the future of the Middle East, and the fate of the Iraqis themselves depend on the resolve of the U.S. government and the American people in achieving a positive outcome in Iraq. In short, moving the Iraqi people toward a secure, independent state is a vital U.S. national security priority that requires the highest level of national commitment."[22] A vigorous debate in the United States about Iraq was important, Lugar said, but should be constructive. Lugar argued that what happens in Iraq during the next 18 months would help determine whether the United States could begin to redirect the Middle East toward a more productive and peaceful future beyond the grip of terrorist influences.

During the oversight hearings, Lugar took several jabs at the administration but did so in a muted, understated way. He was concerned, even incredulous, that the postwar effort was so poorly planned. "On some occasions during the past year and a half, the administration has failed to communicate its Iraq plans and cost estimates to Congress and the American people," he said, in words that many saw as a massive understatement. He noted that during the weeks leading up to the war in early 2003, the Foreign Relations Committee held multiple hearings in pursuit of answers to basic questions about plans for Iraqi reconstruction. "Administration officials often were unable or unwilling to provide adequate answers," he said. Lugar noted that a key coordinator of the reconstruction effort, General Jay Garner, chose not to testify or send his deputy to a hearing in March of 2003 by the Foreign Relations Committee even though Garner briefed the press at the same time the hearing occurred.[23] Some analysts believe Lugar should have insisted that Garner testify before his panel and question if he would have been so forgiving of Garner's dismissive attitude if it had been a Democratic administration that was in power.

At a May 18, 2004, hearing with Wolfowitz and the Deputy Secretary of State Richard Armitage, Lugar said that a detailed reconstruction plan was needed for Iraq to prove to American allies and Iraqis that the United States had a strategy and was committed to making it work. "If we cannot provide this clarity, we risk the loss of support of the American people, the loss of potential contributions from our allies, and the disillusionment of Iraqis," he declared.[24] He noted that in Iraq the United States was perceived more as an occupation force than as a friend helping to nurture a new nation. Delays in reconstruction undercut U.S. credibility and increased suspicions among Iraqis who were impatient for improvements. Without tangible progress in reconstruction, Iraqis would see little benefit in the U.S. military presence, Lugar said.

In hearing after hearing, he tried to emphasize the high stakes for the United States. And he said that Congress's interest in Iraq was not an academic exercise. He argued that within the bounds of Congress's oversight capacity, he was attempting to illuminate U.S. plans, actions, and options with respect to Iraq both for the benefit of the American people and to guide Congress's policymaking role. "With lives being lost and billions of dollars being spent in Iraq, the American people must be assured that we have carefully thought through an Iraq policy that will optimize our prospects for success. Moreover, a detailed plan is necessary to prove to our allies and to Iraqis that we have a strategy and that we are committed to making it work."[25]

In addition to holding hearings, Lugar tried other ways to get his colleagues to focus on Iraq. In late 2005 and throughout 2006, Lugar sent more than a dozen "Dear Colleague" letters to fellow senators about developments in Iraq. His hope, Lugar said, was to make the debate on Iraq policy as constructive and non-partisan as possible. "We should continually strive to elevate our debate by studying thoughtful sources of information and embracing civility in our discourse," Lugar wrote in his first letter, which reflected lofty sentiments but also sounded preachy, even patronizing.[26] In the 14 letters that followed, Lugar wrote brief commentaries as he passed on reports, essays, and studies from think tanks and independent research groups on various aspects of the Iraq challenge. Lugar seemed to imply that American policy toward Iraq would improve if people of goodwill tried to understand and agree upon the facts. There is, in the letters, little sense of the sharply downward trajectory of the American war effort in Iraq during this critical time.

His hope to shift the Iraq war out of partisan politics did not materialize. By 2005 and especially in 2006, Democrats united behind a sharp, biting critique of the Bush administration's Iraq policy. They argued that Republicans in Congress were more intent on protecting the Bush administration than trying to correct its Iraq policy that was way off course. With Iraq in flames, apparently veering toward civil war, and with American casualties rising, the public's support for Bush's war policy plunged. Democratic leaders took advantage of this surging anger to win back control of Congress in the 2006 mid-term elections.

III

If Republicans used Iraq effectively in the 2002 and 2004 elections to retain control of Congress, the deteriorating situation in Iraq was the central factor in the GOP's crushing defeat in the 2006 midterms. Republicans lost control of both the House and Senate and Lugar had to relinquish his prized chairmanship. As Democrats assumed control of Congress in January of 2007, the party's leadership said that changing

American policy in Iraq was their overriding goal. Just weeks after the mid-term elections and before the Democrats took control of Congress, the Iraq Study Group reported that the war in Iraq was going poorly and required major changes. "The situation in Iraq is grave and deteriorating," the report began. It called for greater emphasis on regional diplomacy and redeploying American forces out of combat roles.[27]

After the 2006 electoral pummeling and with grim reports on the ground, President Bush decided that he needed a new Iraq strategy. He fired Defense Secretary Donald Rumsfeld, hired Robert Gates to succeed him, and sought a new military approach to Iraq. After extensive consultations within the White House, with conservatives at the American Enterprise Institute, and with key military advisors, Bush settled on a new "surge" strategy that called for the introduction of 21,500 additional combat troops into Iraq, primarily Baghdad. Two days before announcing that strategy on January 7, Bush invited Lugar and Republican senator John Warner to the White House for a meeting. National Security Advisor Steven Hadley took notes. According to Lugar, he suggested to the president that the administration reduce America's presence in Iraq and redeploy many of its troops to safer places outside of Baghdad. He said that he feared that if Bush's proposed surge failed, America's political environment might force the total withdrawal of U.S. forces from Iraq. Lugar said the president listened carefully to the two senators but had clearly made up his mind to go forward with the surge. The president told Lugar that Secretary of State Condoleezza Rice would intensify American diplomacy in the region, an apparent acknowledgement that he agreed with Lugar that more vigorous diplomacy in the region was required.[28]

Bush's announcement of the surge ignited a fierce debate between the administration and many of its allies on Capitol Hill and Democratic leaders over Iraq policy. Democrats, led by House Speaker Nancy Pelosi and Senate Majority Leader Harry Reid, said they would press for a change of direction in Iraq. But they took off the table an effort to cut off funding for the war. This was a critical step, because it signaled that Democrats were not going to use the single most powerful tool in their arsenal and arguably the only one that would alter American policy in Iraq: the power of the purse. Senate Armed Services Committee Chairman Carl Levin declared flatly "we're not going to cut off funding to the troops. No one wants to do that." And Pelosi agreed, saying, "Congress will fund our troops as long as they are in harm's way."[29]

The early congressional battle in 2007 focused on non-binding resolutions that would formally reject Bush's new strategy. In the Senate, Foreign Relations Committee Chairman Joe Biden worked with Republican senator Chuck Hagel on a resolution disapproving of the surge. That panel considered the Biden-Hagel resolution on January 24, 2007, in a combative, contentious meeting. Lugar was sharply critical of the resolution, saying it was a waste of time. His statement at the beginning of the session was one of his most passionate and wide ranging about the war in Iraq and Congress's role in trying to alter its direction.

He began with an admission that startled many. "I am not confident that President Bush's plan will succeed. Militarily, the plan may achieve initial successes. But the premise that clearing and holding high-risk areas of Baghdad will create enough space for an effective political reconciliation is dubious," Lugar said bluntly. He said he was concerned the surge would not solve the underlying problems that had bedeviled American policy in Iraq for years: the Iraq government wouldn't confront Shiite militias, the uncertain loyalty of many Iraqi army and police units, the seemingly implacable Sunni insurgency, Iran's meddling in Iraqi affairs, the ineffectual history of American economic aid, and the political and military limits of American forces being able to hold large areas of urban landscape under hostile circumstances.

Lugar said the United States should be reluctant to send any more troops to Iraq except in support of a clear strategy for getting a negotiated reconciliation. It should not depend on theories or hope that something good would happen if violence were reduced in Baghdad. But the senator said the Biden-Hagel resolution was "the wrong tool" at this stage in the Iraq debate. "It is unclear to me how passing a non-binding resolution that the President has already said he will ignore will contribute to any improvement or modification of our Iraq policy. The President is deeply invested in this plan and the deployments opposed by the resolution have already begun. The non-binding resolution before us has political utility, but its passage will not benefit U.S. policy and it may actually harm the policy making process."

The Biden-Hagel resolution, Lugar argued, would further divide the executive and legislative branches even though that gap was already "unacceptably wide." Passage of the resolution would raise the probability that both branches would write off the other when it came to Iraq, he warned. "Though there can only be one commander in chief, American foreign policy is strengthened when the executive and legislative branches work together. With the passage of this resolution, I believe we would be letting our frustration get the better of us," Lugar said.

A resolution of disapproval would express and even quantify U.S. disunity on Iraq, he said, arguing that roll call votes carry a unique message and foreign audiences do not always understand the difference between non-binding resolutions and binding votes. "In this case, we are laying open our disunity without the prospect that the vehicle will achieve meaningful changes in our policy. This vote will force nothing on the President, but it will confirm to our friends and allies that we are divided and in disarray."

Lugar said the resolution didn't deal with the complexity of Iraq, asserting that a non-binding resolution reduced discussion of these complexities to the "legislative equivalent of a sound bite." Congressional input should be more sophisticated and prescriptive than a non-binding resolution allowed for, he charged. Nor did the resolution advance the policy debate regarding Iraq, he said, as it failed to reflect the range and depth of opinion on Iraq in Congress. There were congressional advocates for the president's plan, for troop increases larger than the president's, for partition of Iraq, for an immediate withdrawal of American forces, for a phased withdrawal, for recommendations of the Iraq Study Group, and for other alternatives.

The resolution, in his view, would be selling Congress's powers short. "We do not need a resolution to confirm that there is broad discomfort with the President's plan within Congress. In fact, a vote on this resolution is likely to reveal far less discomfort than actually exists, since some members will vote against it because of its format."[30] After a stormy meeting, the Biden-Hagel resolution was approved 12 to 9 by the Foreign Relations Committee. But Senate Republicans later blocked consideration of the resolution on the Senate floor.

The debate over Iraq shifted to a $124 billion emergency spending bill, with $95 million allocated for the wars in Iraq and Afghanistan. In this bill, Democratic leaders inserted language calling for U.S. troop withdrawals from Iraq. The House voted 218 to 212 on March 23 in favor of a bill that required most troops to leave Iraq by August 2008. The Senate passed a version of the bill that would have set goals for withdrawal rather than requiring it. It was passed 51 to 47 on March 29. Congress sent a compromise version of the bill to President Bush, who vetoed the measure because of the troop withdrawal language. Democrats tried to override Bush's veto in the House but failed. Both chambers then passed a bill that gave Bush virtually all the funds he requested. The final version of the bill included 18 benchmarks for the Iraqi government to meet and required the president to report progress on Iraq meeting them.

Later in the summer, in one of the most forcefully contested votes of the year, Senate Republicans blocked an amendment by Democratic senators Carl Levin and Jack Reed that would have required the redeployment of U.S. troops to begin within 120 days and the withdrawal of most troops by April 30, 2008. Then in the early fall, Democratic senator Jim Webb tried to pass an amendment that would have required minimum rest times between deployments for U.S. troops serving in Iraq and Afghanistan, including National Guard and reservists. The measure would not have explicitly mandated troop redeployments, but it would have resulted in a drawdown in forces. This amendment was also blocked by a Republican filibuster.

Lugar did not actively participate in these debates and tactical skirmishes. Noting that congressional Democratic leaders were not willing to cut off funds for the troops, he said the legislative battle over troop deployments was largely a sideshow. He believed that it made more sense for him to monitor the war in Iraq, offer concrete suggestions, and make his case for major changes to administration officials privately.[31]

But he later acknowledged that his private overtures were not successful. On Monday, June 25, 2007, Lugar came to a nearly deserted Senate floor to give a speech about Iraq. For nearly 5 years, Lugar had quietly voiced his concerns about the U.S. war in Iraq. While he spoke about it frequently in public, his remarks were restrained and muted. But the senator now concluded that his various statements of concern were not resonating in the White House. He decided that a sharper, more comprehensive critique of American policy in Iraq was needed.

"In my judgment, our course in Iraq has lost contact with our vital national security interests in the Middle East and beyond. Our continuing absorption with military activities in Iraq is limiting our diplomatic assertiveness there and elsewhere in the world. The prospects that the 'surge' strategy will succeed in the way originally envisioned by the president are very limited within the short period framed by our own domestic political debate," he said.

"Unless we recalibrate our strategy in Iraq to fit our domestic political conditions and the broader needs of the United States national security, we risk foreign policy failures that could greatly diminish our influence in the region and the world," the senator declared. Lugar said the current course the United States was on in Iraq was not likely to be successful. "In my judgment, the costs and risks of continuing down the current path outweigh the potential benefits that might be achieved. Persisting indefinitely with the surge strategy will delay policy adjustments that have a better chance of protecting our vital interests over the long term."

Political fragmentation in Iraq, an overstretched and overstressed American military, and sharp divisions within the United States made it imperative for American policymakers to craft a new strategy. The Bush administration should not be so focused on Iraq that it missed other opportunities to protect vital American interests in the Middle East. The United States, he argued, had four primary objectives in the region: to prevent Iraq or any part of it from being a terrorist base, to prevent Iraqi sectarian disorder from spilling into the wider region, to prevent Iranian dominance of the region, and to limit loss of U.S. credibility. The stakes were enormous, he said. "Our subsequent actions in Iraq may determine how we are viewed for a generation." Lugar argued that American security interests called for a downsizing and redeployment of U.S. military forces to more sustainable positions in Iraq or the Middle East.

Speaking on the Senate floor to a national audience on c-span, Lugar did not try to sidestep the enormity of American policy errors in Iraq. "The United States has violated some basic national security precepts during our military engagement in Iraq. We have overestimated what the military can achieve, we have set goals that are unrealistic, and we have inadequately factored in the regional consequences of our actions. Perhaps most critically, our focus on Iraq has diverted us from opportunities to change the world in directions that strengthen our national security," he said. "Our struggles in Iraq have placed U.S. foreign policy on a defensive footing and drawn resources from other national security endeavors, including Afghanistan. With few exceptions, our diplomatic initiatives are encumbered by negative global and regional attitudes toward our combat presence in Iraq."

It was now time, he argued, for a sustained and ambitious set of initiatives to repair alliances and demonstrate American staying power in the Middle East. Vigorous and creative regional diplomacy was needed in which the United States worked with Saudi Arabia, Jordan, Egypt, Turkey, and the Gulf States to contain Iran's disruptive agenda in the region. And there was further need to address two critical issues that were less directly related to Iraq: the Arab-Israeli conflict and U.S. dependence on Persian Gulf oil. American forces should be deployed to targeted terrorist enclaves, to deter Iran, to provide a buffer against regional sectarian conflict, and to reassure friendly states that the United States is committed to Middle East security.[32]

Lugar's remarks were a frontal challenge to the Bush administration's strategy in Iraq. After years of softening his criticisms and hedging his words, Lugar decided to go public with his frustration. After Lugar concluded his remarks, Senator Richard Durbin, the second ranking Democrat, rose from his desk on the Senate floor to praise Lugar's remarks as being "in the finest tradition of the Senate." Durbin recalled that 40 years earlier he sat in the Senate visitor's gallery and watched Robert Kennedy give a speech about ending the war in Vietnam. "I believe the speech that was given tonight by my colleague from Indiana, Republican senator Richard Lugar, is that kind of speech. I think it is the starting point for a meaningful debate, a debate which looks at the Middle East in a new context and in a realistic context and realizes that it is time to change direction in our course in Iraq."[33]

That evening, cable T V news shows described Lugar's comments as a critical development in the American war in Iraq. The nation's major newspapers gave his remarks significant coverage the following day. The

New York Times described the speech as a potentially important development. One leading Democrat, Carl Levin, chairman of the Senate Armed Services Committee, praised Lugar's remarks but did so with a caveat. "I am encouraged by what he said and it just adds to the momentum for change. Hopefully, he'll take some very specific steps to implement what his words mean. They are powerful words."[34]

A few weeks after his speech, Lugar teamed up with Senator John Warner, a former chairman of the Senate Armed Services Committee, to introduce an amendment requiring the administration to begin planning for a revised strategy after the surge ran its course. Lugar said that it was essential to move beyond the "binary choice between surge and withdrawal." It was critical for the administration to develop a more sustainable policy in Iraq that reduced troop commitments and transitioned away from the mission of interposing the United States between sectarian factions. He acknowledged that there had been some military progress, but there was no evidence of political agreements in the short term. "I believe that continuing with the surge delays policy changes that have a far better chance of protecting our vital interests in the region over a sustained period."

He and Warner said it was important to ensure that the U.S. military and diplomatic policy was prepared for change when General David Petraeus's report arrived in September. Lugar argued there was a need for a "constructive bipartisan attempt to prepare for whatever policy follows in the coming months." The Lugar-Warner amendment mandated that the administration immediately begin planning for post-September contingencies, including a drawdown or redeployment of forces. It required these plans be presented to Congress by October 16 of that year and be executable beginning no later than December 31. "The surge must not be an excuse for failing to prepare for the next phase of our involvement in Iraq, whether that is withdrawal, redeployment or some other option. We saw in 2003 after the initial invasion of Iraq, the disastrous results of failing to plan adequately for contingencies," Lugar said.

The Lugar-Warner amendment also called the 2002 war authorization "obsolete" and said it required revision. Many of the conditions and motivations that existed when Congress authorized force almost 5 years earlier no longer existed or were irrelevant to the current situation. The amendment said that Congress expected the president to send a new rationale for the authorization at the time of the Petraeus report. There was, Lugar argued, a need for a "more forward looking congressional debate" on Iraq, including exploration of issues that Congress had not debated, including the missions of a residual force, the redeployment of units to other countries, and the role of U.S. troops as it relates to the broader Persian Gulf.

The amendment spelled out the need for an urgent diplomatic effort in the region to repair alliances, recruit more international help, deal with refugee flows, prevent aggression, generate basing options, and prepare for other future developments. Lugar said there was a need for a consistent diplomatic forum related to Iraq that was open to all parties in the Middle East. This could facilitate a more regular contact with Syria and Iran "with less drama and rhetoric." This would help ease refugee problems, regulate borders, explore development programs, and prevent conflict between Kurds and Turks. "We need to lay the groundwork for alternatives, so that as the President and Congress move to a new plan, it can be implemented safely, effectively, and rapidly," Lugar said.[35]

The Lugar-Warner amendment was in effect a policy memo to the Bush administration, urging it to lay the groundwork for alternatives, so that as the president and Congress moved to a new plan it could be implemented safely, effectively, and rapidly. The amendment by the two senior Republican senators attracted considerable press attention but not the interest of the Bush administration.

The president was more focused on the September testimony of General David Petraeus and U.S. ambassador to Iraq Ryan Crocker. When they delivered their report in September of 2007 to several congressional committees, Petraeus and Crocker asserted that the surge was working militarily and that it provided a context for broader political agreements to be reached in Iraq. When Petraeus appeared before the Foreign Relations Committee on September 11, 2007, Lugar acknowledged there had been a reduction in the violence in Iraq partly because of the surge and also because better training of Iraqi forces was occurring. He said that he still didn't believe the American strategy in Iraq was sustainable. "But the greatest risk for U.S. policy is not that we are incapable of making progress, but that this progress may be largely beside the point given the divisions that now afflict Iraqi society," he told Petraeus and Crocker. "The risk is that our efforts are comparable to a farmer expending his resources and efforts to plant a crop on a flood plain without factoring in the probability that the waters may rise."

He said the surge should not be an excuse for failing to prepare for the next phase of U.S. involvement in Iraq, whether it was partial withdrawal, a gradual redeployment, or some other option. Bold and creative regional diplomacy was a precondition for the success of any policy in Iraq. "The pace and intensity of American regional diplomacy related to Iraq has failed to match the urgency and magnitude of the problem. . . . We still lack a formula with which to engage Iraq's neighbors on a constant basis. We are allowing conditions in which miscalculation can thrive," he said.[36]

But as Lugar anticipated, the Petraeus-Crocker testimony shifted the political debate on Capitol Hill. The Bush administration seized on their findings of progress to convince Republican allies in Congress to hold firm and resist Democratic efforts to end the war. And Democratic leaders, weary and frustrated after nearly a year of fighting the president, lost their desire for continued battles with the White House.

Now convinced that a change in Iraq policy would only come with a Democratic occupant in the White House, Democrats shifted their attention to the 2008 presidential race. With conditions on the ground in Iraq seeming to improve and the American economy beginning to struggle badly, Democrats turned their attention to domestic matters.

IV

If most lawmakers lost interest in Iraq after the battles of 2007, Lugar remained informed and engaged. He followed events carefully and spoke frequently about America's challenges in Iraq and in the region. He acknowledged that the surge, coupled with the key policy shifts by Sunni and Shiite leaders, helped lessen the volatility in Iraq. But he worried that the necessary political reconciliation was still not occurring. And he was frustrated that America's diplomatic resources were not unleashed in the region to bring together the many affected parties.

Conditions in Iraq had stabilized enough in 2008 for the U.S. and Iraqi governments to sign a Status of Forces Agreement under which U.S. combat forces would be pulled out of all cities and towns in favor of bases. The agreement set a December 31, 2011, deadline for the complete withdrawal of U.S. combat forces from Iraq.

After the election of Barack Obama to the presidency and his administration's decision to focus on Afghanistan, Lugar told the U.S. ambassador to Iraq, Christopher Hill, in September of 2009 that he was concerned that the United States was at risk of "taking our eyes off the other ball" in Iraq. There is some irony in this statement, for many warned in 2002 and 2003 that the United States was in danger of losing its focus on Afghanistan when it launched its invasion of Iraq.[37]

The interest of American policymakers and the public regarding Afghanistan had faded soon after the United States toppled the Taliban in the late fall of 2001. The Taliban government in Afghanistan had protected and sponsored al-Qaeda as it plotted the 9/11 attacks, and it refused to turn over leaders of the terrorist group after the attacks in the United States. Small numbers of U.S. troops and CIA special forces, working with Afghan anti-Taliban forces, drove the Taliban from power in late 2001. On December 6, 2001, the Taliban leadership fled Kandahar, a crucial stronghold for them. On the same day, the UN Security Council approved a provisional government headed up by Hamid Karzai. The Bush administration decided on a "light footprint" strategy for Afghanistan, sending in only a small number of troops to secure the nation. There were fewer than eight thousand American troops in Afghanistan in the summer of 2002. This approach, they believed, would avoid stirring nationalist anger in Afghanistan and would also allow them to gear up for the Iraq war. A senior State Department official at the time, Richard Haass, said the Bush administration was never confident that it could succeed in bringing about political stability or economic development in Afghanistan and decided not to try. Haass's suggestion of sending in between twenty-five thousand and thirty thousand U.S. troops into Afghanistan was rejected by senior administration officials.[38]

In the early years of post-Taliban governance, Afghanistan showed progress. In early 2004, Afghans voted for a new constitution and in October of that year they elected Karzai as president. In 2005, they voted for a parliament that included some ex-Taliban ministers. And in that year about 4.5 million Afghan children, including a million girls, attended school.[39]

But the Taliban gradually rebuilt its strength and launched attacks from the east and south on American and NATO troops, and Western causalities began to mount. By 2008, it was widely acknowledged that the Taliban was a much-revived force within Afghanistan. During his presidential campaign, Obama pledged to draw down American troops in Iraq and shift more resources to Afghanistan, which he said had been badly neglected.

Throughout the decade of American involvement in Afghanistan, Lugar warned repeatedly that the United States was failing to devote sufficient attention and resources to bringing about stability in Afghanistan. In a hearing in 2003 before the U.S. invasion of Iraq, Lugar said that as the United States was gearing up for key challenges in Iraq and North Korea, it should not lose focus on Afghanistan. "The international community will take notice of our staying power in Afghanistan. If we are able to help Afghanistan transition into a secure democracy, we will bolster our ability to attract allies in the war against terrorism. Our commitment to Afghanistan is also a demonstration of how we will approach post-conflict Iraq. American credibility is on the line in these situations, and we must understand that failure to follow through could have extremely negative consequences on the war on terror," he said.[40] Speaking weeks later at a Foreign Relations Committee hearing with Karzai, Lugar said "the fate of your country is a bellwether in the global campaign against terrorism." The United States, he said, should not let budgetary incrementalism or policy inattention weaken its commitment to governments and peoples "who have joined us in the war against terror."[41]

Several years later, in November of 2006, Lugar spoke at a German Marshall Fund conference in Riga, Latvia, before a NATO summit. He said that NATO was not succeeding in Afghanistan and that failure there would be a crushing blow to the alliance. "Afghanistan has become a test case for whether we can overcome the growing discrepancy between NATO's expanding missions and its lagging capabilities."[42]

But as Afghanistan drifted off the policy radar in Washington. Lugar repeatedly urged policymakers to pay more attention to Afghanistan and focus sufficient resources into it. But few were listening. Lugar urged the Obama administration to decide what it wanted to achieve in Afghanistan—but also to be realistic. During a high-profile hearing in the summer of 2010, Lugar told Richard Holbrooke, the administration's special envoy to Afghanistan, that the United States needed to define and explain its goals in Afghanistan. He said to Holbrooke that both civilian and military operations in Afghanistan were proceeding without a clear definition of success. At times, he said, it seemed as if the United States was trying to remake the political, economic, and social life of Afghanistan. "But these grand ambitions are beyond our resources," he said. At other times, American goals seemed far narrower, limited to preventing the Taliban from taking over the country and allowing Afghanistan to be a terrorist safe haven. But Lugar added that even this narrow definition required elaboration. How much Taliban military capability and territorial control was acceptable? How should American policymakers judge success? What time constraints did the administration perceive given resources and alliance pressures? How did the dynamics in Pakistan figure into the Afghanistan calculus?

The senator said that he understood why the administration didn't want to be pinned down on an ironclad definition of success in Afghanistan. But he said it was imperative to decide what missions are critical. "It is up to the President to define success and delineate how much time and how many resources should be devoted to achieving it," he said.[43] Lugar continued and even intensified his criticisms of Obama's policy on Afghanistan in 2011. He accused the administration of devoting enormous resources for the war in Afghanistan while neglecting the threat of terrorist havens in Yemen, Somalia, and Pakistan.[44]

V

Lugar's legacy on the wars in Iraq and Afghanistan is complex. As one studies his statements on both Iraq and Afghanistan, it is clear that Lugar was characteristically well informed. Regarding Iraq, as the nation moved toward war in 2002, he understood how consequential it was likely to be for American foreign policy. In speeches, statements, and private conversations, he pleaded with the Bush administration to approach any war carefully and to develop clear and detailed plans for postwar Iraq. He grew impatient and critical when these plans were never outlined. He asked hard and probing questions as the nation was moving toward war—an important responsibility for a legislator.

Lugar's comments, while often perceptive, were also complex, hedged in nuanced language, and difficult for the layperson to comprehend. They were not presented in a way that intensified public pressure on the administration to reassess its strategy. Lugar opted to focus heavily on influencing the administration in private, confidential discussions behind closed doors. When it became clear in the summer of 2007 that he was not getting through, he decided to voice his reservations forcefully and publicly. But by then, the train had already left the station. Bush was committed to a course of action and was not going to back down or reverse course.

One of the great unknowns is what might have occurred if Lugar had voiced his concerns and reservations more forcefully in the summer of 2002, as Brent Scowcroft did. Lugar was willing to raise questions about the coming war in Iraq but declined to forcefully emphasize his many concerns about the war.

Some believe that Lugar could—and should—have done more in 2002 and 2003 to slow the nation's rush to war. Senator Chuck Hagel, the second most senior Republican on the Foreign Relations Committee at that time, said Lugar's stature and reputation for thoughtfulness could have affected the debate. Hagel blames the Bush administration for not seeking out Lugar's counsel in the run-up to the war, because Lugar would have been an invaluable sounding board. "The Bush administration made a number of tragic mistakes regarding Iraq. I think it was a tragic mistake they didn't listen to him. I went to the President and to Condi Rice and urged them to have Lugar sit down with the president—without Dick Cheney—and listen to him. But they never did. They didn't use him. It was a terrible, terrible squandering of a resource. And Lugar wanted to help. It was a great waste," Hagel said.

But Hagel also believes Lugar should have been more outspoken in outlining his concerns, especially about the absence of a postwar strategy. "I went to him a number of times and urged him to get more out front on Iraq. I told him that he had a stature that no one else had in the Congress. I told him that I didn't think that anyone's voice was more powerful than his on this matter. I strongly encouraged him to speak out more forcefully and publicly."

"Dick opted to do it his way—quiet, private. I told him the White House wasn't going to listen to him that way. By his style, he marginal-ized himself. I think he could have done more. If you had Dick Lugar ratcheting it up on the Sunday shows, questioning everything with a little sharper verbiage I think it would have had an effect. I think Dick was too much under the thumb of the Republican leadership in Con-gress and the White House. I don't think he was near active enough and so the Congress was marginalized."[45]

Richard Armitage, the former deputy secretary of state, agrees that Lugar should have been more forceful in expressing his reservations regarding Iraq, adding that it might have affected the policy debate. "He should have stood up to the president a little more," Armitage said.[46]

As for the war in Afghanistan, from the early days of the war, Lugar said that American credibility was on the line and a successful effort to secure and rebuild Afghanistan was critical and would have captured the world's attention. But as a supporter of the American invasion of Iraq, Lugar backed a policy that had an outcome that he anticipated and warned against: a loss of American focus in Afghanistan and a ten-dency of American policymakers to see it as "the other war."

Lugar understood the deeply disruptive consequences that the wars in Iraq and Afghanistan had on American foreign policy. He believes the wars consumed much of the nation's attention and many of its re-sources. It was with this in mind that Lugar became a vocal and early critic of the Obama administration's decision to intervene in Libya in the spring of 2011. Speaking in the spring of 2011, Lugar said the United States should not "launch military intervention into yet another Mus-lim country, without thinking long and hard about the consequences and implications." He added that the American experience in Afghan-istan and Iraq, and earlier in Somalia, made it clear that the burden of proof should be on those who supported a military intervention as in the national interest of the United States.[47]

7

✤

Fixing Foreign Aid

I

When Richard Lugar delivered a major foreign policy address at the National Defense University a few weeks before the 2008 presidential election, his remarks attracted attention for the balanced way he discussed the agendas of the two presidential candidates—Barack Obama and John McCain. He applauded McCain's hard-nosed assessment of the world's problems but also credited Obama for his willingness to launch diplomatic initiatives toward nations that the United States was at odds with such as Iran and North Korea. With the presidential campaign in high gear, some Republicans grumbled that Lugar did not hit Obama hard enough. Many Democrats were quietly pleased that Lugar seemed to consider the foreign policy credentials of both candidates on equal footing.

The central theme of Lugar's speech, however, was lost by the partisan politics of the moment. It was that the United States urgently needed to get its foreign policy back on track and this required both advancing large and creative ideas and paying careful attention to the mechanics of implementing these policies. America's foreign policy, he told the group, had become too reactive in recent years, as it got bogged down in real and rhetorical battles with Iran, North Korea, Iraq, Russia, Cuba, Venezuela, and other nations. Lugar warned that if U.S. foreign policy attention is constantly consumed by crises with hostile regimes, it loses the initiative and limits its capacity to lead the world in constructive ways. While it would be wrong, he acknowledged, to ignore threats from countries like North Korea and Iran, American policymakers shouldn't allow their concerns with these regimes to "shorten our strategic horizon, militarize our foreign policy, unjustifiably concentrate our resources, or rob us of our strategic initiative."[1]

If the United States is to remain secure and prosperous, it must shape the diplomatic and economic conditions in the world, regaining the strategic initiative, he argued. This in turn requires both large and compelling ideas and careful attention to the "fundamental building blocks of U.S. foreign policy." These building blocks include strong alliances, solid trade relationships, well-functioning embassies, reliable intelligence, broad humanitarian contacts, effective treaty regimes, and a positive reputation abroad. "If this preparation has been neglected no amount of charisma, bravado, or diplomatic skill by the commander in chief and the national security team will make up the deficit. Attending to the building blocks of national leverage not only increases our opportunities for foreign policy success, it decreases the chances that we may be cornered in a position where military force becomes necessary," he said.[2]

Lugar, in his long Senate career, has championed consequential policies related to energy, non-proliferation, global food production, arms control, and adherence to international law. But he has also been a relentless advocate for paying attention to the basics of foreign policy and ensuring that good policy is delivered on the ground. Relatively few lawmakers take much interest in the plumbing of American foreign policy. It is not glamorous work, but it's important to the success of foreign policy.

II

When assessing U.S. national security programs, analysts often divide them into three broad categories: defense, diplomacy, and development. Most defense programs are managed by the Department of Defense and represent by far the largest portion of national security expenditures. Diplomacy refers primarily to the programs run by the

State Department. Development is the effort by the United States to help other nations improve their economies and health care and education systems and to respond to humanitarian needs. Many of these programs are funded through the U.S. Agency for International Development, but dozens of other federal agencies are also involved.

With his three decades on the Senate Foreign Relations Committee, Lugar has been primarily focused on diplomacy and development. He has been a champion of America's diplomats, pushing to make sure they are adequately funded, trained, and supported. And he has been a strong, but not uncritical, advocate of the nation's foreign assistance programs. Unlike some Republicans who are adamantly opposed to foreign aid, Lugar believes that these programs, when carefully developed and well managed, can benefit the United States and the nations that receive American assistance. He has disagreed fundamentally with the view of one prominent Republican, Senator Jesse Helms, who charged that foreign assistance is little more than "throwing money down foreign rat holes."[3]

Lugar believes the U.S. government has been too inclined to look at its national security structure from the narrow perspective of each of these three categories and not sufficiently attentive to constructing a coherent national security strategy to tackle threats and take advantage of opportunities the country faces now and will likely face in the future. Too often, he has argued, Congress and the White House focus on specific elements of national security without developing an integrated national security strategy. Once a strategy is in place, Lugar said, the nation should determine what structural reforms are needed and how to better coordinate defense, development, and diplomatic programs.[4]

As he surveyed the U.S. national security apparatus, Lugar identified two areas of concern: the heavy imbalance toward defense programs and the lack of coordination between the various civilian agencies that allocate U.S. foreign assistance. Lugar frequently observed that the country's military and civilian capabilities are out of balance; he has joined others in warning about the militarization of American foreign policy. In a July 2008 hearing of the Senate Foreign Relations Committee on the increasing role of the military in American foreign policy,

Lugar said the expanding prominence of the Pentagon required urgent reassessment. Especially since 9/11, the Pentagon's role has increased markedly in stabilization and reconstruction, foreign assistance, and public information programs. There has been increased funding and new authorities even though many experts do not consider the military well suited to be running these programs. Nevertheless, Congress granted new authorities to the Defense Department because civilian agencies lacked the capacity to provide needed services.

"It is clear that our military and civilian capabilities are severely out of balance," Lugar said at the hearing. "While Congress maintains generous levels of funding for our military, funding for our diplomacy and foreign assistance persistently falls short." The expanded role of the Pentagon in national security raised fundamental questions, Lugar said.[5] Should the Pentagon be involved in programs of a purely civilian nature? What are the consequences of U.S. engagement in the world that is "fronted by a military program"? Does the United States, through its generous support of military programs in some nations, risk professionalizing foreign militaries to the extent that they overshadow the capacities of civilian governments? If the State Department's assistance programs are sometimes cumbersome and slow, shouldn't this be addressed directly rather than by creating competing programs in other agencies? Lugar said it was necessary to develop an integrated national security strategy that assigned roles and allocated resources according to the strength of each foreign policy agency. It's critical to avoid "mission creep" by the Pentagon in ways that had not been carefully considered by all the relevant policy actors.[6]

One analyst said the emergence of the Pentagon as the supreme national security agency challenges long-standing American traditions. "When the Pentagon has a much greater overseas presence than the State Department, we have traveled a long way from the early days of the Republic, when the writers of the Constitution did not even anticipate the existence of a Department of Defense," the analyst wrote. "With jobs to be done that no one else wanted, the military became the executive branch's go-to institution.... Unlike every other liberal democracy in the world, America today clothes its lead diplomatic team in a military uniform," she added.[7]

Lugar's effort to rethink the role of the Pentagon in national security was strongly supported by Defense Secretary Robert Gates, who made this case forcefully and repeatedly. Gates argued that if the United States hopes to tackle the difficult challenges around the world in the coming decades, it needs to strengthen other components of national power both institutionally and financially and to create the capacity to integrate and apply all of the elements of national power to problems and challenges abroad. Gates argued that one of the key lessons to emerge from the wars in Iraq and Afghanistan was that military success is not sufficient and that economic development, institution building, the rule of law, promoting internal reconciliation, good governance, providing basic services, training and equipping indigenous military and police forces, and strategic communications are critical to long-term success. These require competent and adequately funded civilian agencies. There was a pressing need, Gates argued, to increase spending on "the civilian instruments of national security: diplomacy, strategic communications, foreign assistance, civil action, and economic reconstruction and development."[8]

The Pentagon chief noted that the Pentagon's budget, even without calculating spending for the wars in Afghanistan and Iraq, is more than $550 billion a year, while the State Department's budget is under $40 million. This $40 billion is less than what the Pentagon spends on health care each year. And the nation's 6,600 foreign service officers are fewer than it takes to operate one aircraft carrier strike group. Using an even more striking example, Gates observed that there are as many people in Pentagon marching bands as in the entire U.S. diplomatic corps.

While concerned about the large and growing role of the Pentagon in U.S. national security programs, Lugar also lamented the confusing sprawl of civilian programs involved in foreign aid. This created ambiguity about what entities are developing aid policy and raised questions as to whether there is sufficient coordination, not just between the State Department and the U.S. Agency for International Development but among the two dozen or so government department, agencies, and offices that provide some type of foreign aid.[9]

The senator has observed that there are many entities within the U.S. government involved in the dispensation of development assistance. These programs support economic development, humanitarian assistance, disaster relief, security and military initiatives, governance and rule of law, health, and trade development.

The USAID was created in 1961 to be the nation's lead agency in dispensing U.S bilateral economic aid as well as disaster relief programs. It was created to separate long-term development from military and security aid. It was designed to serve the cause of development independent of strategic concerns. Since results were never immediate, USAID's performance has been under constant debate, and efforts to either refine or fundamentally overhaul its operations have been a permanent feature of policy debates. In 2006, Secretary of State Rice created the position of director of foreign assistance, who also served as head of USAID. This move essentially absorbed USAID into the State Department.[10] The State Department runs several assistance programs dealing with weapons of mass destruction, narcotics, refugee relief, and law enforcement. The Department of Defense, in addition to its programs to project American military strength, runs or co-runs programs such as foreign military financing and international military education and financing. The Treasury Department manages three foreign assistance programs and oversees the U.S. contributions to the World Bank, International Monetary Fund, and other multilateral development banks.[11]

The Bush administration, while at least rhetorically elevating development to the status of defense and diplomacy, created a number of agencies that appeared to undermine USAID's role. For example, Bush created the Millennium Challenge Corporation in 2004 to manage a program that concentrated resources on a small number of lower- and middle-income nations that adopted political and economic reforms. The Bush administration also created other programs for delivering foreign assistance outside the ambit of USAID, such as the Middle East Partnership, the President's Emergency Plan for AIDS Relief, and the Malaria Initiative. In addition to these new entities, other agencies such as the Peace Corps, the Overseas Private Investment Corporation, and the African Development Foundation are involved in dispensing various types of assistance around the world.

While all of these agencies vie for scarce funds and clear missions, the 1961 Foreign Assistance Act, the main law that is supposed to guide

American foreign assistance programs, has become an unwieldy mess. And it began with enormous complexity; one scholar points out that in its original form it outlined 33 goals, 75 priority areas, and 247 directives.[12]

For years, American policymakers interested in development have debated a number of issues such as the appropriate level of U.S. official assistance, the growing prominence of the private sector in overall assistance, the best way to coordinate foreign assistance among the various domestic agencies, the optimum balance between bilateral and multilateral aid, and the most effective way to coordinate American efforts with other those of other nations.

III

To help Congress sort through these and other issues and begin to create a coherent foreign assistance strategy, Lugar commissioned two studies by the Senate Foreign Relations Committee's staff. He wanted to understand how these complicated and sometimes theoretical issues affected the actual delivery of aid on the ground. Before embracing specific reforms, Lugar wanted to have a clear factual record to consult.

In 2006, Lugar sent a committee investigative team to visit 20 countries in Latin America, Africa, Asia, and the Middle East to examine the relationships between the State Department and the Defense Department in American embassies. He wanted them to assess the agencies' cooperation on counterterrorism strategy and foreign assistance programs. The report was to examine how the U.S. government could strengthen its posture overseas and provide a more effective response to terrorism.

The report, *Embassies as Command Posts in the Anti-terror Campaign*, was released in December of 2006. It found that the number of military personnel and Defense Department activities in non-combat countries was increasing significantly. It warned that blurred lines of authority between the State Department and the Defense Department could lead to interagency turf wars that undermined the effectiveness of the overall U.S. effort against terrorism.[13]

The staff investigative report said that as a result of inadequate funding for civilian programs, U.S. defense agencies were increasingly being granted authority and funding to fill perceived gaps. The rise in funding, self-assigned missions, and realigned authorities for the Secretary of Defense and the combatant commanders were creating new strains on interagency coordination in the field. It found evidence that some host countries were questioning the increasingly military component of America's presence overseas. Some foreign officials questioned what they saw as a new emphasis by the United States on military approaches to problems that did not have military solutions.

The report noted that some countries were receiving between a quarter and a half of their U.S. foreign aid in the form of military assistance. In one country visited by the staff, security assistance was the only form of foreign aid provided by the U.S. government. The report concluded that the military had taken on a number of new tasks in the war against terror and had a greater presence in embassies. The study recommended a more prominent role for ambassadors, saying that in the campaign against terror, the leadership qualities of the U.S. ambassador have become a critical factor in victory or failure. Additionally, it recommended that the administration develop a comprehensive budget for foreign assistance that incorporated economic, development, humanitarian, security, and military assistance.

In a follow-up study the next year, Lugar directed his staff to examine how American embassies actually dealt with foreign assistance overseas. He sent the panel's staff to 24 countries in Latin America, Africa, Eastern Europe, Asia, and the Middle East to assess how increased funding and new programs were being implemented in the field. The staff was also asked to examine how a new foreign assistance management process created by Secretary of State Rice was working. The report, *Embassies Grapple to Guide Foreign Aid*, was released in November of 2007. In his transmittal letter, Lugar said there was a need to prioritize U.S, goals and design strategies so they were transparent to policymakers, legislators, and recipients. It was necessary to be able to measure, analyze, and assess outcomes so that policymakers could tell what programs are working and making a positive difference.[14]

Lugar said the U.S. policy community naturally focused on events in Washington, but it was necessary to pay attention to the countries where foreign aid programs are actually carried out. It was essential to know if U.S. embassies were up to the task of managing new programs and the increased funding. It was critical to see how the proliferation of programs and the new management process were affecting operations overseas and to gather new perspectives from American staff working overseas.

The report found that many of the personnel in embassies felt the U.S. government and the community of international development supporters failed to agree on either the importance or the content of foreign aid strategy. There was a striking lack of common purpose. The study concluded that agreement between headquarters and the field on foreign assistance was minimal and communications were complicated rather than improved by the State Department's efforts to provide strategic direction from Washington. From the perspectives of those running assistance programs, policymakers in both the executive and legislative branches often seemed demanding and inconsistent. New interests, from democracy promotion to HIV-AIDS prevention, appeared to surface regularly even though they had long been a priority for those actually running programs.

The report recommended that the president craft a foreign assistance strategy that spelled out the humanitarian and security rationales for foreign assistance. The president should instruct the Secretary of State to work with the USAID administrator to implement the president's foreign assistance strategy, giving the Secretary of State the explicit authority to ensure that all foreign assistance to individual countries and regions be in the foreign policy interest of the United States. The Secretary of State should partner with the USAID chief and Congress to secure the foreign assistance funding needed to carry out the president's strategy. The Secretary of State should provide strategic direction, transparency, and accountability to foreign aid. The USAID should be recognized for its central role in U.S. development policy. The position of administrator of USAID should be restored to its former status as a position separate and distinct from the State Department.

The staff report recommended that foreign assistance functions and authorities should not be migrating to the Department of Defense because of inadequate executive branch requests for funding in the proper budget account. Congress should use its oversight power to ensure that foreign aid spending is carefully and purposefully spent. Lawmakers should also overhaul the 1961 Foreign Assistance Act, and the congressional panels should take up and pass a foreign aid authorization bill at least every 2 years.

IV

These reports confirmed for Lugar that a major overhaul effort was needed for U.S. foreign aid programs. Such an effort, Lugar argued, must recognize that development and diplomacy were complementary but also "distinct disciplines." Diplomacy is more concerned with solving immediate problems, while development takes a wider and even less strategic view. "These differences underscore why development must be an independent partner of diplomacy and not merely its servant," he said. Lugar argued that American development policy should focus on large issues such as food scarcity, poverty, disease, and environmental degradation.[15]

Lugar said that as the United States rediscovered the importance of foreign assistance, it needed a stronger foundation to support a more effective development strategy. The nation had increased funds for development and elevated its priority but had allowed USAID to wither. Many new programs were located outside of USAID, with roughly two dozen departments and agencies involved with some aspects of foreign assistance, including the Pentagon. Each of these agencies naturally considered itself the lead agency in its sector, provoking competition among agencies rather than coordination and coherence.

Lugar joined about a dozen members of the Senate Foreign Relations Committee in a yearlong effort to develop legislation that would begin to bolster USAID. The bill, introduced in July of 2009, reestablished a bureau for policy and strategic planning within USAID, created a council on research and evaluation of foreign assistance, mandated a comprehensive review of all aspects of USAID's human resources, and set up a high-level task force on personnel issues.[16]

Lugar said the bill was a "relatively modest proposal" but he applauded the measure's broad support with nearly two dozen Senate sponsors. "This level of backing for a bill related to foreign assistance is extremely rare," Lugar said. The senator said it was essential to give

USAID basic budget, policy development, and evaluation tools. "Our development efforts will never be as effective as they should be if the agency that houses most of our development expertise is cut out of relevant policy, evaluation, and budgetary decisions," he said.[17]

He envisioned the bill as the first step in a two-step process. Congress should pass the measure to bolster USAID and then consider broader structural reforms to achieve fundamental changes in U.S. foreign aid and development programs. For the broader package, Lugar said he was eager to review several Obama administration studies on foreign assistance and development that were released in 2010. In September of 2010, the president pledged a new American approach to development, with an intense focus on boosting economic growth by strengthening multilateral programs, encouraging the work of nongovernmental development actors, and working in better alignment of the priorities of developing nations.[18] The president's plan said it was important to elevate development as a pillar of U.S. national security and to reestablish the United States as the global leader in international development. The State Department issued a separate report in December of 2010, the first Quadrennial Diplomacy and Development Review. The report underscored many of the themes that Lugar had been advancing, including the need to expand the country's civilian power and to upgrade USAID. The report emphasized the critical roles played by ambassadors in overseas embassies and said U.S. development funds should focus on food security, global health, climate change, sustainable economic growth, democracy and governance, and humanitarian assistance. Under the State Department plan, USAID would be in charge of two new important Obama programs: the Feed the Future program and the Global Health Initiative.[19]

V

While working on the broad overhaul of foreign assistance programs with Foreign Relations Committee Chairman John Kerry and several members of the House of Representatives, Lugar also teamed up with Kerry in 2009 on a shorter-term but urgent priority to provide aid to Pakistan. This assistance was badly needed for a nation that was struggling with economic and security challenges and appeared perpetually on the verge of unraveling.

The Lugar-Kerry bill provided about $1.5 billion a year and $7.5 billion over 5 years to Pakistan for non-security programs. This was about triple what the United States typically sent to Pakistan each year for non-security assistance. The purpose of the legislation, the senators said, was to establish a "deeper, broader, long term strategic engagement" with Pakistan, a long-term relationship built on mutual trust and cooperation.[20] Their bill delinked military from non-military aid. In the past, security assistance dwarfed development aid, so the military could bypass the civilian government. Now American economic assistance to Pakistan would no longer be the neglected cousin to military aid.

The Kerry-Lugar bill required the American president to submit a detailed plan on American assistance to Pakistan, describing key objectives of the United States, the role of Pakistani institutions, and the amounts allocated to specific projects. It stipulated that non-security assistance should be used for projects that benefit the people of Pakistan such as police reform, independent judicial systems, political pluralism and rule of law programs, investments in children and women, education, and food security. The bill set up benchmarks for measuring the effectiveness of the U.S. strategy, focusing on outcomes. It required the president to submit a semi-annual report to Congress that described in detail the aid provided to Pakistan. It required the secretary of state, in consultation with the Pentagon and the director of national intelligence, to submit an annual report on progress of Pakistani security forces. The bill left the level of security aid to be determined each year. The Kerry-Lugar package conditioned military aid on certification that the Pakistani military was making a concerted effort against al-Qaeda and the Taliban and was not blocking the political or judicial process in Pakistan.

After Congress approved the bill and it was signed by President Obama, military and opposition political leaders in Pakistan blasted the new American aid package, charging the United States with trying to meddle in Pakistan's internal affairs by imposing conditions on assistance. No sooner had these tensions eased than devastating floods in the late summer of 2010 ravaged Pakistan, forcing Kerry, Lugar, and others to reassess how the United States could help its beleaguered ally. Adding further complexity to the American-Pakistan relationship, U.S special forces killed Osama Bin Laden in Pakistan in the summer of 2011, raising the suspicions of many Americans that at least some Pakistani leaders were aware that Bin Laden had been hiding in their country.

The difficulty of developing an effective assistance plan for just one nation underscored how challenging it will be to fix the nation's overall foreign assistance programs. After the 2010 mid-term elections, one of Lugar's allies in the foreign assistance reform effort, House Foreign Affairs Committee Chairman Howard Berman, lost his chairmanship in the Republican sweep of the House. The new chairman of the panel, Congresswoman Ileana Ros-Lehtinen, made it clear that she had no interest in foreign aid reform. She said the focus should shift to cutting foreign assistance programs and making sure that those that remained were run efficiently.[21] But Lugar vowed to stay involved and wait for another opportunity to press ahead with a foreign assistance overhaul that he believes is critical for American foreign policy. Taking a long-term perspective, Lugar is convinced that strengthening the building blocks of American foreign policy, including foreign assistance, must remain an important priority.

8

Combatting the Global Food Crisis

I

Richard Lugar is not usually one for superlatives. But when he speaks about Norman Borlaug his words are full of admiration, even awe. They reflect both the senator's idea of what constitutes a valuable career and also the importance of bold American-supported efforts to help feed the world. In a tribute to Borlaug given shortly after the scientist's death in 2009, Lugar lavished praise on the man who is widely credited for launching the Green Revolution that boosted agricultural productivity with especially profound consequences for the developing world. Lugar credits Borlaug's pioneering work on plant research with transforming the lives of hundreds of millions of people, adding that Borlaug saw more clearly than almost anyone the connection between agriculture and a prosperous and peaceful world.

Lugar is impressed by Borlaug's towering professional accomplishments in agriculture as well as his cast of mind. "He was a man of vision but also one of great practicality," Lugar said. When studying Borlaug's early writings, Lugar was struck by the scientist's "acute perception of the future and his ability to see past the pressing problems of finding the right wheat or rice variety to grasp firmly the larger dimensions of his work."

The senator was especially impressed that the creative thinker who helped launch the Green Revolution also considered more prosaic issues to help feed people, such as building sound infrastructure, irrigation, and food distribution systems. Borlaug also stressed the importance of sound economic, trade, property, education, and agricultural policies. Describing Borlaug in words that many use to describe him, Lugar said the scientist was a man "whose optimism never flagged and who believed that constant striving would eventually wear down all obstacles."[1]

II

Lugar's interest in agriculture goes back to his youth. His grandfather, Riley Webster Lugar, farmed in Morgan and Marion Counties in Indiana and his father, Marvin, purchased a farm in 1931 that Lugar still owns. Lugar worked on the farm during summers as a boy, pulling corn from fields of soybeans. He frequently tells stories about the lessons he learned from working on the farm and the enormous challenge of running a successful farm.

Lugar begins most days in his Senate office by checking crop prices online. And he proudly observes that he helps design the crop plan for his farm each year. For most of his adult life, Lugar has a deep interest in American agricultural policy and the global challenges facing agriculture. Lugar chaired the Senate Agriculture Committee from 1995 to 2001 and used his leadership position to write a farm bill that many described as bold. His Freedom to Farm legislation sought to replace the New Deal–era regime of crop subsidies with a 7-year schedule of fixed payments, moving farmers toward a free market system. Much of the law was later overturned by the Bush administration and Democratic and Republican lawmakers who were comfortable with the country's elaborate and expensive farm subsidy programs.

Lugar lamented the demise of his reforms, arguing that traditional American agriculture policy distorts food prices, hamstrings innovation, limits product diversity, and offers subsidies to a select group of farmers at enormous public cost.[2] The protectionist bent of American farm policy, with heavy domestic subsidies and import barriers, also disrupts global markets and punishes farmers in the developing world. He has observed that the United States shuts out poor nations' farm exports while subsidizing its own farmers to sell abroad at below cost. Other analysts have noted that the United States, Europe, and Japan spend about $350 billion a year subsidizing their own farmers while negotiating trade deals with nations requiring them to drop their own farm subsidies.[3]

After his Freedom to Farm bill was dismantled, Lugar continued offering alternative agriculture policies as amendments on the floor of the Senate. Under one of Lugar's most recent plans, a safety net would be provided for all farmers, regardless of where they live or what they grow. He sought to cap annual farm assistance at $30,000 per recipient and pushed to end crop-specific subsidies in favor of an income insurance program for all farms. He proposed making all farmers eligible for risk management accounts.[4]

While battling to overhaul American farm subsidy programs, Lugar also emerged as one of Congress's leading champions of federal child nutrition programs. He fought off an attempt by House Speaker Newt Gingrich in 1995 to turn a federal school lunch program into a state block grant program. Lugar called this one of his proudest legislative achievements. "This was an important moment in public policy," he said.[5]

III

As a former chairman of both the Senate Agriculture and Foreign Relations committees, Lugar has studied the connection between U.S. agriculture and foreign policies for decades. The senator has long observed that the global food situation is highly precarious; about 2 billion people live on less than $2 a day. A sudden increase in food prices can plunge millions into malnutrition and threaten starvation.

Lugar has been talking about America's opportunity—and even responsibility—to help feed the world since 1996, and he has used his chairmanship of the Agriculture Committee to advocate for expanded agriculture research and innovation. In a major speech on the challenges of feeding the world in October of 1997, the senator outlined the essence of the challenge facing the United States and the world. He said that the world's population was poised to increase from about 6 billion to more than 9 billion people by 2050. To feed this huge increase in the world's population, global farm production would have to triple on about the same acreage. The "only hope" to accomplish this would be major advances in agriculture productivity prompted by a significant infusion of research funds, especially in the area of biotechnology. Lugar said he was confident that historic advances could be achieved in developing drought-resistant crops and high-yield seeds that revolutionize agriculture. The other critical element to being able to feed the world was a major effort to dismantle tariff and non-tariff trade barriers that badly distorted agricultural trade.[6]

For a decade, Lugar's work in this area proceeded quietly and attracted relatively little notice. But beginning in 2006, a combination of high oil prices, weak harvests in important exporting nations, and rising global demand pushed up food prices around the world, causing a food panic that shook a number of governments and caused riots overseas. The steep jump in commodity prices in 2007 and 2008 helped ignite food-related demonstrations in 30 countries during the spring and summer of 2008.[7]

As the crisis worsened in the summer of 2008, Lugar urged the Bush White House to pay close attention to the situation and pressed it to take steps to alleviate the short-term crisis while also addressing its structural causes. Lugar sent a letter to President Bush, politely urging greater high-level attention to the crisis. He delivered a speech about global hunger at the American Enterprise Institute and organized his summer overseas travels to explore the issue in greater depth.[8]

Lugar argued the 2008 food crisis was driven by increasing demand for food from growing populations in emerging countries, soaring energy prices that drove up costs all along the farm-to-market chain, increased demand for bio-fuels, droughts in several important exporting nations, cutoffs in grain exports by major suppliers, market-distorting subsidies, and the falling U.S. dollar. Looking at the big picture, Lugar said it was important to consider how the international community could improve its ability to anticipate and respond effectively to future food problems. It was also critical to determine how to achieve open trade in support of food security when the United States and European Union continued to fund large agriculture subsidies for their domestic farmers. The senator also said that policymakers around the world needed to promote greater agriculture productivity from improved farming methods, even when some opposed genetically modified seeds.[9]

Focusing on the crisis at hand, he urged Bush to emphasize food issues at a coming G8 summit and support policies such as reconstituting the Food Aid Convention that expired in 2003, using the convention to manage regionally placed supplies of food stocks, establishing a mechanism that monitors food shortages, doubling international assistance for agriculture productivity, cutting back farm subsidies to remove market distortions, and backing a strong G8 statement to invest in the next generation of bio-fuels made from non-food stocks.[10]

As Lugar pondered the food crisis, he was convinced that it was both a huge challenge for American foreign, trade, and agricultural policies and an opportunity to rehabilitate the nation's battered global image given the controversial war in Iraq and tensions on other matters. The nation, he said, had an opportunity to demonstrate its technological prowess and humanitarian leadership. There was, he said, an opening to launch a "new era in diplomacy" through enlightened food policy.[11]

"In the best case, the cause for ending hunger worldwide would become a pillar of U.S. foreign policy, and it would be recognized as such by nations around the world. Such an effort could build relationships with nations where, up to now, we have had few mutual endeavors. It could help solidify our global image, improve our trade relations, and serve as a model for similar efforts in the areas of energy and scientific cooperation," he said in remarks to the Alliance to End Hunger.[12]

IV

The Center for Strategic and International Studies, a respected think tank based in Washington, had been studying the global food crisis, and its leaders decided they wanted to elevate the issue and help frame the debate. In May of 2008, CSIS created a task force to assess the rising humanitarian, security, developmental, and market impacts of rising food costs and shortages.

They asked Lugar and Senator Bob Casey to serve as the co-chairs of the task force. Casey was a freshman Democrat on the Foreign Relations Committee. Though he had no specific expertise on the issue, he had a reputation as a serious-minded problem solver. Lugar is known as a heavyweight on agriculture and foreign policy, having studied global food problems for decades. Lugar took advantage of the opportunity to co-chair the CSIS task force. It allowed him to dig deeper into the issue, expand his network of contacts, and take advantage of a new platform to make a major push for new policies.

Stephen Morrison, the CSIS project director, said later he was delighted that Lugar was available to co-chair the task force. Lugar had considerable standing in the Congress and across the world on international affairs and a special expertise on this issue. Morrison added that Lugar spoke with "pragmatism and vision," noting that during the deliberations of the task force, Lugar pressed for a concrete action plan.[13]

When the task force's first report was unveiled in June of 2008, Lugar attended the briefing held in the Senate Russell Building. Speaking to a packed room of policy analysts and food activists, Lugar defined the global food problem and made the case for a vigorous American response. Forceful and coherent American policies directed at the global food crisis would bolster the country's standing in the world and repair some of the damage to America's reputation that occurred in recent years. The world's view of America would shift, he argued, if the United States led a bold response to a problem in which nearly one billion suffer from chronic food insecurity and about twenty-five thousand die every day from malnutrition-related causes.

"One of today's big ideas should be the eradication of hunger worldwide. We can bring America's dedication to science, innovation, technology, and education to bear on expanding the global food supply and helping others feed themselves. It is in our own interest to lead the world in developing and disseminating innovative solutions to ensure that food scarcity does not hold back human potential," Lugar said.[14]

Lugar said the current food crisis was triggered by a complex web of factors that converged at the same moment: government mismanagement, flawed food distribution systems, insufficient investments in agricultural research, and the failure of many countries to embrace credible science. The situation threatened to increase global hunger but also to undermine many of the development and health gains that had been achieved over the previous decade. The U.S. response needed to be as multifaceted as the cause. Lugar directly confronted a controversy that he believes is critical to the global food problem: the taboo in Europe and some developing nations against genetically modified crops. He lamented that conventional biotechnology and sustainable farming techniques had not been universally accepted around the world. "In some parts of the world, farmers are trying to feed their families with technology that would not seem out of place in biblical times." He observed that of the 23 countries that used genetically modified crops, nearly all were food exporters. "Not surprisingly, the nearly 40 countries that are threatened by the recent spikes in food prices and by increases in the number of undernourished are not on this list," he said.[15]

Lugar then came to another controversial aspect of the crisis: the view that the increasing use of bio-fuels, such as corn for ethanol, was partly responsible for the crisis. Many believe the diversion of some crops into the production of ethanol has boosted food prices. Lugar has been a dogged champion of ethanol and has vigorously supported various tax and subsidy programs to promote it, a policy that has caused some to question how complete his faith in free market agriculture really is.

Lugar said that food and energy security should be goals pursued simultaneously, arguing that overcoming energy scarcity is one of the central ways to ensure an affordable and transportable global food supply. Abandoning bio-fuels ultimately would reduce the planet's ability to feed itself. He said he was confident that the science that had taken the world to this point would also take it beyond the use of food crops for bio-fuels. Major progress has been made in accelerating advanced bio-fuels derived from agriculture, forest, and municipal waste and from special energy crops like switchgrass.

The CSIS report released by Lugar and Casey outlined modest but tangible reforms. The report recommended modernizing and doubling emergency assistance, elevating rural assistance and agricultural productivity to major foreign policy priorities, and revising the U.S. approach to bio-fuels so that fuel and food security objectives are jointly addressed.

For Lugar, the CSIS task force was the beginning of a more intense effort to tackle the global hunger crisis. Teaming up with Casey, the two senators introduced the Global Food Security Bill in the fall of 2008 and then reintroduced it early in 2009 for a new Congress and a new president. The package was a 5-year plan offering modest solutions that would have a concrete impact. It created a special coordinator in the U.S. government for global food security who would be in charge of developing a food security strategy for the nation. In addition, the plan authorized about $10 billion over 5 years for agricultural productivity and rural development based on the experience of American land grant universities, and it bolstered U.S. emergency response by creating a separate emergency food assistance fund that could make local and regional purchases of food.[16]

Trying to keep a clear focus on the problem and educate Congress and the American public on the global food challenge, Lugar commissioned a special report by the staff of the Senate Foreign Relations Committee. He sent a team of committee staffers to visit ten countries to investigate the causes of food insecurity and outline practical steps the United States and other countries could take to tackle this problem. The report, Lugar hoped, would keep the issue before Congress and provide a factual foundation to make an aggressive legislative push to deal with the crisis in the coming year. The Senate Foreign Relations Committee staff traveled to Costa Rica, Ethiopia, Guatemala, Indonesia, Laos, the Philippines, South Africa, Uganda, Vietnam, and Zambia and met with officials from governments, non-governmental organizations, universities, research institutions, the World Bank, the International Monetary Fund, the World Food Program, the U.S Department of Agriculture, and the U.S. Agency for International Development.

Released in February of 2009, the committee report found that high food prices imperiled recent advances in alleviating extreme hunger. It said the demand for food from growing and wealthier populations would continue to test the world's ability to feed itself. The staff report also found that some populations such as children, women, and the sick are more vulnerable to undernourishment and that the burden of food insecurity falls hardest on women who are the heads of households. It noted that wealthy countries have based their development on a strong agriculture sector. Greater attention to small and medium-sized land holders could produce high rates of return, and basic investments in better fertilizer, seed, and irrigation could improve productivity.

It also concluded that trying to support a growing population by expanding land under cultivation would have negative environmental effects. Rather, the focus should be on getting more production from existing land. The staff report, reflecting Lugar's views, argued that fighting hunger should be a centerpiece of U.S. foreign assistance policy and that the eradication of global hunger served U.S. national security interests and reflected the humanitarian impulse of the American people. The international community had failed to understand the importance of keeping up investments in agriculture for both food production and poverty alleviation. It argued that people had been lulled into complacency by decades of low food prices and hadn't prepared for growing population, urbanization, environmental degradation, and energy supply disruptions. It predicted that unless there is more focus on the problem the world would likely experience frequent and intense crises that increase migration, stimulate conflicts, intensify pandemics, and exacerbate poverty. The report ended with a quote from Lugar: "The United States cannot feed every person, lift every person out of poverty, cure every disease, or stop every conflict. But our power and status have conferred upon us a tremendous responsibility to humanity."[17]

Lugar urged the new chairman of the Senate Foreign Relations Committee, John Kerry, to hold a hearing in March of 2009 on global food issues with a panel of experts to keep the challenge alive before Congress. During that hearing, Lugar said the package that he and Casey developed was a practical starting point for improving American and global efforts to confront hunger. It was not perfect, Lugar acknowledged, but a clear place to begin. On the last day of March 2009, the Senate Foreign Relations Committee approved the Lugar-Casey bill. President Obama endorsed the essence of the legislation a few days later.

At least partly in response to Lugar's prodding, the State Department released policy papers on global hunger in the early months of 2009 and then outlined the key elements of the Global Hunger and Food Security Initiative in September of 2009. "More than one billion people—nearly a sixth of the world's population—suffer from chronic hunger," the State Department paper began. While more of a discussion of the problem of global hunger than a policy plan, the State Department papers said the U.S. government supported a comprehensive approach to food security that focused on advancing agricultural-led growth to reduce undernutrition. It would also be necessary to increase the impact of humanitarian food assistance. The State Department said the United States needed to develop a "whole of government strategy" to attack this problem and endorsed the idea pushed by Lugar and Casey of a U.S. global food security coordinator.[18]

Lugar was pleased the Obama administration was focusing on the global food challenge. He said that the administration, led by Secretary of State Hillary Clinton, had done "its own intensive study of food security" and reached some of the same conclusions as he and Casey had about the importance of boosting agricultural productivity and incomes, promoting research and technology, focusing on the special role of women farmers, and the nutritional needs of children.

Both his plan and the State Department papers supported developing partnerships with host country governments, the private sector, and universities. Lugar vowed to keep working for legislation that represented a consensus among Congress, the administration, and the NGO community. "We are in reach of unified government action on the difficult issue of food security," Lugar said.[19]

Lugar was encouraged when the administration unveiled a sweeping Feed the Future program at the end of 2010 that reflected ideas he had been advancing for several years, including placing a greater emphasis on helping poor farmers in 20 developing nations in sub-Saharan Africa increase production, market their goods, and earn a greater income.[20]

9

❦

Transforming America's Relationship with India

I

The first day of October 2008 was not a typical day in the U.S. Senate. With the global economy melting down and the U.S. presidential race heating up, the attention of most of the country and much of the world was focused on Washington and on Congress's upper chamber. Senate leaders had scheduled a vote that evening on a controversial $700 billion financial rescue package. An earlier version had failed in the House and a new package had been assembled. Financial markets around the world waited for the Senate vote with jittery anticipation. Senate passage was critical, and both Barack Obama and John McCain left the campaign trail and returned to Washington to vote on the plan. Majority Leader Harry Reid and Minority Leader Mitch McConnell, working closely with the Bush administration, also scheduled a Senate vote that evening on a nuclear agreement between the United States and India.

While Richard Lugar was keenly interested in the fate of the financial rescue legislation, he was not directly involved in developing it. However, the nuclear accord was something he had worked on for more than 3 years and was dear to his heart. The landmark nuclear agreement between the world's two largest democracies would open U.S. nuclear trade with India after a 30-year freeze and could reshape the country's often troubled relationship with India into a strategic partnership.

The agreement was very consequential but also mind-numbingly complex. Submitted by the Bush administration and reworked by Congress, Lugar was one of a handful of legislators who understood its big picture consequences and its thousands of intricate details. The three other lawmakers who had worked on the accord with Lugar were no longer involved. Congressmen Henry Hyde and Tom Lantos, former chairmen of the House Foreign Affairs Committee, had died. Hyde died in 2007 and Lantos passed away earlier in 2008. Joe Biden, Lugar's Senate partner on the bill, was spending the fall of 2008 on the campaign trail as Obama's running mate.

With the Senate vote on the rescue package set for the evening, a portion of the day was allocated for debate on the nuclear agreement. Lugar managed the bill on the Senate floor with Democratic senator Chris Dodd, who was standing in for Biden. Most senators paid little attention to the discussion about the nuclear agreement. This legislation, however consequential, was not the day's main event and even seemed peripheral given the collapsing global economy.

During his remarks on the Senate floor, Lugar tried to explain to his weary and distracted colleagues the significance of what they were about to vote on. "This is, indeed, a historic day and a historic moment in the relationship between the United States and India, a very important partnership for world peace," he said.[1] "This is one of the most important strategic diplomatic initiatives undertaken in the last decade. By concluding this pact, the United States has embraced a long-term outlook that will give us new diplomatic options and improved global stability."

The senator said the legislation would allow the United States to engage in peaceful nuclear cooperation with India, while advancing its national security and non-proliferation goals. "It is an opportunity to build a strategic partnership with a nation, India, that shares our democratic values and will exert increasing influence on the world stage," he declared.

Lugar said it would usher in a new, more constructive relationship with India, while easing disagreements over non-proliferation challenges. Under the accord, India could purchase nuclear fuel technology and reactors from the United States that were previously denied it because of its status outside the Nuclear Non-Proliferation Treaty. In return, India agreed to create a new national export control system, maintain its unilateral nuclear testing moratorium, work with the United States to stop the spread of enrichment and reprocessing technologies, and separate its civilian and military facilities under safeguards established by the International Atomic Energy Agency. "The benefits of this pact are designed to be a lasting incentive for India to abstain from further nuclear weapons tests and to cooperate closely with the United States in stopping proliferation," Lugar said.[2]

Most senators who spoke on the Senate floor that afternoon supported the agreement. But there were a smattering of critics, skeptics, and even a few fierce opponents. Democratic senator Byron Dorgan said passing the accord would be a "grievous mistake" that would come back to haunt the United States. "We are taking apart the basic architecture of nuclear non-proliferation that has served us many decades. We are saying to India, who has never signed the Nuclear Non-Proliferation Treaty: it is okay if you produce additional nuclear weapons we can't see and we don't know about. We are going to sign an agreement that allows you to do that. That is almost unbelievable," he said.[3] Lugar disputed Dorgan's interpretation of the agreement, insisting that protections had been written in to the bill to prevent the scenario Dorgan described.

As the debate drew to a conclusion, Lugar was allowed to make a brief summary statement. Speaking with rare emotion, Lugar said the Senate had an opportunity to put American foreign policy on a different and better path. "I ask all senators to participate in a historic moment. This is an opportunity for the United States and India to come to come together in a way that historically is important for the world," he declared.[4] The Senate passed the agreement, 86 to 13, with both Obama and McCain voting for it.

The U.S.-India civilian nuclear pact was a major event whose significance, for good or bad, may come to equal or even surpass the financial rescue legislation. Conceived of by the Bush administration and pushed mightily by the increasingly powerful American-Indian lobby, the accord had many champions. But Lugar played a pivotal role. Working in his painstaking way, the senator spent hundreds of hours studying the proposal, listening to both supporters and critics, modifying the plan to tighten its requirements, and ensuring a role for Congress in approving the final package and monitoring its implementation. It was an initiative outlined by President George W. Bush but ushered through the complex legislative process by Lugar and a few other lawmakers.

Lugar's work on the U.S.-India agreement illustrates how Congress is able to shape a critical foreign policy. And it shows how the fate of legislation often requires a dogged and determined lawmaker to move it through Congress.

II

The United States and India have had a complicated, even difficult relationship over the last half century, and nuclear issues have often been at the heart of the tensions. The United States actively promoted nuclear energy cooperation with India beginning in the mid-1950s under the Atoms for Peace Program. The program was designed to halt the proliferation of nuclear weapons by offering access to civilian uses of nuclear technology in exchange for pledges not to use the technology to develop weapons. The United States helped India build nuclear power reactors, provided heavy water for a critical research reactor, and allowed Indian scientists to study at American nuclear laboratories. The understanding was that India would use American technology and expertise to build nuclear power plants for its energy needs. It insisted it was not interested in building nuclear weapons.[5]

Both the United States and India were active in negotiations in the late 1960s on what became the Nuclear Non-Proliferation Treaty. India ultimately decided not to join the treaty, arguing that it was discriminatory. The NPT was opened for signature in 1968 and entered into force in 1970. It seeks to contain the spread of nuclear weapons. Its 189 signatories fall into two categories. First, there are the nuclear weapons states consisting of the United States, the United Kingdom, Russia, China, and France. The treaty defines nuclear weapons states as nations that detonated a nuclear explosion before January 1, 1967. In the second category are all the other nations, deemed non-nuclear weapons states. Under the treaty, the five nuclear weapons states commit to work toward disarmament and the non-weapons states agree not to develop or acquire nuclear weapons. The nuclear weapons states agree not to help the non-weapons states develop or acquire nuclear weapons and the non-weapons states agree not to pursue these weapons. The treaty also charges the IAEA with inspecting the non-nuclear weapons states' nuclear facilities and establishing safeguards for the transfer of fissionable materials between the weapons and non-weapons states. The NPT has the largest membership of any arms control agreement, with only India, Israel, and Pakistan remaining outside the treaty. For these three nations, joining the treaty as non-weapons states would require that they dismantle their nuclear weapons and place their nuclear materials under international safeguards. The situation regarding North Korea is complex. It joined the NPT in 1985 and sought to withdraw from the treaty in 2003. There is still a dispute as to whether North Korea has legally withdrawn from the NPT. In any event, most experts agree the NPT has been successful in containing the number of states with nuclear weapons.[6]

The world's nuclear tranquility was shaken in 1974 when India used American and Canadian nuclear materials to conduct an underground nuclear test. India described the test as a "peaceful" one, but the international community viewed it as an ominous and unwelcome indication that India now had a nuclear bomb. The Indian tests reinforced the concern of many that nuclear technology designed for peaceful purposes could ultimately be used to produce nuclear weapons. The U.S. Congress responded to that test by creating the Nuclear Suppliers Group in 1975, an organization of nuclear supplier states that voluntarily agreed to coordinate export controls to prevent the transfer of nuclear material and nuclear-related technologies to states that might use them in a nuclear weapons program.[7]

A few years later, Congress passed the Nuclear Non-Proliferation Act of 1978, which imposed tough new requirements for U.S. nuclear exports to non-nuclear weapon states. The law called for full-scope safeguards and termination of exports if a country detonated a nuclear explosive device or engaged in activities related to acquiring or manufacturing nuclear weapons. All nuclear exports from the United States to India were cut off in 1980 under the strictures of the law.

The Clinton administration sought both a tougher set of global rules on nuclear weapons and a better relationship with India, two goals often in tension. To achieve the former, the president pushed for the indefinite extension of the NPT in the 1995 review conference. He also signed the Comprehensive Test Ban Treaty on September 24, 1996, the first day it was open for signature. President Clinton called it "the longest-sought, hardest-fought prize in the history of arms control."[8] The CTBT prohibits nuclear test explosions of any size and establishes a rigorous global verification system to detect violations. For the treaty to go into force, all nations that are considered "nuclear capable" must sign and ratify it. This means that India and its rival Pakistan could prevent it from coming into force by refusing to sign it and ratify it, which they've done. Other nuclear-capable countries have also failed to sign and ratify the CTBT. In a crippling blow to the treaty, the U.S. Senate voted not to ratify it in 1999.

Indian leaders opposed both the permanent extension of the NPT and the CTBT. Both efforts, they argued, were part of an American effort to keep them from developing their own nuclear weapons and to extend a nuclear monopoly that excluded India. From India's perspective, the permanent extension of the NPT drastically reduced the chance that the treaty might be amended some day to allow India to join as a nuclear weapons state. And becoming a party to the CTBT would foreclose India's option of further nuclear testing.[9]

The American-Indian relationship shifted from tense to contentious in May of 1998 when India stunned the United States by conducting five underground nuclear tests. Prime Minister Atal Bihari Vajpayee sent a letter to Clinton and other world leaders insisting the tests were necessary because India faced threats from China, an overt nuclear state, and Pakistan, a covert nuclear weapons state that had fought three wars with India. Pakistan, to no one's surprise, responded to India's nuclear tests with nuclear tests of its own. Southwest Asia was viewed in Washington as an increasingly dangerous region, due to the dueling nuclear tests that India began.

The United States imposed tough sanctions on both India and Pakistan. Those directed at India halted defense sales, export licenses for munitions, and military financing. They denied American government credit and loan guarantees to India and opposed loans and technical assistance to India from international financial institutions. They also prohibited most loans from American banks, blocked Export-Import Bank loan guarantees for U.S. exports to India, and ended or suspended most assistance programs. In response to India's nuclear program and test of nuclear weapons, the United States denied broad categories of sensitive technology to India, including supercomputers, missile and space technology, satellites, advanced fighters, microelectronics, and fiber optics.[10]

Despite this tough sanctions regime, the Clinton administration tried to reach out to India. Strobe Talbott, the deputy secretary of state, held a series of meetings with a senior Indian diplomat, Jaswant Singh, to ease tensions and search for areas of agreement. Enough progress was made for Clinton to visit India in 2000 and receive a warm greeting while still expressing his concern about India's nuclear program. The tone and substance of the U.S.-India relationship shifted dramatically when George W. Bush came to office. He wanted to ease American sanctions on India and develop a better relationship with that nation. After the 9/11 terrorist attacks on the United States, the Bush administration lifted the sanctions on India and Pakistan that were imposed in the wake of their nuclear tests, arguing the country needed these two nations as allies in the fight against terrorism.[11]

Bush met Vajpayee in November of 2001 and both leaders said they wanted to improve the bilateral relationship and build a strategic partnership. Several years of diplomatic work ensued. In September of 2004, a major U.S.-Indian agreement was reached on bilateral cooperation on commercial space programs, missile defense, and high-technology trade. It eased some American export controls that were imposed in 1998. India agreed to address some U.S. concerns and comply with American export controls on some sensitive items.

Then in July of 2005, Bush hosted the new Indian prime minister, Manmohan Singh, in Washington. During that visit, Bush and Singh issued a joint statement that pledged bilateral cooperation on a range of issues, including terrorism, trade, investment, agriculture, energy, the environment, HIV-AIDS research, space, and high technology. But the initiative that captured the most attention and came to define the new bilateral relationship was a commitment to reestablish civil nuclear commerce between the United States and India. To achieve this, India pledged to take steps that would bring it into closer adherence to the global non-proliferation regime. Bush pledged to make administrative adjustments to begin this new relationship and then to request Congress to rewrite American laws to allow the country's new nuclear relationship with India to go forward.[12]

III

Richard Lugar did not receive advance notice before Bush made his blockbuster proposal to overhaul America's nuclear policy toward India. As the chairman of the Foreign Relations Committee and a self-described friend of the Bush administration, this was an oversight that would anger the most placid of lawmakers. While not pleased by the failure to receive a heads-up from the White House, Lugar set aside his frustration and plunged into the substance of the proposal before him. The senator vowed to examine the initiative carefully. He instructed his staff to set up comprehensive hearings to examine the matter in detail. He understood that it would be difficult to reject a signature foreign policy initiative from the Bush administration but was also unwilling to just rubber stamp the administration's plan. Lugar decided it was essential to work with Biden, the top Democrat on the panel, to examine the administration's proposal and craft a congressional response.

The Foreign Relations panel held its first hearing on the administration's U.S.-India initiative on November 2, 2005. Sitting in the chairman's seat, Lugar offered a detailed and balanced review of the Bush initiative and the issues it raised. Lugar said the joint statement by Bush and the prime minister of India on July 18, 2005, represented a sea change in the relationship between the two nations. "This document stands as a milestone in the U.S.-Indian relationship," he said, adding it was clearly in the interest of the United States to develop a better relationship with India.[13] But the senator did not try to downplay the scope of the changes contemplated or the necessity of carefully thinking through their implications, especially for the global non-proliferation regime. And he did not try to sugarcoat India's less than stellar record in this area.

"India has never signed the Nuclear Non-Proliferation Treaty, the foundation of international efforts to stop the spread of nuclear weapons. India has developed a nuclear weapons arsenal, in conflict with the goals of that treaty. New Delhi in 1974 violated bilateral pledges it made to Washington not to use U.S.-supplied nuclear materials for weapons purposes. More recently, Indian scientists have faced United States sanctions for providing nuclear information to Iran," he said. "India's nuclear record with the international community also has been unsatisfying. It has not acknowledged or placed under effective international safeguards all of its facilities involved in nuclear work, and its nuclear tests in 1998 triggered widespread condemnation and international sanctions."

Lugar noted that India had repeatedly, but unsuccessfully, tried to gain recognition as an official nuclear weapons state. The senator acknowledged that many questioned if the nuclear accord would undermine non-proliferation efforts. "Opponents argue that giving India this status will undermine the essential bargain that is at the core of the NPT—namely, that only by foregoing nuclear weapons can a country gain civilian nuclear assistance. They observe that permitting India to retain nuclear weapons while it receives the same civilian nuclear benefits as nations that have foresworn weapons programs would set a harmful precedent that would encourage other nations to take India's path. New Delhi has long claimed that the NPT is discriminatory and that the international community has instituted what it calls a 'nuclear apartheid' against it."

The senator said that transforming the joint statement into a reality would require changes to non-proliferation laws by Congress and also an American commitment to work with allies to adjust international rules to enable full civil nuclear energy cooperation and trade with India.[14] Lugar called on Nicholas Burns, the undersecretary of state for political affairs, to explain the initiative. Burns, a smooth-talking career diplomat, was the administration's point person on the accord. Burns argued that the initiative was an important way to recast the relationship between the two nations. He said that the administration decided that it was in the American interests to bring India into compliance with the standards and practices of the international non-proliferation regime. It had concluded that the only way to reach that goal was to end India's isolation and begin to engage it. India would soon have the largest population in the world, and to consign it to a place outside that system did not appear to be strategically wise and had not proven effective, Burns said. He added the agreement would also help the United States and India work together on energy, environmental, and other critical matters. He pledged to work with Congress to help put the agreement into acceptable legislative form.[15]

Lugar, eager to hear a different perspective, then called on Ashton Carter, a Harvard University professor who co-chaired the senator's policy advisory group, a team of security experts who brief Lugar regularly. Lugar said he wanted Carter's views on the agreement—and he got them. Carter told the panel that the U.S.-India initiative was a bold step, but mostly in the wrong direction. The professor said that when viewed only as a nuclear deal, the accord was bad for the United States. Washington recognized New Delhi's nuclear status in return for little in the way of additional restraints on India's nuclear arsenal or help in confronting nuclear proliferation and terrorism beyond what India was already poised to provide. And he said the agreement would impose serious costs on U.S. nuclear non-proliferation objectives in other critical regions. Carter said the agreement gave India what it sought for 30 years, nuclear recognition, in return for a strategic partnership with the United States. The U.S.-India strategic partnership would seem to be in India's interest as well as America's, he noted. So why should the United States offer a major concession to secure something that India also wanted? He added that the accord was unbalanced in its specifics; American concessions were spelled out clearly, while India's were much more vague.[16]

The professor said that going forward the United States should rebalance the agreement rather than reject it. The country, he declared, could get more from India, including immediate diplomatic support to curb Iran's nuclear program, help from India to balance China in the region, a pledge to work better with Pakistan, joint action with the U.S. military in operations, military access and basing privileges, preferential access for the U.S. industry in India's civil nuclear expansion, special access for the U.S. defense industry to the India market, and a contribution to nuclear non-proliferation from India's nuclear program. And Carter said that there are others things that could "even up" the deal. These included India agreeing to stop production of new fissile material for weapons as the nuclear weapons states have done, agreeing to forego indigenous enrichment and reprocessing for its civil nuclear program in favor of the international fuel cycle initiative proposed by Bush in 2004, and separating its civil and military nuclear facilities permanently.

IV

Lugar set up a rigorous process to review the U.S.-India nuclear initiative. Over the course of 6 months, he presided over four hearings in which virtually every aspect of the agreement was scrutinized. Secretary of State Condoleezza Rice was one of 17 witnesses who came before the panel to discuss the accord. Lugar set up classified briefings for lawmakers and exhaustive presentations by nuclear experts to congressional staff. He kept in touch with Burns and with Biden to discuss technical issues and gauge political support.

Kenneth Myers III, then a Lugar staff member who worked on the issue, said the senator plunged into the arcane elements of the agreement while considering larger strategic questions and practical political considerations. A veteran of dozens of treaties and executive agreements, the senator wanted the review process to be methodical and meticulous. "This was vintage Lugar. There were terribly complicated policy issues. Nothing was black and white. He wanted it reviewed carefully. He had us go through it line by line by line. He wanted to clearly understand the pros and the cons. He wanted everyone to be comfortable with this. He wanted Senator Biden to be a full partner. He instructed us to work very closely with Biden's staff. His instructions to us were, 'I want this done right. I don't care how long it takes.' And it took a long time. He would have been personally disappointed if the process had been acrimonious and people felt they weren't treated fairly," Myers said.[17]

"Senator Lugar understood the tensions and the trade-offs. He cares deeply about non-proliferation. At the same time, he cares deeply about the U.S.-India bilateral relationship. He wanted to improve the bilateral relationship with India while preserving, protecting, and promoting non-proliferation," he said. Myers said that Lugar tried to weigh a complex mix of factors: the Bush administration's desire for a strategic breakthrough with India, the views of the increasingly powerful Indian-

American community, the skepticism of the arms control community, and even the stance of his long-time ally Sam Nunn, who opposed the agreement.

Lugar methodically considered the agreement, dealing with its substance but also weighing how possible changes would affect supporters, opponents, and the administration. He wanted to hear all sides and to see if there were matters he hadn't considered. After intense consideration, Lugar decided to come out in support of the agreement. He announced his views at the commencement speech of the Naval War College on June 16, 2006. Speaking in broad terms, Lugar said the United States had for too long abandoned strategic thinking for crisis management. And crisis decision making, he said, tends to limit options and foreclose broader strategies that require more time.[18]

"A successful foreign policy depends much more on how well a nation prepares to avoid a crisis. When a nation gets to the point of having to make tactical choices in a time of peril, it almost always faces a choice between a bad option and a worse option. Crisis decision making is to foreign policy what a surgeon is to personal health," he said. The senator said that no amount of skillful decision making can make up for the failure to attend to the fundamentals of U.S. foreign policy. A vibrant and successful foreign policy, he said, focuses on building alliances, expanding trading relationships, honing diplomatic capabilities, creating exchange programs, securing international agreements, and earning global respect.

Turning to the U.S.-India nuclear agreement, Lugar said it represented the kind of strategic thinking that has been far too rare in American foreign policy. The accord allowed the United States to pivot from its cold war alliance structure and embrace a rising, dynamic nation with whom American interests are compatible. Lugar said it was appropriate to be concerned about the precedent set by this agreement, adding the United States needed to ensure the agreement did not sabotage America's responsibilities under the NPT. He said he was confident that Congress and the administration could agree on an approach to India that was strategic and innovative while preserving the U.S. non-proliferation agenda. "I believe we can help solidify New Delhi's commitments to implement strong export controls, separate its civilian nuclear infrastructure from its weapons program, and place civilian facilities under IAEA safeguards," he said. The agreement would be a powerful incentive for India to cooperate closely with the United States in stopping proliferation and abstaining from further nuclear weapons testing.

"We should not see India as a card to play in balance of power games. Alliances based on shared dangers can have a long shelf life if the threat is intense enough but rarely are transformational. We need more from India than security cooperation. We need a partner that sits at the intersection of several strategic regions that can be a bulwark for stability, democracy, and pluralism," he concluded.[19]

V

Lugar convened the Foreign Relations Committee on June 29, 2006, to formally consider the U.S.-India civilian nuclear agreement. The meeting was called a mark-up, which takes place when a committee, usually after a number of hearings to examine legislation, formally considers the bill. The chairman of the panel offers a detailed proposal and other members of the panel are allowed to offer amendments to modify the chairman's mark.

Lugar had taken the legislation submitted by the administration and, working with Biden, made some changes. The Lugar-Biden version gave the president the authority to complete the civilian nuclear cooperation agreement with India. It allowed the president to waive parts of the 1954 Atomic Energy Act to permit exports of nuclear materials, equipment, and technology to India. In return, India promised to open up its civilian nuclear sites to inspection by the IAEA for the first time and to continue negotiations with the United States on a fissile material cutoff treaty.

Lugar said he believed that he and Biden assembled a good package that preserved the main elements of the administration's proposal but made important adjustments. The Lugar-Biden bill was the first step in a complex process. Their bill authorized the administration to proceed with negotiations with India to craft the nuclear agreement. But any agreement would then require the approval of a special exemption for India from the IAEA and the Nuclear Suppliers Group. Finally, Congress would then vote on the final agreement, called a 123 Agreement. This is the term for a peaceful nuclear cooperation agreement with a foreign nation under the conditions in section 123 of the Atomic Energy Act. Under the administration's proposal, the 123 Agreement that it negotiated with India would go into force 90 days after it was submitted to Congress, unless both houses of Congress voted against it and then overcame a near-certain presidential veto.[20]

Lugar and other lawmakers told the administration that this limited role for Congress was not acceptable and persuaded the administration that the accord needed to secure a positive vote by both the House and Senate before it went into effect. They also added reporting and certification requirements to keep Congress informed of the final negotiations and the status of India's nuclear programs.

The bill also preserved a section of the Atomic Energy Act that would terminate nuclear cooperation if India conducted a nuclear test, proliferated weapons or materials, and broke its agreement with the United States or the IAEA. "In our view, this fully protects Congress's role in the process and ensures congressional views will be taken into consideration," Lugar said. "I believe we have constructed a bill that allows us to seize an important strategic opportunity while ensuring a strong congressional oversight rule and reinforcing U.S. non-proliferation efforts," he said.[21]

Speaking next, Biden cited Lugar's skillful leadership for creating a bill that earned the support of a large bipartisan majority of the committee. Biden said Lugar could have taken the administration's proposal and rammed it through the Foreign Relations panel on a party line vote. But he credited Lugar for soliciting the views of Democrats and crafting a bill that would stand the test of time. Biden said the agreement would be seen a half century into the future as the historic turning point in which the relationship between India and the United States improved. Biden added that he and Lugar crafted a bill that would preserve important progress on non-proliferation. "We've worked very hard over the past few months to ensure that Congress develops legislation that allows civil nuclear cooperation in India to proceed and ends India's nuclear isolation. But which does so without seriously jeopardizing the hard won non-proliferation gains of the past four decades."

Biden said the bill preserved the rights of Congress to conduct a meaningful review of the peaceful nuclear cooperation agreement that India and the United States ultimately negotiated. "The administration initially presented us with a Hobson's choice. You could accept their initial approach at the price of limiting congressional power and shortchanging a non-proliferation interest or you could reject the deal entirely, at the risk of doing terrible damage to the relationship with a close friend and rising power," he said. "Mr. Chairman, it has been an honor to work with you on this bipartisan bill. I think it is absolutely vital to make sure that on an issue this important, we gain the educated, informed and ungrudging support of the overwhelming majority of our colleagues."[22]

Senator Chris Dodd, the second ranking Democrat on the panel, also lavished praise on Lugar and his partnership with Biden. He heralded the agreement as creative and strategic. "The involvement of the Congress and the involvement of this committee—this is an example of how it ought to work. I know it is a little more cumbersome to go this route but in the long run, you build a kind of base of support, the public support of these agreements that are critically important, so that the opportunity that I'm going to have to actually vote on something, because it has a huge impact," he said. "It's a bit labor intensive to go that route, I think we get a much better result, one that has broader support and deeper support for the long term."[23]

Democratic senator Barbara Boxer also offered praise to Lugar and Biden but continued to oppose the overall initiative. "The bill before us today is a dramatic improvement over the legislation we received from the Bush administration. The administration's proposal, in my view, didn't have any merit from a non-proliferation standpoint and I believe it showed contempt for the role of Congress," she said. Boxer said Lugar and Biden had worked hard to improve the package but didn't address her continuing concerns that providing nuclear assistance to India's civilian program would free up India's limited domestic resources for use in its nuclear weapons program.[24]

As the mark-up proceeded, Democratic senator Russ Feingold offered an amendment requiring the president to certify that no form of American nuclear assistance would help India's nuclear weapons pro-

gram. Lugar said the president would never be able to offer such an as-
surance and called the amendment a "killer condition." It was defeated
13 to 5. The panel accepted by voice vote an amendment by Republican
senator Lincoln Chafee that said that American exports of nuclear fuel
to India should not contribute to, or encourage, increases in India's production of fissile material for its nuclear weapons program. The committee also accepted an amendment by Barack Obama that said that if the
United States cut off nuclear exports to India it should not encourage
the continuation of nuclear exports to India by any other nations.[25]

After an hour of deliberation, the Lugar-Biden bill was passed 16 to
2, with 15 of the panel's members joining the bill as co-sponsors. The full
Senate approved the bill in the fall and a final version of it was approved
by both the House and Senate in December.

VI

After Congress approved the bill at the end of 2006, the Bush administration and Indian officials plunged into intense talks to nail down
the details of the treaty. The two nations announced a final text in July
2007.

A period of deep political turmoil then engulfed India, with an
intense debate over the merits of the nuclear agreement. Part of the
controversy was due to differences in how the Bush administration and
Indian leaders described the final package. The two sides made differing
statements about issues such as whether the agreement would guarantee
India a fuel supply or if India was allowed to maintain a strategic reserve
of nuclear fuel. Of even greater importance, there were differing statements about whether the agreement would cease if India conducted
another nuclear test. Prime Minister Singh insisted the treaty would not
limit India's nuclear options. "The agreement does not, in any way, affect
India's right to undertake future nuclear tests, if it's necessary in India's
national interest," Singh declared. That was not the American view.[26]

The Indian government survived several no-confidence votes and
had to reconfigure its coalition before it was able to go forward. India
then negotiated a safeguards agreement with the IAEA, which was approved by the IAEA's Board of Governors on August 1. Intensive nego-

tiations with the Nuclear Suppliers Group resulted in the granting of a waiver for India on September 6, 2008. The final step in the process was for the U.S. Congress to consider the 123 Agreement.

The president formally sent the agreement to Congress on September 10, 2008. The legislation before Congress approved the 123 Agreement, but it also required additional safeguards and congressional oversight, especially on any subsequent agreement with India on reprocessing nuclear fuel. The bill also gave Congress the right to review and disapprove any future agreement to permit India to extract plutonium and uranium from spent reactor fuel that originated in the United States.

Additionally, the president agreed to inform appropriate congressional committees at the earliest possible time after any request by the Indian government to negotiate reprocessing agreements. The bill specified that Congress could reject a presidential decision to resume nuclear trade with any country that had detonated a nuclear explosive device by adopting a joint resolution of disapproval within 60 days of decision.

With the November elections approaching in the United States and the congressional session winding down, it was far from clear that the agreement could be approved by the time Congress adjourned for the year. If it was not approved by then, the legislation would have to be re-introduced in the new Congress. With the Bush administration pressing hard for a vote and the Indian-American lobby working frantically, the bill was put on a fast track. The House passed the legislation on September 27 on a 298 to 117 vote; the Senate passed the same bill on October 1, 86 to 13. In both chambers, the debate was brief and superficial. Neither chamber reviewed the package with the kind of care and consideration that many experts said was necessary.

In the final phase of the legislative rush, Lugar played a critical role, defending the accord during the deliberations on September 18 in the Foreign Relations Committee and during the floor debate on October 1. He conferred with Rice and kept in touch with key Democrats in the House and Senate.

Speaking 2 weeks after the final congressional vote at the National Defense University on a range of foreign policy matters, Lugar acknowledged past failures in American foreign policy. But he said the U.S.-India agreement was an example of Congress and the administration working successfully to advance a major strategic goal. "The benefits of this pact are designed to be a lasting incentive for India to abstain from further nuclear weapons tests and to cooperate closely with the United States in stopping proliferation. But the strategic benefits of the relationship extend far beyond the nuclear agenda," he said.[27]

"The bottom line is that American efforts to shape the world are unlikely to succeed fully without the cooperation of India. Its sheer size ensures that it will have an enormous impact on the global economy. The agreement gives us a better chance to cooperate with the Indians on limiting carbon emissions. We have a strong interest in expanding energy cooperation with India to develop new technologies, cut greenhouse gas emissions, and prepare for declining global fossil fuel reserves. The United States's own energy problems will be exacerbated if we do not forge energy partnerships with India, China, and other nations experiencing rapid economic growth."

While Lugar was proud of the nuclear agreement with India, many analysts were far less supportive. A number of long-time allies in the non-proliferation movement praised Lugar for improving an agreement they believed to be fundamentally bad for the United States. But they said the final package was still a step in the wrong direction that could unravel the precarious non-proliferation regime. They noted that several countries have cited the deal and argued this precedent should enable them to have the non-proliferation rules relaxed on their behalf. They were parties to the NPT and lived within the constraints of the NPT. Yet India hadn't joined the NPT, has nuclear weapons, and the United States provided relief for it. How was this fair?

Sharon Squassoni, a security expert at the Carnegie Endowment for International Peace, said the U.S. decision to make a special exception for India on nuclear policy "overturned decades of U.S. and global non-proliferation policy" and has caused fundamental damage to the global non-proliferation regime.[28] She said that at the 2010 NPT Review Conference, nearly 120 nations complained about the special agreement with India, which the United States championed. Squassoni argues that "small scale revisions to the non-proliferation regime will not be able to repair the damage that the India deal has caused."[29]

Most analysts agree that as of autumn 2011, the nuclear agreement between the United States and India has fallen short of expectations. No American companies have sold nuclear reactors or equipment to India, largely because the Indian Parliament passed a law in 2010 that would have made suppliers of nuclear equipment liable for potentially costly claims in the event of a nuclear accident during the reactor's lifetime. State-owned companies from Russia and France, which are less concerned with this liability issue, have signed lucrative nuclear contracts with India. And the overall relationship between the United States and India remains wary and sometimes tense.[30]

10

❧

Sisyphus on the High Seas

I

Richard Lugar's long advocacy of the Law of the Sea Treaty has not earned him many headlines in Indiana, or any other place in the United States for that matter. But he has fought hard for the treaty because he believes it's in the nation's security, economic, and political interests. As a former naval officer knowledgeable about maritime issues, Lugar is convinced the treaty is an important instrument for the United States to project its power on the high seas and to demonstrate its commitment to global leadership.

But Lugar's fight for the Law of the Sea Treaty has been a complicated and difficult struggle as the senator has tried to build support for an arcane treaty whose provisions seem far removed from the daily concerns of most Americans. Partly through his patient construction of a detailed public record, much of the American foreign policy community and most military, business, and environmental groups back the treaty. But a small group of passionate Republicans continues to block the Senate's consideration of the treaty. This group has threatened a filibuster if the treaty is ever brought to the Senate floor, and these threats have dissuaded Senate leaders from presenting the treaty to the full Senate for its consideration. It's been a classic story of the power of a small, passionate, and vocal minority prevailing over the preferences of a broad bipartisan majority.

But Lugar, like a modern-day Sisyphus, has continued to push ahead, hopeful and even confident that one day the Law of the Sea Treaty will be adopted by the Senate and the United States will be a full participating member of the treaty.

Lugar's relentless advocacy of this issue shows the senator's tenacity when he believes an important matter is at stake. A lawmaker who dislikes confrontation, Lugar has been willing to challenge the conservative wing of his party on this treaty, arguing that the nation has much to gain by fully joining the treaty regime. His work on this matter shows the essence of Lugar's legislative approach: carefully assembling a record, trying to broaden and deepen the treaty's base of support, challenging the claims of those who oppose the treaty, and arguing that support for the treaty would reflect enlightened international leadership by the United States. He has been relentless and persistent but also patient. He has pushed ahead when the legislative environment seemed conducive to Senate action but then pulled back when he became convinced that the environment had changed and a premature Senate vote might result in a defeat for the treaty.

II

The 1982 Convention on the Law of the Sea created the governance framework for nearly three-quarters of the earth's surface and what lies above and beneath it. It has been signed and ratified by nearly 160 countries and the European Union. The United States has signed but not ratified the treaty.[1] The treaty is the result of centuries of evolving sea practices and the work of three conferences sponsored by the United Nations; one in 1956, another in 1960, and one that began in 1973 and concluded in 1982. This last conference continued for nearly a decade as it sought to create a comprehensive framework for managing ocean uses that would be acceptable to the international community. The Law of the Sea Treaty was agreed to in 1982 and came into force in 1994 when the 60th nation, Guyana, signed it.[2]

The treaty set out global rules for navigation and overflight rights, created a legal framework for the commercial use of the sea, and established rules to protect the marine environment. Among other things, the treaty established exclusive economic zones in which coastal nations, such as the United States, have the sole exploitation rights for 200 nautical miles from their coasts over all natural resources. Nations can also claim rights to any of their continental shelf beyond that 200-mile zone.

When the international agreement on the Law of the Sea Treaty was reached in 1982, President Reagan declined to sign it, citing concerns about the new regime for governance over the international seabed. Reagan was concerned by a number of issues related to the seabed including the lack of U.S. representation in decision making about deep seabed mining, requirements for industrialized nations to transfer technology related to deep seabed mining, rules that provided for artificial limits on production of deep seabed minerals, and rules that imposed regulations and financial costs on private companies seeking to conduct deep seabed mining. However, Reagan, in a detailed statement on ocean policy in 1983, said the United States would adhere to all aspects of the treaty, except for those pertaining to the seabed.

President George H. W. Bush authorized negotiations to address these areas of concern regarding the international seabed. President Bill Clinton signed the implementing agreement for the Law of the Sea Treaty on July 29, 1994, arguing that the Reagan administration's objections had been addressed in a supplemental agreement. He sent the treaty to the U.S. Senate in October of that year. A month later, Republicans won control of the House and Senate and Jesse Helms became the new chairman of the Senate Foreign Relations Committee. He refused to even hold hearings on the treaty.[3]

Helms and other conservatives cited Reagan's initial decision not to sign the treaty in 1982 as evidence that the treaty was a bad deal for the United States, even with the 1994 revisions. In speeches, articles, and eventually in congressional testimony, the opponents of the Law of the Sea Treaty developed a withering critique to explain their opposition. Most fundamentally they charged that the treaty undermined America's sovereignty by accepting treaty obligations to international bodies within the UN system. The accord, they charged, created a raft of supranational bodies to develop and enforce its provisions, complete with an executive branch, legislature, and judiciary. If the United States acceded to the Law of the Sea Treaty, they warned, the pact's new agencies would wield their powers in ways that would prove harmful to American interests. Frank Gaffney, a conservative foreign policy analyst, said U.S. adherence to the treaty "would entail history's biggest and most unwarranted voluntary transfer of wealth and surrender of sovereignty." He warned of a "supranational government for 70 percent of the world's surface."[4]

Gaffney and other conservative critics of the Law of the Sea Treaty seized on the accord's genesis in a UN-sponsored conference as evidence that it was an instrument of the UN, which, they alleged, had a long track record of supporting policies that were contrary to the interests of the United States. They cited the treaty's dispute resolution mechanisms as an important reason why the United States would be better served by voluntarily observing those parts of the treaty it found acceptable but not becoming encumbered by the treaty's full array of obligations. They said the treaty also set a bad precedent for supervision of other elements of the so-called international commons such as space and the Internet. They argued that many of President Reagan's chief lieutenants remained opposed to the treaty after Reagan left the White House—and even after the 1994 changes were made. Opposition to the treaty by William Clark, Edwin Meese, Casper Weinberger, Jeane Kirkpatrick, John Lehman, and other Reagan administration alumni was cited as an indication that the treaty was anathema to Reagan's world view.[5]

III

When Lugar assumed the chairmanship of the Senate Foreign Relations Committee in 2003, he was determined to put the Law of the Sea Treaty on the committee's agenda. He felt the treaty had languished for too long without a review. It was critical, Lugar believed, to create a clear and accurate record about the treaty. In his view, too many myths and half-truths had been asserted about the treaty. He was confident that a fact-based assessment of the treaty would assuage skeptics and fortify support by its advocates.

In the first hearing held by the Senate Foreign Relations Committee on the treaty on October 14, 2003, Lugar invited the testimony of experts in national security and maritime law, including Admiral Joseph Prueher, former commander in chief of the Pacific, and Admiral James Watkins, chairman of the U.S. Commission on Ocean Policy. In his opening statement, Lugar made it clear that the treaty would benefit the United States and deserved the support of the Senate. "This treaty represents the culmination of decades of work to produce a comprehensive international framework governing the use of the world's oceans. The Law of the Sea has great potential to advance United States interests related to the navigation of the seas, the productive use of their resources, and the protection of the marine environment," he said. "The absence of American leadership in the convention diminishes its effectiveness and our own influence over international ocean policy. As a maritime state and the world's only superpower, the United States has vital economic and security interests in preserving freedom of navigation of the oceans and in preventing piracy, smuggling, terrorism, and other criminal activity from occurring off our shores."[6]

In a second hearing by the Foreign Relations Committee the following week, Lugar called experts from the State and Defense Departments and representatives from the maritime business community. All made strong arguments for American support of the treaty. Lugar said he was convinced the treaty offered important benefits for U.S. national security, including freedom of navigation and overflight across the world's oceans. The treaty, he argued, offered important economic benefits to the United States by establishing its ability to explore and exploit natural resources of the ocean for 200 miles from its shore. Additionally, the treaty would open up access to the continental shelf of the United States, which encompasses 370,000 square miles. "These are compelling arguments in favor of ratifying the convention, and I believe that the Senate should move swiftly to do so," he said.[7]

After these two public hearings in October of 2003, Lugar invited experts, including an interagency team from the Bush administration, to conduct more extensive briefings with committee staff and the personal staff of members on the Foreign Relations committee. With this foundation in place, Lugar brought the treaty up before the Senate Foreign Relations Committee in February of 2004, and a motion to accede to the convention was approved on a 19 to 0 vote.

Seeking to build even stronger support for the treaty from senators who were not on the Foreign Relations Committee, Lugar sent out 20 "Dear Colleague" letters in the spring and summer of 2004, making the case for full Senate support of the treaty. In these letters, Lugar cited the treaty's national security, economic, and environmental benefits. With an eye toward possible opposition from the Helms wing of the party, Lugar addressed the issue of Ronald Reagan and the Law of the Sea Treaty. He said the historical record showed that Reagan accepted and embraced most of the treaty. The one part to which he objected—the international seabed provisions—had been comprehensively renegotiated, and each of Reagan's objections had been resolved. "President Reagan was right to insist on these changes to the Convention. Now they have been made, the time has come for the Senate to finish the job that Reagan started and ratify the Convention," he said.[8]

Then the senator released a question-and-answer document about the treaty, explaining its history, central provisions, and major benefits for the United States. It explained what the treaty did, how it advanced the nation's interests, why it should be approved promptly, which industries supported it, and why the Bush administration supported its immediate approval.[9]

IV

In organizing committee hearings, sending letters to colleagues, and a releasing a Q&A document on the Law of the Sea, Lugar developed a formidable public record. But he learned that some conservative Republicans were mounting an effort to derail the treaty. Gaffney warned other conservatives that Lugar was trying to "ram" the treaty through the Senate.

Taking advantage of an opportunity to pull together his arguments and articulate them in a comprehensive way, Lugar gave a speech on May 4, 2004, at the Brookings Institution on the treaty. It was arguably the most wide-ranging and persuasive defense of the treaty any American lawmaker had given. The treaty, Lugar said, established a comprehensive set of rules governing the uses of the world's oceans, including the airspace above and the seabed and subsoil below. It carefully balanced the interests of states in controlling activities off their own coasts and the interests of all states in protecting the freedom to use the oceans without undue interference. The United States had the most to gain from the establishment of order and predictability with respect to the oceans, he said.[10]

There was strong support for the treaty from the military and the private sector, Lugar said, noting that every major ocean group supported the treaty, including shipping, fishing, oil and natural gas, drilling contractors, ship builders, and telecommunications firms that use underwater cables. He acknowledged that when the treaty was first concluded in 1982, it had seabed mining provisions that President Reagan opposed. But these had been fundamentally amended. Lugar said the revisions negotiated by the Clinton administration in 1994 had "comprehensively revised the regime and resolved each of the problems" that Reagan cited in 1982.

Lugar then tackled a central issue surrounding the treaty; he charged that the strong opposition among some Republicans was less about the treaty and more about the very nature of multilateral agreements. Opposition to the treaty, Lugar said, was rooted in "vague and unfounded concerns" about the treaty's effects. These concerns were being expressed primarily by those who opposed virtually every multilateral agreement. Many of their arguments, he said, were "patently untrue." Others were outdated and applied to the treaty of 1982 before it had been revised. American negotiators had prevailed in rewriting the treaty in 1994, and the United States was only hurting itself by failing to exploit this hard-earned diplomatic victory. He dismissed as false assertions by the treaty's critics that it would give the UN control over oceans, put production limits on seabed minerals, institute mandatory technology transfers, hinder U.S intelligence, and inhibit a Bush administration initiative to seize weapons of mass destruction that were being transported over the seas.

Some Republicans, Lugar said, were reflexively opposing a treaty that advanced the nation's interests. "The vast majority of conservative Republicans would support, in prospect, a generic measure that expands the ability of American oil and natural gas companies to drill for resources in new areas, solidifies the navy's right to traverse the oceans, enshrines U.S. economic sovereignty over our Exclusive Economic Zone extending 200 miles off our shore, helps our ocean industries create jobs, and reduces the prospects that Russia will be successful in claiming excessive portions of the Arctic. All of these conservative-backed outcomes would result from U.S. ratification of the Law Sea Convention. Yet the treaty is being blocked because of ephemeral conservative concerns that boil down to a discomfort with multilateralism," he said.

Lugar said there was no unilateral option with regard to ocean policy. "The high seas are not governed by the national sovereignty of the United States or any other country. If we are to establish order, predictability, and responsibility over the oceans—an outcome that is very much in the interest of the United States—we have to engage with other countries." The senator noted that the Commission on the Limits of the Continental Shelf, a body created by the treaty, would soon begin making decisions on claims to continental shelf areas that could impact the United States's own claims to the area and resources of its broad continental margin. Russia was already making bold claims in the Arctic.

"Opponents seem to think that if the U.S. declines to ratify the Law of the Sea, it will evaporate into the ocean mists," Lugar said. But he observed that unlike some treaties, such as the Kyoto Protocol on climate change and the Comprehensive Test Ban Treaty, which required U.S. acceptance to work, the Law of the Sea would continue to form the basis of maritime law regardless of whether the United States was a party. Critical international decisions related to national claims on continental shelves beyond 200 miles from national shores, resource exploitation of the open ocean, navigation rights, and other matters would be made in the context of the treaty whether the United States joined or not, he said.

Lugar said that he was troubled that the sweeping and erroneous charges that had prevented American acceptance of the treaty for more than a decade were indicative of a wider skepticism about cooperative global arrangements. If this treaty could not be approved, he said, there was little reason to think that any multilateral solution to any international problem was likely to be accepted by the United States.[11]

Despite Lugar's arguments, intra-GOP politics blocked a Senate vote on the treaty in 2004. Senate Majority Leader Bill Frist bowed to pressures from conservative Republicans and kept the treaty off the Senate floor. Frustrated and disappointed, Lugar saw no practical opening in which to push the treaty. He had to hold back and wait for a better moment. That moment appeared to have arrived after Democrats won control of the Senate in 2006 and a vote on the Law of the Sea was part of their international agenda. Lugar issued a strong statement in May of 2007, saying that U.S. absence from the treaty caused the country to forfeit its leadership in oceans policy. He charged that "ideological posturing and flat-out misrepresentations by a handful of amateurs have sought to cast a shadow over the treaty by suggesting that we are turning over our sovereignty to the United Nations. Their criticisms simply don't hold water."[12]

The Senate Foreign Relations Committee began hearings in October of 2007 on the Law of the Sea Treaty. Once again, Lugar implored action, repeating the arguments he had been making for years on the treaty. He noted that President Bush was strongly supportive of the treaty. Lugar compared U.S. absence from the Law of the Sea Treaty to the Soviet Union's decision to boycott the UN during consideration of the Korean War resolutions. In both cases, Lugar said, these were "self-inflicted wounds" that did not advance their agendas.[13]

On October 31, 2007, the Senate Foreign Relations Committee voted 17 to 4 to approve the treaty. Lugar wanted a strong committee vote to take the treaty to the Senate floor. But the opposition of four Republican senators in the committee signaled that a filibuster was awaiting the treaty. With this opposition in place and with Congress worried about Iraq, Afghanistan, and increasingly the economy, the treaty languished once again.

V

Lugar remained hopeful. At Hillary Clinton's confirmation hearing to be secretary of state in January of 2009, Lugar asked her to describe the new administration's stance toward the treaty. She said that joining the treaty would advance the interests of the U.S. military and the United States more broadly. As the world's leading maritime power, a nation with the world's largest navy, extensive coastline, an expansive continental shelf, and substantial commercial shipping and marine environmental interests, the United States had as much as any nation to gain from joining the convention, Clinton said.[14] Later that year, Clinton sent a letter to Lugar and Senator John Kerry, the chairman of the Foreign Relations Committee, that the administration wanted to assist the Senate in passing the treaty.[15]

In a wide-ranging speech in September of 2009 on the United States and international treaties, Lugar cited the stalled Law of the Sea Treaty as an example of a Senate treaty process that was deeply flawed. The Law of the Sea Treaty remained blocked, he observed, despite "repeated statements by successive presidents, defense secretaries, secretaries of state, and chairmen of the Joint Chiefs of Staff that the treaty is an urgent priority. It has happened despite virtually unanimous support from ocean industries, environmental groups, and international legal scholars."

The unwillingness of Senate leaders to spend time to debate treaties has meant that treaty opponents have been able to delay indefinitely Senate action on significant treaties, even when those treaties had the support of more than two-thirds of the Senate. In the case of the Law of the Sea Convention, this delay had extended for more than 6 years. Too often, Lugar lamented, treaties languished in the Senate without getting up or down votes. There was a need, he said, for a reinvigorated Senate commitment to the treaty process. Regardless of the causes, U.S. estrangement from multilateral treaty regimes had serious costs, for both the United States and the international community.[16]

Lugar said later that he was hopeful that after the Senate finished work on an arms control agreement with Russia, there might be an opportunity to consider the Law of the Sea Treaty soon. With huge economic, environmental, and security stakes on the line and with new challenges on the oceans ranging from pirates, oil spills, the melting of the Arctic ice cap, and a global scramble for the Arctic's mineral riches, he said it was long past time for the United States to act on the treaty.

11

❧

Arms Control in the Twenty-First Century

I

Richard Lugar has made a career of measuring his words carefully, of expressing even frustration and anger with restraint and understatement. But in November 2010, Lugar decided he had had enough and that it was time to speak out forcefully to his fellow Republicans. He had been consulting closely for almost a year with the Obama administration regarding the New START treaty. For more than 6 months, from March through September, he had been the only Republican senator to publicly declare his support for the arms control treaty with Russia.

Even though he is the acknowledged arms control expert in the Senate, Lugar's role within the Senate Republican caucus on the arms control treaty had been eclipsed by Senator Jon Kyl of Arizona, a hard-edged conservative with a history of disliking most arms control treaties. Kyl, the second ranking Senate Republican with close ties to Senate Republican leader Mitch McConnell and the party's conservative base, was designated by McConnell as the Senate GOP's lead negotiator with the White House on the treaty. But Lugar, given his senior position on the Senate Foreign Relations Committee and experience on arms control issues, remained very involved in helping the Obama administration devise a strategy to win approval of the treaty in the Senate.

The Obama administration consulted closely with Lugar throughout 2009 and 2010 about moving the treaty through the Senate, but they negotiated with Kyl, especially regarding Kyl's demand for additional funds to modernize the U.S.'s nuclear weapons infrastructure. Modernization consisted of allocating more money to upgrade the country's nuclear laboratories, nuclear weapons, and delivery systems. Given his long history of opposing most arms control treaties, some questioned whether Kyl really wanted to reach an agreement with the Obama administration. And throughout the administration's lengthy negotiations with Kyl on modernization funds, it was never clear if Kyl would agree to support the treaty even if he won commitments for the funding level he wanted for modernization.

Then on November 16, the day after Congress's 2010 lame duck session began, Kyl confirmed the suspicions of many when he said the New START treaty should be set aside. Too many other issues had to be resolved in the relatively brief postelection session, and the treaty was too complex to deal with and accomplish anything during the short session, Kyl said in a statement after participating in a meeting with Senate Majority Leader Harry Reid. Kyl said the Senate should take up the treaty in 2011.[1] Kyl's call to delay the treaty until the following year was seen by many, including Lugar, as a backdoor attempt to kill it. With a larger conservative group of Republican senators coming to Washington in the next Congress, the administration appeared to have little chance of securing the 67 votes required to pass a resolution of ratification in the next Congress.

Kyl's comment, after months of assiduous courtship by the Obama administration, was widely interpreted as a bombshell that would derail the president's top national security goal. Reeling from the Kyl statement and trying to reshape the debate, Secretary of State Hillary Clinton traveled to the Capitol on November 17 to meet with a bipartisan group of senators and congressmen in the ceremonial suite of the Senate Foreign Relations Committee on the first floor of the Capitol, ostensibly for a wide-ranging discussion of foreign policy. But Clinton was there to talk about arms control and to jump-start the beleaguered New START treaty.

After the closed door meeting with the lawmakers, Clinton, Senate Foreign Relations Committee Chairman John Kerry, and Lugar stepped before a large throng of reporters and TV cameras to make a public case for Senate approval of the treaty in the coming weeks. Both Kerry and

Clinton said it was imperative to pass it before the end of the year. "This is not an issue that we can afford to be postponed. Once we take that message with the urgency you've heard from the three of us, we will get the votes and we will pass this treaty," Clinton said. Kerry remarked that there was "no substantive opposition to the treaty" and said it was time to move ahead.[2]

Lugar spoke last. "We're talking today about the national security of the United States of America," he said, observing that about 20 years earlier the Soviet Union had more than thirteen thousand nuclear warheads aimed at the United States, any one of which could have destroyed Indianapolis. America's relationship with Russia was far less confrontational now, but thousands of Russian warheads were still pointed at the American homeland. "The American public might have forgotten about it. The senators may have forgotten about it," Lugar said, observing that policymakers seemed deeply concerned about small nuclear programs in North Korea and Iran rather than that of Russia with its thousands of nuclear weapons. "But we're talking about thousands of warheads that are still there, an existential problem for our country. To temporize at this point I think is inexcusable," Lugar said.[3]

After deflecting several specific questions about legislative tactics, Clinton and Kerry left the briefing and went off to other appointments. But Lugar strolled into a Capitol hallway and spoke bluntly to reporters about Kyl's attempt to block the treaty. He said the Republican leadership was preventing a debate on the treaty because they didn't want to force their rank-and-file membership to take a position on the agreement.

"At this moment, the Republican caucus is tied up in a situation where people don't want to make choices. No one wants to be counted. No one wants to talk about it," he said. But Lugar argued that every senator had an obligation to take a stand on this critical national security matter. "Sometimes when you prefer not to vote, you attempt to find reasons not to vote," he said accusingly. And Lugar went further, urging the Democratic leadership in the Senate to set aside the objections of Kyl and other Senate Republicans and move forward with the treaty. "I'm advising that the treaty should come on to the floor so people will have to vote aye or nay," he said, adding he was confident that if the treaty came to a vote, "we have a sufficient number of senators who do have a sense of our national security. This is the time; this is the priority. Do it."[4]

Lugar's forceful words surprised reporters and garnered headlines in Capitol Hill publications and foreign policy blogs. Press accounts remarked that Lugar, the Republican loyalist, was urging the Obama White House and Democratic leaders in the Senate to press ahead, ignoring the pleas of the second ranking Senate Republican to set the treaty aside. And Lugar vowed not only to help them bring the measure to the floor but also to round up enough Republican votes to pass the treaty.

His comments helped trigger a 5-week battle on arms control that angered some Republicans but won the praise of foreign policy leaders in the United States and around the world. It was described as an act of brave statesmanship. The battle over the New START treaty was one of the defining battles of Lugar's Senate career, says Vice President Joe Biden, who was a colleague of Lugar's for 30 years. "This was one of Dick's finest moments. Dick was the guy saying, 'Push, Push, Push. Move. Dick has always underestimated his clout. In fact, the first time he really exercised it was with START. And it mattered," Biden said.[5]

II

Arms control has been one of the defining features of Richard Lugar's Senate career, but this was not necessarily his plan when he first entered the Senate in 1977. However, when he joined the Senate Foreign Relations Committee in 1979, he was thrust headlong into the world of arms control. The Foreign Relations Committee has jurisdiction over all treaties that are submitted to the Senate. And arms control treaties between the United States and the Soviet Union dominated the agenda of the committee in the last 2 decades of the cold war, recalls Biden, who joined the Senate Foreign Relations Committee in 1977, 2 years before Lugar did. "Dick and I earned our spurs dealing with arms control. It was what the committee primarily did back then," Biden says.[6]

Shortly after joining the Foreign Relations Committee, Lugar plunged into the Senate's consideration of SALT II, an arms control treaty submitted by President Jimmy Carter. The treaty, first contemplated by President Gerald Ford and concluded by Carter, was an agreement with the Soviet Union that set ceilings on strategic offensive weapons systems and imposed qualitative restraints on existing and future strategic systems.[7] Lugar approached the treaty skeptically, arguing, as did many congressional Republicans, that the Carter administration was not adequately funding U.S. defense needs and was too eager to strike an arms control deal with the Soviet Union. Lugar blasted the Carter administration for underfunding or discontinuing important defense programs. "We are in danger because President Carter has unilaterally killed the B-1 bomber program, killed the deployment of the neutron bomb, and delayed development of the MX missile system for 2 and a half years," he said in July of 1979.[8]

Lugar argued that the SALT II treaty the Carter administration submitted to the Senate wouldn't reduce the Soviet nuclear threat to the United States or inhibit a single weapons system the Soviet Union was trying to develop. But he charged that it would constrain U.S. deployment of MX missiles, the development and deployment of ground-based cruise missiles, and possibly U.S. air- and sea-based cruise missile development. Lugar said any U.S.-Soviet arms control treaty that came before the Senate should provide for "weapons destruction on a large scale." But he seemed mainly to be referring to the Soviet weapons. The United States, he said, should commit to a 5-year defense spending plan that would boost real defense spending by between 4 percent and 5 percent a year over 5 years. He was fearful that the "the tide of strategic balance" had shifted to the Soviet Union and there was a troubling "security gap" between the United States and the Soviet Union that needed to be addressed.[9]

When the SALT II treaty came before the Foreign Relations Committee in October of 1979, it was approved by the panel on a narrow 9 to 6 vote. Joining Lugar in voting against the treaty were Republican senators Howard Baker, Jesse Helms, and S. I. Hayakawa and two Democratic senators, John Glenn and Richard Stone. "We are headed for a security gap which needs the attention of strong presidential leadership," Lugar said in explaining his no vote. "The SALT Treaty does not reduce nuclear arms, it schedules their increase. And it does so in a way which assures the supremacy of Soviet forces." He called the treaty a "blueprint for U.S. inferiority."[10] Carter ultimately withdrew the treaty when the Soviet Union invaded Afghanistan in December of 1979. So a full-scale debate on the treaty on the Senate floor never occurred.

If the SALT II debate showed a hawkish side to Lugar, it also revealed his commitment to learn about the arcane details of arms control and meet Soviet leaders who dealt with security matters. In August of 1979, Lugar was part of seven-member Senate delegation to the Soviet Union to discuss SALT II and other foreign policy and agriculture issues. Lugar was the only Republican senator on the trip, joining Democratic senators Joe Biden, David Boren, Bill Bradley, Carl Levin, David Pryor, and James Sasser.[11]

Lugar's interest in discussing arms issues with international leaders was apparent several years later when he led an arms control delegation to Europe in May of 1983. As the chairman of the European Affairs subcommittee of the Senate Foreign Relations Committee, Lugar led the bipartisan delegation to Western Europe to discuss nuclear arms control. Lugar said it was important for European leaders to hear from non-administration officials about the 1979 NATO decision to pursue arms control talks with the Soviet Union while also deploying new missiles in Europe if no agreement was reached with the Soviets. Arriving during a tense time between the Reagan administration and European leaders and publics, Lugar said the trip was designed to affirm that if the Soviet Union refused to accept substantial reductions in its intermediate-range nuclear weapons the scheduled NATO deployments would take place.[12]

While much of Lugar's work in arms control was due to his membership on the Senate Foreign Relations Committee, Lugar was also selected in 1985 to be part of a team of Senate observers to arms control talks between the United States and the Soviet Union taking place in Geneva. The group, first called the Senate Observers Group, was created by Senate leaders and the Reagan administration to supplement the work of the Foreign Relations Committee and provide more regular and systematic involvement of the full Senate in arms control negotiations between the two superpowers. The members of the Senate Observers Group were not participants or negotiators in the talks, but monitored the deliberations, consulted frequently with the administration's negotiators, and met with Soviet negotiators and leaders.

Senate Majority Leader Robert Byrd said that while the Foreign Relations Committee would continue to primarily oversee arms control negotiations, the observers group would help focus the Senate's attention on arms control earlier in the process. He noted that the Senate had failed to approve three successive arms control treaties signed by three presidents: the Threshold Test Ban Treaty in 1974 submitted by President Nixon, the Peaceful Nuclear Explosions Act submitted by Ford, and the SALT II treaty that was submitted by Carter but never voted on by the Senate. This suggested an institutional chasm between the executive and legislative branches that needed to be bridged.[13]

Byrd and Senate Minority Leader Robert Dole led the group's first trip to Geneva in March of 1985, and the group returned regularly to Geneva to consult with U.S. negotiators and exchange views with Soviet negotiators in subsequent negotiating rounds. The Senate Observers Group included prominent and respected senators such as Lugar, Ted Stevens, John Warner, Claiborne Pell, Ted Kennedy, Al Gore, and Sam Nunn. Lugar was one of four co-chairmen of the group along with Pell, Stevens, and Nunn.

While the observer group's name and composition changed over the years, it remained part of the arms control debate, and Lugar stayed on the panel for more than 20 years. He said it allowed him to meet with the U.S. negotiating team and also with members of the Soviet delegation. These experiences, Lugar says, have been critical to the development of his professional life. He learned about the details of arms control and developed critical contacts with first Soviet and then Russian officials. These perspectives persuaded him that arms control should be seen as a blend of high statecraft and hugely complex and consequential technical details, especially as it pertained to implementing and verifying agreements.[14]

Lugar became a supporter of arms control but not an uncritical one. He voted for Senate consent to the ratification of the Intermediate Nuclear Forces Treaty, which banned intermediate-range nuclear weapons in Europe; the Conventional Forces in Europe Treaty, which created limits on the number of tanks, helicopters, and armed personnel carriers in Europe; the START I treaty, which limited the United States and Soviet Union to 6,500 nuclear warheads; the START II treaty, which limited the United States and Soviet Union to 3,500 nuclear warheads;

and the Chemical Weapons Convention, which outlawed offensive chemical weapons.

But Lugar joined with most other Senate Republicans in opposing the Comprehensive Test Ban Treaty in the fall of 1999. While he cited specific objections to the treaty, many believe he bowed to pressure from GOP leaders to oppose the deal during a particularly tense period between the Clinton administration and Republicans in Congress. Lugar said the CTBT's goal to ban all nuclear explosions worldwide was probably impractical. The CTBT, he charged, was not of the same high caliber as other arms control treaties. He believed the United States might have to do some limited nuclear testing, which would not have been allowed under the treaty. In Lugar's view it was wrong to support an ineffectual treaty, because this would undercut support for more substantive and proven arms control measures.[15]

III

Lugar was a strong supporter of the START process that was launched by President Reagan and Mikhail Gorbachev and concluded by President George H. W. Bush and Gorbachev in 1991, just months before the Soviet Union collapsed. Its ratification and eventual implementation was delayed by the implosion of the Soviet Union. The treaty entered into force in 1994 and extended for 15 years, until December of 2009. The treaty set an aggregate limit of 1,600 delivery vehicles and 6,000 warheads for each country. To verify compliance with START I, each side monitored the numbers and locations of ballistic missiles, launchers, and heavy bombers deployed by the other country. The treaty required the two nations to exchange data on locations, operations, and technical characteristics of the treaty-limited items that allowed the parties to remain confident in each other's compliance with key provisions. It also provided for on-site inspections to verify the accuracy of data provided by the other country. Some were short notice while others were announced in advance. The treaty also called for the exchange of telemetry transmitted from ballistic missiles during test launches.[16]

START I was the first treaty to provide for deep reductions in U.S. and Soviet strategic nuclear weapons. While some parts of the treaty became outdated, such as limits on warheads and delivery vehicles, its verification and transparency elements were widely praised and cited as valuable until the treaty expired in 2009.

Lugar was a strong supporter of START I, saying it provided for a comprehensive verification regime that allowed each nation to learn a great deal about the nuclear arsenal of its chief adversary. It also created strong working relationships between the political and military leadership in both countries. There were several attempts in the 1990s to replace START I with a successor treaty that would preserve the verification provisions while calling for deeper reductions in the strategic arsenals of both nations. START II was concluded in 1993 by President Clinton and Russian president Boris Yeltsin. The treaty, which was ratified by both nations but never went into force due to a complex procedural dispute, required both nations to reduce their strategic nuclear warheads to between 3,500 and 3,000. At a March 1997 meeting, Clinton and Yeltsin agreed to reduce their strategic nuclear arsenals to between 2,500 and 2,000 weapons, but no final agreement was signed.[17]

President George W. Bush entered office in 2001 deeply skeptical about formal arms control treaties and never really changed that view. In 2002, Bush and Russian President Vladimir Putin first agreed to make unilateral statements that each country would reduce its strategic nuclear arsenal to between 2,200 and 1,700 weapons. They later decided to sign a formal treaty, the Moscow Treaty, in which the countries pledged to reduce their warheads to between 2,200 and 1,700. But the treaty contained no verification mechanisms, relying on the verification regime established in the START I treaty.[18]

During consideration of the Moscow Treaty by the Senate Foreign Relations Committee in 2003, Lugar asked Secretary of State Colin Powell and Defense Secretary Don Rumsfeld about the gap in verification that could occur given that the Moscow Treaty extended to 2012, while the START treaty's verification provisions were set to expire at the end of 2009. In other words, it was possible that there would be no way to verify the treaty from the end of 2009 until 2012. Powell told Lugar that this gap "did not seem to be something pressing at the moment," adding the United States and Russia had "some 7 years to find an answer to that question." Lugar accepted the answer with some reluctance but accurately anticipated the problem when START I expired in December of 2009 without a successor treaty with verification mechanisms in place.[19]

The senator had hoped the Bush administration would work with Russia on codifying a verification regime under the Moscow Treaty, either by continuing the START I verification regime beyond 2009 or through other measures. The United States and Russia began informal talks in 2006 on what to do after START I expired, but they made little progress. Neither party wanted to extend START I in its current form because some of its provisions interfered with military programs on both sides. Russia wanted to replace START I with a new treaty that would further reduce deployed forces while using many of the same definitions and counting rules of the treaty. The Bush administration was divided on what to do, but the president had little interest in negotiating a new arms treaty with Russia.

With few signs of Bush administration interest in a new treaty, Lugar grew frustrated. In the spring of 2007, Lugar sent a letter to Secretary of State Rice in which he expressed concern about press reports that the United States would not enter into negotiations with Russia on extending the verification regime of START I or additional measures under the Moscow Treaty aimed at verification of that agreement. He cited comments by Robert Joseph, a former State Department official for arms control, who said the Bush administration didn't want to participate in any more cold war–style arms control. "Such a statement appears at odds with both the formal record of the administration's policy and with the specific assurances provided to the Committee on Foreign Relations in the past," Lugar wrote.

He noted that administration officials testified before the Foreign Relations Committee and said that while the Moscow Treaty did not have a verification regime, the United States could rely on the START I verification regime for transparency. He cited Rumsfeld's testimony in July of 2002. "This testimony led the Committee to conclude that the absence of verification provisions in the Moscow Treaty made extension of START, as well as confidence and transparency measures under the Moscow Treaty, high priority issues for bilateral arms control between the United States and Russia."[20]

"I would appreciate learning what steps the administration has taken regarding either extension of the START verification regime beyond 2009 or specific verification measures under the Moscow Treaty. United States goals and interests are not advanced by placing the strategic relationship with Russia in cold storage for the last two years of this administration nor by permitting the START I verification regime to collapse," he wrote.

When he traveled to Russia in September of 2007 to celebrate the 15th anniversary of the Nunn-Lugar program, Lugar was asked by a number of Russian officials and journalists why the Bush administration appeared disinterested in negotiating a follow-on treaty replacing START I. He did not have a good answer. Shortly after returning from his trip, Lugar wrote again to Rice about his concerns. "In private as well as public gatherings, Russian and American experts both noted with concern the policies the administration is employing in the areas of non-proliferation and arms control. Numerous officials report that the administration refuses as a matter of principle to consider or discuss legally binding arms control proposals. In the meantime, existing treaties are foundering because of U.S. policies and funding shortfalls— namely the Fissile Material Cutoff Treaty and U.S. voluntary contributions to the Comprehensive Test Ban Treaty Organization. This course of action is counter to U.S. national security interests and introduces elements of strategic uncertainty into the international community and increases existing strains in the U.S.-Russian strategic relationship," he wrote.[21]

He noted that administration officials had said they wouldn't negotiate a legally binding treaty with Russia nor support the continuation of a formal verification regime. He questioned the utility of having a verification regime without the force of law. "But what is the rationale for abandoning a legally binding START Treaty? The predictability and confidence provided by effective verification reduces the chances of misinterpretation, miscalculation and error. While concluding such a regime is challenging and time consuming, it is worth the effort and commitment needed to reach an agreement."

Lugar said it would be a mistake to permit the START I treaty to expire, arguing that such a decision would be seen as weakening the international nuclear non-proliferation regime. START I, he argued, should be viewed as an integral part of U.S. non-proliferation policy and the Bush administration should work with Russia on a legally binding document to replace START I and revive U.S. leadership on non-proliferation and arms control in its final 2 years.

Despite Lugar's plea for action, little arms control activity occurred during the final years of the Bush administration. After the 2008 presidential election, Lugar took a December trip to Russia at the suggestion of several American diplomats who believed Lugar might be able to bridge the two administrations and lay a foundation for the Obama administration to hit the ground running with Russia on arms control issues. Lugar met with Russian Foreign Minister Sergei Lavrov and others and then sent a letter to President-elect Obama urging him to move ahead on a replacement to START I. In his December 22, 2008, letter, Lugar lamented that START I would expire in less than a year. He urged Obama to engage Russia in negotiations that would return the U.S.-Russian strategic relationship to firmer footing based on international legal obligations that reduced the prospects of misinterpretation and provided verifiable outcomes in which both sides could have confidence.[22] Lugar then offered the incoming president several specific recommendations that included nominating an ambassador-at-large for strategic talks with Russia and committing to ensure START I did not expire. He also said the United States should insist that tactical nuclear weapons be made part of the negotiations.

During her confirmation hearing in January of 2009 to be secretary of state, Hillary Clinton said negotiating a successor to START I was an important and time-sensitive priority.[23] And the new administration put an arms control agreement with Russia on a relatively fast track. Obama met Russian President Dmitry Medvedev on April 1, 2009, to discuss, among other things, arms control issues. Then a few days later he delivered a major speech in Prague, committing to work for a world without nuclear weapons. An arms control treaty with Russia "that is legally binding and sufficiently bold" was a critical first step toward this goal.[24]

The United States and Russia began formal talks on what became the New START treaty in May of 2009. Obama and Medvedev met in Moscow in July and set broad parameters for an agreement: between 500 and 1,100 strategic delivery vehicles and between 1,500 and 1,675 nuclear warheads. When the talks bogged down in the fall, Obama and Medvedev issued a joint statement on December 4, 2009, saying they were still committed to working toward an agreement. On March 26, 2010, Obama announced that an agreement with Russia had been reached and he traveled to Prague on April 8 to sign it with Medvedev. It was sent to the Senate about a month later, on May 13.[25]

Lugar praised the signing of the agreement, issuing a brief statement on March 26, 2010. "I commend the U.S. and Russian delegations for months of dedicated effort. I look forward to the president's submission of the new treaty, its protocols, annexes, and all associated documents to the Senate for advice and consent on ratification. I also look forward to working with Chairman Kerry to begin scheduling hearings and briefings for the Foreign Relations Committee so that we can work quickly to achieve ratification of the new treaty."[26]

Under New START, each side is allowed 1,550 deployed warheads, 700 deployed delivery vehicles, and 800 deployed and non-deployed launchers. To ensure compliance, the two nations agreed to exchange data about force size and structure, notify each other of changes, and permit 18 short-notice inspections each year to verify the accuracy of claims. It required for the first time that all delivery vehicles have a unique identifier number.

The only binding limit on missile defense was a provision that the United States and Russia can't use existing ICBM silos or SLBM launch tubes to house missile defense interceptors. The treaty's preamble contained language acknowledging the "interrelationship" between strategic and defensive systems. Russia also issued a unilateral statement saying it would be monitoring the development of the American missile defense system carefully and said there must be "no qualitative or quantitative build-up in the missile defense capabilities" of the United States.[27]

IV

Lugar believed the treaty was a modest but important achievement that deserved Senate approval. However, even before the treaty was signed by Obama and Medvedev in May of 2010, Lugar was concerned that Republicans in the Senate would not be eager to give the new president a foreign policy victory. Lugar said that after Obama received the Nobel Peace Prize in December of 2009, he anticipated that many Republicans were bracing to battle the president over the treaty.[28]

While many of the most consequential arms control agreements since World War II have been negotiated by Republican presidents, many Republicans in Congress have been deeply skeptical of arms control agreements between the United States and the Soviet Union and then with Russia. They argued that arms control agreements have too often been unbalanced accords in which Moscow has pocketed American concessions, secured agreements to their advantage, and then adhered to them selectively. The skepticism of George W. Bush toward arms control was broadly shared by many modern Republicans, leaving Lugar as something of an outlier in his party.[29]

As the Obama administration proceeded with negotiations with Russia on the follow-up to START in 2009, there were many signs of GOP unrest. In September of 2009, the U.S. Senate Republican Policy Committee released a report regarding a successor treaty that signaled deep skepticism if not outright opposition to any treaty.

The Senate GOP report argued that if the treaty required any reductions in the U.S. nuclear arsenal, Obama would have to explain "what beneficial geopolitical developments compel such cuts." The report asserted that U.S. nuclear reductions had no effect in slowing nuclear programs in Iran and North Korea, observing that the nuclear weapons programs in these nations had grown as the U.S. nuclear arsenal shrunk. The report said that before any arms control agreement was reached between the Obama administration and Russia, it should be preceded by a rigorous Nuclear Posture Review that set out U.S. nuclear security needs and outlined the rationale for arms reductions. U.S. military requirements should determine the size of the American nuclear arsenal, not a political desire to secure an agreement with Russia, it said.[30]

The Senate GOP report argued that any U.S.-Russian arms treaty should deal with tactical weapons in which Russia had a large numerical advantage over the United States. The report also argued that any treaty must not limit the U.S. missile defense or the deployment of the prompt global strike system in which conventional weapons could be launched on ICBMs or SLBMs. It said that a comprehensive American nuclear modernization plan had to accompany any new treaty with Russia. "It is difficult to overstate the dire condition of the U.S. nuclear weapons complex: its physical infrastructure is crumbling and its intellectual edifice is aging," the report said.

As the Senate GOP policy committee was laying down its markers for any future arms control treaty, conservative groups outside of Congress were also bracing for a fight—even before they knew exactly what they were going to be fighting about.

After the treaty was concluded, Heritage Action for America, a political unit of the conservative Heritage Foundation, began preparing a strategy to defeat New START and tried to identify senators who could be persuaded to oppose it. It organized more than 60 briefings on Capitol Hill and told senators that the treaty severely weakened U.S. national security by restricting U.S. missile defense capabilities and limiting non-nuclear weapons. The treaty's verification provisions were called "wholly inadequate." The Heritage group said the treaty would prevent future advances in U.S. missile defense and doubted the United States would be able to verify Russian compliance or non-compliance of the treaty. It also said the treaty ignored more pressing threats posed by Iran and North Korea. Once the debate over New START heated up, the Heritage Action Fund sent mailers to 10 states, including Arizona, Kentucky, and Tennessee, where key Republican senators had not yet declared if they would support the treaty. The Heritage mailer said the treaty failed to protect U.S. security interests. Another conservative group, Liberty Central, also went after the treaty, attacking it for undermining American national security. Members of the Tea Party wing of the GOP joined in attacking the treaty throughout 2010. In Senate Republican policy meetings, Senator Jim DeMint, a Tea Party favorite, lambasted the treaty and called for its rejection.[31]

But the real focal point of GOP skepticism was Jon Kyl, the Republican senator from Arizona who has been a vocal skeptic of arms control ever since he was elected to Congress in 1986 and especially since winning election to the Senate in 1994. He opposed the Chemical Weapons Treaty in 1997 and played a leading role in defeating the Comprehensive

Test Ban Treaty in 1999. Without a seat on either the Senate Foreign Relations or Armed Services Committees, Kyl insinuated himself into arms control debates by sheer doggedness. He is a member of the Senate Intelligence Committee and is a co-chairman of the Senate's National Security Working Group, the successor to the Senate Arms Control Working Group.

A lawyer by training and sometimes described as a more polished version of former Senate Foreign Relations Committee Chairman Jesse Helms, Kyl is a leader of a faction in the Republican Party that one analyst describes as the hawk-nationalist alliance. This group champions missile defense, more spending on virtually all defense programs, and an aggressive American foreign policy. It is skeptical of arms control and international agreements more generally.[32]

Lugar and Kyl have a cordial but also wary relationship. They are in basic agreement on many domestic issues but differ fundamentally on foreign policy. Lugar has long supported arms control and American cooperation with international bodies. He sees the American relationship with Russia as a complex blend of cooperation and competition. Kyl, on the other hand, frequently speaks of Russia as a hostile nation that can't be trusted.

Kyl flew to Geneva in November of 2009 to monitor the U.S. talks with Russia on a successor to START. After he returned to Washington, Kyl gave a speech on the Senate floor that signaled that he would approach any new treaty skeptically. He said somewhat unpersuasively that he hoped to support the treaty that was being negotiated, but then he added that "as I learn more about what has been negotiated thus far, and the general process this treaty negotiation has taken, I grow more concerned."[33]

Once the treaty was signed, Kyl sharpened his attack on New START, first in a May 19, 2010, speech at the Nixon Center and then in a lengthy speech on the Senate floor on May 24. In the Senate speech, Kyl said there were a number of issues that had to be examined carefully. First was modernization. He noted that the previous year's Defense Authorization Act required the administration to submit a nuclear modernization plan when New START was sent to the Senate. The administration submitted its modernization plan, called a 1251 report, on May

13, 2010, along with the START treaty. It laid out a funding plan of $80 billion for the modernization of the nuclear arsenal and related facilities over 10 years and another $100 billion for nuclear delivery systems. But Kyl refused to say if this would be enough to win his support. America's weapons must be safe, secure, and reliable, he said, adding that current American weapons were about 30 years old and in poor condition. He acknowledged that the administration had proposed substantial funds for these programs, but he was still skeptical if these were new funds or largely money that had already been committed.[34]

Kyl also questioned how the treaty limited U.S. nuclear forces and specifically if it would constrain U.S. missile defense systems. He said the treaty put a "direct restriction" on U.S. missile defense activities in Article V, blasting the administration for not disclosing this clearly. "This concession to the Russian Federation will establish a dangerous precedent with respect to including missile defense limitations in future offensive arms control agreements," Kyl charged.

Regarding missile defense, Kyl said he was alarmed by the reference to it in the treaty's preamble, the Russian unilateral statement on missile defense, and remarks by unnamed Russian officials saying they might try to blackmail the United States from increasing its missile defense capabilities by threatening to withdraw from the treaty. "There is something fundamentally disturbing about entering into a treaty with the Russians when we have such a divergence in view over a substantial issue like missile defense," Kyl said.[35]

Kyl also questioned if the new treaty could be verified and focused on the treaty's impact on the "disparity" between U.S. and Russian nuclear forces, especially Russia's large numerical advantage in tactical nuclear weapons. Kyl also charged the treaty could hamper the development of the global strike system. He summarized his concerns in terms that some found alarmist: "So our stockpile is aging, refurbishments are behind schedule, the Cold War infrastructure is falling apart, and the critical science and technology skills that underwrite our nuclear deterrence are atrophied." But Kyl insisted that he would await the careful Senate examination of the treaty before deciding to support or oppose it.[36]

Many Senate Republicans were prepared to take their cues on the arms control treaty from Kyl. Senator John Thune called him the "resident expert" on arms control, while Senator Sam Brownback called him "the man" on nuclear arms issues. "Everyone kind of turns to Senator Kyl because he has been so keyed up on the issue," said Senator Lisa Murkowski.[37]

As Republicans geared up to debate the treaty, analysts noted a striking difference between current Republicans lawmakers who were very skeptical about the treaty and a long list of former Republican law-makers and foreign policy experts who strongly supported the treaty. Republican foreign policy veterans from the Ford, Reagan, and George H. W. Bush administrations made frequent statements supporting the treaty.[38] By contrast, some current Republican lawmakers and a number of Republicans eyeing a 2012 bid for the Republican presidential nomination for president came out in opposition to the treaty.

V

As Kyl and other conservative Republicans were expressing their skepticism about the New START treaty, Lugar was working with the Obama administration and Senate Foreign Relations Committee Chairman John Kerry to build support for it. Even before the administration formally submitted the treaty to the Senate on May 13, Lugar considered what hearings would be most useful in explaining the treaty and forging a large bipartisan consensus behind it. Kerry at that time was working nearly full time on what turned out to be a futile effort to negotiate climate change legislation, so he deferred much of the organizing work to Lugar. For his part, Lugar wanted to make sure the hearings answered basic questions about the treaty, built a comprehensive record, and demonstrated the treaty was part of a series of arms control treaties that Republican administrations and lawmakers had supported. "One of our goals was to show that this wasn't a Barack Obama disarmament treaty," said one Republican staffer.[39] Lugar felt it was substantially and politically important to show that the treaty was supported by America's military leaders.

The Senate Foreign Relations Committee's first hearing related to the treaty was held April 29, 2010, a few weeks before the treaty was signed in Prague. The hearing considered the historical and modern context of U.S.-Russian arms control. It featured two former Defense secretaries, William Perry and James Schlesinger, who also wrote a key report on the future of America's nuclear arsenal. In his opening statement, Lugar observed that only 26 members of the current Senate were in the upper chamber in 1992 for the debate on the START I treaty and only 6 members of the Foreign Relations Committee were senators when the Senate dealt with the Moscow Treaty in 2002. Lugar then discussed themes he would develop in the coming months.

New START, he said, was clearly in the country's national security interests. It would reduce American and Russian strategic nuclear launchers and warheads and replace the 1991 START treaty that expired the previous year. Equally important, it would provide forward momentum to the U.S. relationship with Russia, which he saw as vital to U.S. policy goals related to Iran's nuclear program, nuclear non-proliferation, and global energy security and to stability in Eurasia. He lamented that the United States now lacked both the ability to carry out on-site inspections in Russia and the formal consultation mechanisms that monitor the Russian strategic nuclear program. "It's essential that a verification system be in place, so we have a sufficient understanding of Russian nuclear forces and achieve a level of transparency that prevents miscalculations," he said.[40]

There were, he acknowledged, significant issues to address during the Senate's review of the treaty. First, there was the matter of missile defense. Lugar said that the first START treaty had acknowledged the link between strategic offensive and strategic defensive systems and the preamble to the New START treaty similarly acknowledged this link. He said the administration did need to explain why it accepted in Article V a restriction on the deployment of U.S. interceptor missiles in existing strategic missile launchers. The Senate debate should consider in what specific instances conventional capability could replace nuclear capacity, he said. The Senate should examine modernization challenges and do all that it could to ensure the continued safety, security and reliability of American nuclear weapons. The administration needed to explain how American weapons would perform their missions over the 10-year life of the treaty. The senator said the administration should also articulate how it wanted U.S. and Russian strategic forces to look at the end of the new treaty's lifetime.

Perhaps trying to nudge senators toward a predisposition to support the treaty, Lugar noted the Senate had approved other arms control treaties by large bipartisan votes: START I was approved in 1992 93 to 6; START II was approved in 1996 87 to 4; the Moscow Treaty was approved in 2003 by a 95 to 0 vote. Since the new START treaty combined concepts from START I and the Moscow Treaty, he said that he hoped a thorough and detailed debate could achieve similar levels of support in the Senate.

The Senate Foreign Relations Committee held a dozen hearings from April through July of 2010 on the New START treaty. Witnesses supporting the treaty included Secretary of State Hillary Clinton, Secretary of Defense Robert Gates, Chairman of the Joint Chiefs of Staff Mike Mullen, former secretaries of state Henry Kissinger and James Baker, former secretaries of defense James Schlesinger and William Perry, and former national security advisors Brent Scowcroft and Stephen Hadley. Additionally, the panel received testimony from those officials who negotiated the treaty, including Assistant Secretary of State Rose Gottemoeller and Edward Warner, a senior Defense Department official who would implement it. The committee also heard from another key Defense Department official, James Miller; General Kevin Chilton, commander of the U.S. Strategic Command; and Kenneth Myers III, the director of the Defense Threat Reduction Agency. The panel heard from the directors of the nation's nuclear laboratories, Mike Anastasio from Los Alamos National Laboratory, George Miller from Lawrence Livermore National Laboratory, and Paul Hommert from Sandia National Laboratories. And it listened to the views of several skeptics of the treaty from the George W. Bush administration, including Robert Joseph, a former State Department official, and Eric Edelman, a former Defense Department aide.[41]

During the hearings, Kerry and Lugar built a record they hoped would give the treaty momentum. Schlesinger said it was "obligatory" for the United States to ratify the New START agreement. Perry said that failure to ratify the agreement would cause the United States to "forfeit any right to provide leadership" in arms control. Baker said the New START treaty was a "modest and appropriate continuation" of the first START treaty. Kissinger said the treaty was part of an "evolution of agreements" that went back to the 1970s. Scowcroft said failure to ratify the treaty would throw "the whole nuclear negotiating position into a state of chaos."[42]

Lugar attended all of the Foreign Relations Committee hearings. Usually as knowledgeable about the treaty as were the witnesses before the committee, Lugar asked politely worded but probing questions that largely reflected the concerns that other Republicans had about the pact. He understood their reservations and wanted witnesses to address them. Only occasionally did he voice frustration that others had not done their homework and failed to study the history of arms control or the particulars of the treaty.

When Republican senators Jim DeMint and Jim Risch voiced their concerns about a limited American missile defense system, Lugar observed that U.S. presidents and Congresses had made the decision to pursue a limited system more than 20 years earlier and had dropped aspirations for a total missile defense system, thought to be technologically infeasible and wildly expensive. "I don't know of any serious thinker with regard to missile defense matters, or technical matters, who has envisioned the thought of a comprehensive missile defense system that would stop multiple warheads coming into the United States," he said at one hearing.[43]

After the Foreign Relations Committee hearings concluded and before the September mark-up of the resolution of ratification, Lugar sent more than a dozen "Dear Colleague" letters about the treaty to fellow senators. The letters dealt with all aspects of the New START treaty, including missile defense, tactical nuclear weapons, counting rules, verification and inspection issues, the conventional prompt global strike system, and nuclear modernization. As a package of essays, they constituted a vigorous, technically sound, and powerful defense of the treaty.

In the first letter sent on September 7, 2010, Lugar made a broad case for the treaty that had, he noted, "the unequivocal support from our defense establishment led by Secretary of Defense Robert Gates and our Joint Chiefs of Staff." The treaty, he argued, advanced U.S. security by allowing American technicians on the ground in Russia to collect data on the Russian arsenal and verify its compliance with treaty obligations. Ratification of the New START treaty, he said, was the only way the United States would be able to insert inspectors into Russia to conduct intrusive inspections that are critical to U.S. national security. He observed that since the beginning of the START I regime, the United States had conducted more than six hundred nuclear weapons inspections in the former Soviet Union, which reduced the likelihood the country would be surprised by future advances in Russian weapons technology or deployment. "Rejecting this treaty would inhibit our knowledge of Russian military capabilities, weaken our non-proliferation diplomacy worldwide, and potentially ignite an expensive arms competition that would further strain our national budget," he wrote.[44]

In the letters that followed, Lugar methodically discussed critical and contentious issues, presenting the assertions made by the treaty's critics and his responses. In the letter on missile defense, he observed that critics often noted that the treaty's preamble said there is an "interrelationship" between strategic offense and strategic defense. Lugar said this was accurate but added the preamble is "a nonbinding set of clauses stating the truism that an interrelationship exists between strategic offense and strategic defense." It didn't express rights or obligations, he emphasized. He noted that critics charged the treaty forbids the United States from converting intercontinental ballistic launchers and submarine-launched ballistic missiles into missile defense launchers. Lugar said this was a concession with little meaning because the U.S. military had no plans to do this and concluded it would be both too expensive and strategically unwise to do so. Lugar observed that critics often cited Russia's unilateral statement regarding its possible withdrawal from the treaty if there were qualitative or quantitative expansions of U.S. missile defense programs. But Lugar put this into context. "Unilateral statements are routine to arms control treaties and do not alter the legal rights and obligations of the parties to the Treaty." He added that international law allows nations to withdraw from treaties under "extraordinary circumstances" if they choose to do so.[45]

On the issue of Russian advantages on tactical nuclear weapons, Lugar said the treaty didn't deal with tactical nuclear weapons because both sides agreed their first priority should be to replace the transparency and verification procedures provided by the expired START treaty. The administration decided that it was important to get New START ratified before moving on to negotiations on tactical nuclear weapons.

Lugar noted that the Perry-Schlesinger panel estimated that Russia has about 3,800 deployed tactical nuclear weapons, while the United States has several hundred stored at U.S. and NATO bases in Europe, as well as some sea-launched cruise missiles that are being phased out. He acknowledged that Russia has far more tactical nuclear weapons than the United States but charged that critics distorted their value by implying they constitute a serious missile threat to Europe. "In fact, most of Russia's tactical nuclear weapons either have very short ranges, are used for homeland air defense, are devoted to the Chinese border, or are in storage," he wrote. Lugar added that any future arms deal with the United States and Russia must deal with tactical nuclear weapons but he added the Senate should first ratify New START.[46]

On the issue of modernization that Kyl had been pressing so vigorously, Lugar wrote that the treaty would not directly affect the modernization or the missions of American nuclear weapons laboratories. The treaty explicitly said that modernization and replacement of strategic offensive arms may be carried out. He noted that near the end of the Bush administration, a consensus developed that the United States needed to do more to ensure the vitality of its nuclear weapons complex, even as a framework for a successor to START I was sought. The administration planned to invest more than $100 billion in U.S. nuclear delivery systems to sustain existing capabilities while modernizing strategic systems. The 1251 report submitted by the administration also committed $80 billion over 10 years to sustain and modernize the U.S. nuclear weapons complex. Lugar noted that there was little the Foreign Relations Committee could do to ensure that Congress appropriated these funds in the future since this was under the jurisdiction of the House and Senate Appropriations Committees.[47]

The Foreign Relations Committee had been scheduled to consider a ratification resolution on August 4, but Kerry decided to delay the mark-up until after the Senate's August recess. This delay, which a number of Republican senators requested, would allow senators on his committee to carefully review the committee's record as well as that of the Senate Armed Services and Intelligence Committees. It would also allow the State Department time to respond to more than 900 questions that had been submitted by senators. Lugar opposed delay-

ing the mark-up, saying it was unnecessary and even dangerous given
that American inspectors were no longer in Russia because START had
lapsed. "We ought to vote now and let the chips fall where they may,"
he said.[48]

But Kerry held firm on the delay and began circulating a draft resolution in early September when the Senate returned from its August
recess. The Constitution gives the Senate the power to approve, by a
two-thirds vote, treaties that are negotiated by the executive branch.
The Senate does not ratify a treaty; rather, it considers a resolution
of ratification.[49]

As the September 16 mark-up of the ratification resolution by the
Foreign Relations Committee approached, Lugar decided to offer his
own version, incorporating the suggestions of witnesses before the committee and especially Republicans whom he thought might ultimately
support the accord. Lugar told Kerry that he had his own draft and the
Democratic chairman offered no objections with going forward with
Lugar's resolution since it was similar to his draft.[50]

Lugar's draft, which was modified several times at the request
of Kerry, the administration, and several Republican senators, included
an understanding that the treaty didn't include any limits on U.S. deployment of missile defense. It emphasized that Russia's unilateral statement
on missile defense wasn't binding. The Lugar resolution reaffirmed the
language of the 1999 Missile Defense Act that the United States would
"deploy as soon as technologically possible" an effective missile defense
system.[51]

Lugar's draft conditioned ratification on presidential certification
of U.S. ability to monitor Russian compliance and committed the administration to immediate consultations with Russia should the United
States suspect that Russia was breaking out from the treaty's constraints.
The resolution required a plan from the administration for monitoring
New START. It included an understanding that nothing in the treaty
impeded the research, development, testing, and evaluation of strategic-
range conventional systems. Lugar's resolution committed to ensure the
stability, reliability, and performance of U.S. nuclear forces through a
robust stockpile stewardship program and included a requirement for
the president to submit to Congress a plan for overcoming any future

resource shortfall for modernization programs. It urged the president to negotiate with Russia to reduce tactical nuclear weapons.[52]

Lugar's draft ultimately won the support of two other Republicans on the Foreign Relations Committee, Bob Corker and Johnny Isakson. But strong Republican opposition to the treaty was evident as soon as the mark-up session began. Republican senator Risch tried to postpone the session by citing late-breaking intelligence that allegedly called the treaty into question. This intelligence, he claimed, "directly affects what we're doing here, not only the details of this but actually whether or not we should debate going forward with this." Risch later said he was referring to reports about Russian cheating on other arms control agreements.[53] But Kerry said the intelligence community remained convinced that this information had no material impact on the treaty.

During the deliberations, a handful of conservative Republican senators offered amendments to unravel the treaty. For example, John Barrasso pushed to remove missile defense language from the treaty's preamble, which, if successful, would have required the treaty to be renegotiated with Russia. His amendment failed, as did several other amendments related to missile defense. The amendment prompting the most debate was one by DeMint that, in its original form, expressed the U.S. commitment to layered missile defense and repudiation of the decades-old doctrine of mutual assured destruction. Kerry negotiated a compromise with DeMint that repeated that the United States would go forward with its missile defense programs.[54]

The Lugar resolution was approved by the Foreign Relations Committee on a 14 to 4 vote with all Democratic members of the committee supporting the resolution as well as Republicans Lugar, Corker, and Isakson. But there was still strong opposition from the other Republicans on the committee who offered sharp words during the mark-up session and then filed their dissent in a committee document. The dissent was not a narrow one. In a statement submitted to the committee, Risch, DeMint, Barrasso, Roger Wicker, and Jim Inhofe argued the administration was too focused on resetting relations with Russia and not sufficiently attentive on maintaining multilateral nuclear stability in an uncertain world. "Instead of looking at the new and shifting 21st century challenges, New START embraces the paradigm of the Cold War by focusing only on Russia with its porous limits on nuclear warheads, delivery vehicles and inspection regimes," they charged.[55]

The conservative GOP senators then cited a host of specific concerns. First, on missile defense they said the committee's hearings and debates made clear there was "a fundamental disagreement" between the United States and Russia on missile defense. Regarding tactical nuclear weapons, they raised the familiar issue of the numerical disparity between the U.S. and Russian tactical nuclear arsenals. They also asked why the administration didn't seek a statement in the preamble about the relationship between tactical and strategic nuclear weapons. On the issue of global strike, they argued the treaty would place limits on this potentially important conventional system. They observed that long-range conventional ballistic missiles would count against the treaty's limit of 700 delivery vehicles and their conventional warheads would count against the 1,550 limit.

The conservative Republican senators expressed concerns about the issue of modernization, noting that the United States was the only nuclear nation not pursuing modernization programs. It was important, they declared, to modernize U.S. strategic delivery vehicles and platforms that make up the nuclear triad of land-, air-, and submarine-based weapons. They expressed concern about inspections and verification of the treaty, arguing that it was important to have "absolute confidence in our ability to monitor the Russians and verify compliance." They said the United States couldn't know from so few inspections if Russia was complying with the treaty's central limits. They argued that Russia had a long record of ignoring international agreements that it had signed, charging that Russia repeatedly violated START I from the time it came into force in 1994 until its expiration in 2009. "Russia has a long history of acting in bad faith and violating arms control agreements and commitments," they charged.[56]

VI

With the approval of the treaty in the Senate Foreign Relations Committee in September, the debate quickly shifted to whether the full Senate could consider it before the end of the year. With the 2010 mid-term elections approaching, congressional leaders decided to leave Washington in late September for the campaign trail. Thus, it became clear that if the treaty were to be considered in 2010, it would have to occur in the lame duck session.

As lawmakers campaigned across the country in the fall of 2010, the administration continued to work with Lugar in building support for the treaty among Republicans and to negotiate with Kyl on modernization funding so the Senate could take up the treaty in November or December.

In the view of many, Kyl was in no hurry to reach an agreement with the administration on the nuclear modernization issue, preferring to fight for as many funds as he could secure while also delaying the consideration of the treaty into 2011. The administration continued to court Kyl assiduously. On November 12, just days before the lame duck session was to begin, a high-level team of defense experts from the administration traveled to Arizona and spent 3 hours meeting with Kyl and his staff regarding his concerns about modernization funding. The team walked through a 10-year plan to spend $85 billion on modernization. A senior administration official, Gary Samore, later said he thought there was a "basic agreement" on modernization funding between the administration and Kyl.[57]

But then on November 16, Kyl suddenly announced that he did not think the treaty should come up during the lame duck session given the "complex and unresolved issues related to New START and modernization." He said he hoped to keep working with the administration on the treaty. Stunned by Kyl's statement, Vice President Biden released one of his own saying that passage of the treaty in 2010 was in the national security interests of the United States. "Failure to pass the New START this year would endanger our national security," Biden said. "Without ratification of this Treaty, we will have no Americans on the ground to inspect Russia's nuclear activities, no verification regime to track Russia's strategic nuclear arsenal, less cooperation between the two nations that account for 90% of the world's nuclear weapons, and no verified nuclear reductions."[58]

The next day, after meeting with Kerry and Clinton, Lugar said that he opposed delaying the treaty until 2011, signaling that he was convinced that deferring the treaty was tantamount to killing it. "End-less hearings, mark-up, back to trying to get some time on the floor . . . It will be some time before the treaty is heard from again," he warned in the event of a postponement.[59]

Senate Majority Leader Harry Reid released a statement on November 17, saying there was plenty of time during the lame duck session to consider the New START treaty. The administration, apparently to show that it had been negotiating with Kyl in good faith, released a timeline showing that there were at least 30 high-level administration contacts with Kyl or his staff since August 2009.[60]

President Obama jumped into action after Kyl's comment. He hosted a meeting with Henry Kissinger, James Baker, Madeleine Albright, Brent Scowcroft, and other foreign policy luminaries to call for prompt Senate consideration of the treaty. "It is a national security imperative that the United States ratify the New START treaty this year," Obama said, adding he was confident that the treaty would pass. "This is not a matter that can be delayed. Every month that goes by without a treaty means that we are not able to verify what's going on on the ground in Russia."[61]

The administration then launched a 5-week intensive lobbying effort led by the vice president with frequent statements by Obama, Biden, Clinton, Gates, and others. Lugar urged the White House to intensify its lobbying effort by meeting with key lawmakers and helping organize statements in support of the treaty by foreign policy experts, especially prominent Republicans. Lugar remained steadfast and insisted privately and publicly that the treaty should go forward and predicted that when the Senate vote occurred, it would get the two-thirds majority needed to pass.

Despite threats from Kyl and other Republicans, Majority Leader Reid brought the resolution of ratification to the Senate floor on December 15. On that day, the Senate formally voted to begin consideration of the treaty. The motion passed on a 66 to 32 vote, an indication that the treaty had broad Senate support.

After that procedural vote, Lugar gave his opening speech endorsing New START in a mostly empty Senate chamber. He offered a strong defense of the treaty. "For fifteen years, the START treaty has helped to keep a lid on the U.S.-Russian nuclear rivalry," he said, surmising that the defeat of the new treaty "would be greeted with delight in Iran, North Korea, Syria and Burma." He said the United States "should not be cavalier" about allowing its relationship with Moscow to drift or about allowing its knowledge of Russian weaponry to atrophy. It was imperative, Lugar said, for the United States to manage its relationship with a rival who still had the capacity for inflicting staggering nuclear destruction. The expired START treaty had allowed the United States to manage an adversarial relationship that had been cloaked in uncertainty. It had provided structure and transparency upon which arms control and non-proliferation efforts had been built, such as the Nunn-Lugar program. Its inspections and consultations and the threat reduction activities of Nunn-Lugar had been a constant that had built respect and reduced misunderstandings.[62]

He then reviewed the key issues under debate, such as missile defense, modernization, tactical nuclear weapons, and treaty verification. "Rejecting New START would permanently inhibit our understanding of Russian nuclear forces, weaken our non-proliferation diplomacy worldwide, and potentially re-ignite expensive arms competition that would further strain our national budget," he said.[63]

The next day Kyl offered his critique of New START as Lugar sat a few seats away in the Senate chamber. Kyl argued that it was inappropriate for the Senate to consider the treaty given the raft of other issues that needed to be dealt with during the lame duck and the complexity of the treaty. Speaking to the substance of the treaty, Kyl said the Russians won the negotiations and the pact would require the United States to "cut our forces to the bone." He outlined his views on the need for more modernization funds and lamented the administration's "uncertain commitment to the nuclear triad." He said the treaty was unverifiable and that Russia was an unreliable partner. "Of course, Russia has a history of cheating on every arms control treaty we have ever entered into with them, which amplifies the concern." He said the treaty was a distraction from the "real agenda of proliferation and terrorism."[64]

Over the 8 days of Senate debate, Kyl and Lugar often sat a few seats apart on the Senate floor, but they rarely spoke to each other. Lugar felt that many of Kyl's criticisms of the treaty were inaccurate or hyperbolic, but he declined to get into a back-and-forth exchange. He said that it was better to remain focused on making his main points and helping defeat amendments that would kill the treaty.[65]

Several days into the debate, on Sunday, December 19, both Kyl and Senate Republican leader Mitch McConnell officially confirmed they would vote against the treaty. This caused a flurry of speculation that the treaty might be on its way to defeat. But Lugar remained steadfast and confident, predicting the treaty would prevail when the final vote was cast.

On December 21, the Senate voted 67 to 28 to cut off the debate on the treaty, thus moving into the final phase of the Senate's consideration of New START. Lugar and Kerry held a press conference after this critical procedural vote and said that passage of the resolution of ratification was near. But they refused to take a victory lap, and Lugar sidestepped questions that invited him to be critical of McConnell and Kyl. Lugar said the treaty was a modest but important arms control effort and that, once approved, the leaders from both countries could move on to other issues.[66]

On the final day of debate, the Senate approved several watered-down Republican amendments by voice vote and then moved toward the final vote. Speaking on the Senate floor, Kerry praised Lugar as a "steady, wise and thoughtful collaborator." He later said that Lugar's support for the treaty has been "indispensable." In his final remarks, Kerry spoke poetically of the goals of the treaty, while Lugar spoke more prosaically, referring to arms control as a "technically challenging endeavor" and as a difficult "nuts and bolts enterprise."[67]

The treaty was approved on a 71 to 26 vote. Biden, as president of the Senate, presided over the vote and announced the final tally. Hillary Clinton was on the floor of the Senate during the vote and shook Lugar's hand, thanking him for his long months of work. After the vote, Lugar and Kerry held a press conference in the Senate Radio-Television Gallery and then went down to the Foreign Relations Committee's ceremonial room in the Capitol for a celebration. Biden spoke to the group and effusively praised the work of both Kerry and Lugar.

When Lugar returned to his office in the Hart Building, he received a call from Obama thanking him for his efforts and recalling that his first overseas trip as a senator was to Russia with Lugar. The president said there was a "direct line" from that trip to the passage of the treaty. Speaking several months later, Biden said that Lugar played a central role in Senate passage of the New START treaty. He said Lugar's patient, relentless work on the treaty will be remembered as one of the highlights of Lugar's career.[68]

Lugar believes the passage of New START was an important, even historic moment for the country. It was another step in the long march toward getting nuclear weapons under control. The day after the final Senate vote on New START, with most of the Capitol now empty for the Christmas holiday, Lugar was in his office reading a memo that outlined the technical details of how the treaty would be implemented.[69]

12

❧

Tending to the Homefront

I

In the history of the U.S. Senate, about two thousand people have served in the upper chamber and less than two dozen have been elected to serve six terms. Many of those who have served this long came from states in which one party was in clear ascendancy throughout their political careers, so that once they secured a Senate seat they could keep it until they wanted to leave—or until they died. Senators Edward Kennedy of Massachusetts, Robert Byrd of West Virginia, Strom Thurmond of South Carolina, Richard Russell of Georgia, Claiborne Pell of Rhode Island, and Russell Long of Louisiana are examples of this.[1]

During his more than 35-year career in the Senate, Richard Lugar has represented a state with strong Republican leanings, but it has not been a political lock for the GOP. To stay in Washington, Lugar has had to pay attention to the homefront. His political longevity and success in Indiana politics has not been a fluke. While he has had good luck, he has been a dominant force in Indiana politics as the result of policy accomplishments, careful attention to his state, and diligent attempts to describe what he is doing in Washington in a way that makes sense to his constituents.

While Lugar has unabashedly sought to play the role of a national senator who operates effectively on the global stage, he has stayed close to the people of Indiana. He has always remained mindful that his ability to operate on this larger stage requires Hoosiers to re-hire him every

6 years. He can recite with grim precision the electoral demise of other senators involved in international affairs who lost touch with the people back home—and then lost their jobs. He has worked successfully to connect his work in Washington and overseas to the needs of his constituents in Indiana.

Lugar has developed what political scientist Richard Fenno calls a "home style" that is very effective. While Fenno's original model focused on House members, his central insight is that for lawmakers to win re-election they must secure the trust of their constituents. To do this, they must demonstrate that they are qualified for the job, that they understand their constituents' concerns, and that they can effectively represent their constituents in Washington. In Fenno's view, a home style is how lawmakers present themselves and their records back home.[2]

Lugar's political success is the result of many factors. First, he has a good natural fit with Indiana. Lugar's quiet, substantive, civil approach to public policy and politics is appreciated back home. A conservative Republican, he has not emphasized controversial social issues such as abortion and same-sex marriage and instead has focused on matters that his constituents are the most interested in such as economic growth, agriculture, nutrition, and foreign policy, which he links to trade and export promotion.

Second, Lugar has been attentive to the needs of his constituents. His office responds quickly to questions and helps constituents deal with federal, state and even local governments. Inquiries ranging from how to secure appointments to military academies to the best way to get flags that have flown over the U.S. Capitol are responded to promptly. He has worked to secure federal funds for projects in Indiana but has largely stayed clear of the controversial earmarking excesses of other lawmakers.

Third, Lugar has a strong political operation that works diligently over the full 6 years of his each of his Senate terms, raising funds, monitoring the mood back home, and keeping an eye out for future political challenges. While Lugar always seems calm, his top political people believe it's important to run scared and to assume that tough political challenges are ahead.

Fourth, Lugar has a strong network of former staffers and political supporters back in Indiana who run law firms, foundations, businesses, and think tanks and who promote the senator and provide his office with information about both opportunities and troubles awaiting him back home. He frequently sounds them out, seeking insights or information.

Fifth, the senator's office has done a shrewd and effective job in linking Lugar's name to programs and projects that he supports and that reflect favorably on him. Indiana is full of scholarships, awards, and contests that have been named after the senator. These solidify Lugar's reputation as a public official who supports goals such as effective government, nutrition, education, energy conservation, and principled leadership. While the senator never uses the term "branding" to describe his strategic association with respected causes, this is what it is.

Finally, Lugar has been politically lucky. He has not faced difficult opponents, in part because he has scared off more formidable challenges with high approval ratings and plenty of money in his campaign account. In 2006, Democrats chose not to even nominate a candidate to challenge him. "That doesn't happen very often in this business," said Senate Republican Leader Mitch McConnell.[3] But by the fall of 2010, it was clear that Lugar faced a new political environment in Indiana, at least within the Republican Party. In February 2011, Indiana's treasurer Richard Mourdock announced he was preparing to challenge Lugar in the 2012 Republican primary. Mourdock was endorsed by several Indiana Tea Party groups and claimed to have the endorsements of Republican county chairmen in 67 of Indiana's 92 counties. Polls in the fall of 2011 showed Mourdock and Lugar in a tight race among Indiana Republicans.

II

Some senators fit more easily and naturally into their state's political culture than others. For Richard Lugar, the fit is comfortable. By temperament, demeanor, and political philosophy, Lugar has been at home in Indiana's political life for more than 35 years. He repeatedly notes that he is a fifth-generation Hoosier and identifies with the state in ways that seem plausible, not contrived. When you enter his Washington office, there are two signs on the wall that say "Welcome Hoosiers." On a desk nearby there is an Indianapolis Colts helmet. His campaign ads frequently show him strolling on his farm in Marion County. He returns home often, flying coach on the 2-hour flight from Washington to Indianapolis.

"He is a Hoosier through and through. He is not one of those fly-over senators, who touch base briefly in their states. He travels the state up and down and is so tuned into the issues here. He has an amazing memory, he seems to remember everyone. His attachment to this state is remarkable," said John Tinder, a federal judge and former Lugar staffer.[4]

Lugar's conservative voting record, especially on domestic issues, is widely supported at home, as is his focus on economic and national security issues. His expertise and leadership on agriculture in the Senate has demonstrated to his constituents that he is working on matters that are critical to Indiana's economy.

Lugar's Senate elections tell a good part of the story. Polling results are often interesting, but election results are what counts. After losing in his first run for Senate against incumbent Birch Bayh in the Watergate year of 1974, Lugar won with 59 percent of the vote in 1976, 54 percent in 1982, 68 percent in 1988, 67 percent in 1994, 67 percent in 2000, and 87 percent in 2006, when he did not face a major party opponent.[5]

Members of the House face voters every 2 years and consequently have to stay close to their constituents if they wish to continue to serve. The most politically successful senators stay active and visible in their states, but this is difficult. Senate Historian Don Ritchie argues that senators have often found it challenging to stay plugged into their states without the imperative of facing elections every 2 years.[6]

Marjorie Hershey, a political science professor at Indiana University, said that Lugar, like other senators, has developed a "mental picture" of his state that has inevitably been shaped by past electoral successes. The trick is to keep his picture of the state accurate and up-to-date. "Senator Lugar is viewed with great respect in Indiana. He is seen as an elder statesman. The people are very comfortable with him and very accepting of him." But she adds a caution the Lugar team is well aware of. "You are strong politically—until you aren't. Things can change quickly in your state. The ground can shift under you before you know it. You can't get complacent."[7]

While one should be cautious about offering sweeping generalizations about states and their political leaders, there is clearly a connection between Lugar and Indiana. In his book, *The Indiana Way: A State History*, Professor James Madison of Indiana University says the people of Indiana have "tended to navigate in the middle of the American mainstream, drifting if anywhere a little closer to the more secure edge of the river." Moderation, he said, has been a hallmark of Indiana's political and cultural life. "Evolution, not revolution, was the route taken in Indiana. The state could be backward and out of step, its people close-minded and provincial. But more often Hoosiers navigated in the middle, away from the snags and shallow water, moving slowly but surely, confident that the stream flowed in the right direction, secure that they were on waters others had traveled, and hopeful that still more Hoosiers would follow over the same route," Madison writes.[8]

Madison says Indiana has generally been a politically conservative state since 1940, and Republicans have won more often than Democrats. But, he argues, Democrats have often been competitive, giving Indiana a vigorous two-party system. He argues that Lugar's temperament, cast of mind, and extensive roots in Indiana soil make him a comfortable fit in his state's political life.[9]

"The senator's connection to Indiana is deep and genuine. He loves this state. He loves his farm. He recalls fondly his days as a school board member, mayor, and small businessman. This is where his roots are," said Jim Morris, a former Lugar staffer who once ran the World Food Programme and is now president of the Indiana Pacers basketball team.[10]

While the senator has a natural fit with his home state, it's a connection that he works diligently to maintain. Every weekday morning he reads the *Indianapolis Star* online. Then he turns to a package of news clips that was assembled the previous night comprised of national and local stories in which he is mentioned, a summary of Indiana news, and press releases issued by his office.

Lugar knows the state's 92 counties intimately and can recall his electoral prowess in past elections in virtually every county. He closely follows the state's political, economic, and cultural life—including what sports teams are doing well. He returns to Indiana frequently and tries to meet with as many visitors from home as he can fit into his schedule. He often takes visiting Hoosiers to lunch at the Senate Dining Room. When traveling through Indiana, Lugar enjoys stops at McDonald's to get a cup of coffee and to chat informally with constituents.[11]

III

Richard Lugar has made it a priority to run efficient offices that provide government services to the people of Indiana. Political analysts agree that effective casework is important for successful and durable political careers. Some analysts have argued that good casework is the single most important factor to electoral success. Most agree that it can be, at minimum, very helpful for lawmakers if it's done well. Lugar does it well.

Lugar's various offices in Washington and throughout the state are designed to be advocates for the people of Indiana. In addition to his Washington office in the Senate Hart Building, Lugar's other main office is in Indianapolis. The senator also has smaller offices in Evansville, Fort Wayne, and Valparaiso. The senator expects his staff to treat his constituents with respect and to respond quickly to questions and requests to help them navigate Washington's bureaucracy. Staffers say that Lugar's insistence on providing good casework is rooted in both a sense of responsibility and political shrewdness. As an elected representative he believes it's his duty to help constituents who need help. And as a senator with an ambitious national and international agenda, he believes that good casework is a critical way to show the people of Indiana that he is attentive to their needs, even as he embarks on projects that take him far from the state.[12]

Marty Morris, Lugar's chief of staff and a staffer for more than 30 years, oversees Lugar's governmental and political operations. A large man who played football at Duke University, Morris is forceful and tough. His office is just down the hall from the senator's and is dominated by a large painting of Lugar on the wall. Mitch Daniels, the governor of Indiana and a former Lugar staffer, says Lugar has usually had a strong deputy to run his office and oversee his political affairs, and he observes that Morris now plays this role. "It's been very important for the senator to have somebody to do the difficult things. He doesn't like doing them. He accepts they have to be done. Sometimes people need to be reassigned or fired. The senator is such a nice person. That works fine, but there will be difficult things to deliver, bad news to deliver, and hard decisions to make," Daniels said.[13]

Morris insists the senator's offices project Lugar's best values. "If people come to visit us from Indiana, they've come around 600 miles and expect something of us. They deserve to be treated with respect." He said that when Hoosiers contact Lugar's office they have often been frustrated by their dealings with government agencies. "They want an advocate. You have to recognize that. That comes directly from the senator, not so much by his words but by his actions."[14]

The Lugar office prides itself in doing careful and prompt casework. Morris requires that mail is responded to within 4 days and that requests for information or guidance are dealt with quickly. "When we get contacted by a constituent, I demand that we will answer first. That is the one thing you can control. We can be the fastest. We can work hard and not let things sit. But we have to do what is right and not always what the constituent wants."

Morris said that people working for the federal government usually are trying to fairly apply rules. Occasionally government workers make a mistake that they will rectify once they realize it. There are other cases that are more difficult in which a non-responsive agency is not acting fairly. Morris says the office's casework must be able withstand scrutiny and tells his staff to assume their actions could show up in a front-page story in the *Indianapolis Star*. Lugar's office does its own casework and doesn't coordinate its work with the other Indiana congressional offices or the office of the other senator. Morris said that not all offices approach their dealings with the government in the same way and he wants Lugar's office to follow its own procedures.

Susan Brouillette, the director of casework who is based in the senator's Indianapolis office, said she and her colleagues see themselves as ombudsmen for Hoosiers who need help with the government. They ask their contacts in government agencies to give fair hearings to the matters brought to them by the people in Indiana. "Our job is to advocate for a process, not for an outcome. We treat the people we work with in the government with respect and courtesy and we do the same for the Hoosiers we are trying to help."[15]

Lugar's office is prepared to help constituents communicate with federal, state, and local agencies, identify appropriate resources for assistance, ensure due process of claims with federal agencies, clarify federal regulations and procedures, and obtain general information. Like many Senate offices, Lugar's office gets most of its requests to help constituents deal with questions regarding Social Security, Medicare, Medicaid, veterans benefits, and immigration. On all major policy issues, the office tallies constituent preferences and compiles the results daily and weekly for senior staff to review.

Lugar has never sat on the Senate Appropriations Committee and has little interest in the annual horse-trading that surrounds the allocation of federal funds. He once called work on the Appropriations Committee "boring, boring."[16] Lugar's office does not encourage Hoosiers to seek congressional earmarks to secure federal funds. "Congressional requested funding is the least likely and the most difficult method for obtaining funding for a project. Funding from local revenue, state and federal grants, and existing government funding programs represent the bulk of funding for projects," his website says.[17]

In early 2008, Lugar chaired a five-member Senate Republican working group to develop a party position on the politically volatile issue of earmarks. Lugar helped the group develop a policy that focused on public disclosure and transparency of earmarks requested by senators. His Senate Republican colleagues never formally adopted the policy, but Lugar uses it for his office.

Lugar requires a formal letter of request for each project and a completed internal application. He also expects a request letter written to Lugar and signed by the highest-ranking person of the particular group requesting funds, such as the mayor or college president. The application must include a comprehensive project description, detailed itemization of how the funds would be spent, the purpose of the project, other source of funds, the impetus for the project, and other supporting documents such as pictures and maps. Lugar's staff often meets with groups that are requesting funds, seeking more information. Staff may make site visits to study proposals and arrange conference calls so they fully understand what is being requested. They encourage letters of support from interested parties in the community. After a vigorous internal review, Lugar's office sends its high-priority projects to the Appropriations Committee with a letter from the senator. Lugar rarely lobbies members of the Appropriations Committee directly to push projects. Lugar's staff informs their contacts on the Appropriations Committee what projects are most important to the office.

Lugar's office provides pamphlets and handbooks on a variety of topics of significance to Hoosiers. During the economic crisis of 2008, his office created *The Hoosier Connection* to offer their best contact information for government and social service agencies regarding financial and food assistance, housing, employment, health care, state information, transportation, and veterans issues. The office provides other handbooks for scholarships, seniors, and the federal government. Lugar's office provides information on grants and has a staffer devoted to helping Hoosiers write grant applications.

Senators have smaller offices than people often realize. Even Lugar, a 35-year Senate veteran, has only about 20 staff in his personal office, 20 from the Senate Foreign Relations Committee, and 20 in his various offices in Indiana. By way of contrast, most state governors preside over bureaucracies of thousands.[18]

Lugar's office looks for creative ways to connect with important groups. For example, his office has partnered with the Library of Congress for a decade to help preserve the oral histories of Indiana veterans. The Department of Veterans Affairs estimates that 559,000 veterans live in Indiana. The senator's office has invited veterans of all military branches who served during World War I, World War II, Korea, Vietnam, the Gulf War, and the Iraq and Afghanistan wars to tell their stories. Lugar's office works with more than 230 high schools and other community groups to conduct these interviews. So far, almost ten thousand interviews have been collected by Lugar and has staff, which is more than any other state. Each veteran who participates in the program receives a certificate from Lugar thanking him or her for serving the country and participating in this project. The stories of the veterans become part of the permanent collection at the American Folklife Center at the Library of Congress.

Lugar runs a frugal office and takes pride in returning money every year to the Senate from the amount that is allocated to him for office expenses. "We try to live well within the means the government provides us and send back a portion of it. Sometimes it's tithing. Sometimes it's much more than that," Morris says. Over the years, Lugar has returned more than $5 million to the Senate.[19]

IV

Lugar is a kindly, avuncular man who seems above partisan politics. But he has been a loyal, electorally successful Republican for more than 40 years. And while he does appear to float above most of the day-to-day political machinations in Washington and Indiana, he has a disciplined, even tough, political operation that has kept him politically formidable for a long time.

Morris, his political mastermind, believes in keeping the Lugar political machine running during the senator's full 6-year term. Nothing is taken for granted, and Morris assumes that every election will be tough and the outcome uncertain. Both Morris and Lugar read the various polls in circulation. Most show the senator's favorable ratings consistently above 50 percent. There have been occasional polls that have shown Lugar's favorable rating even among Democrats nearing 70 percent.[20]

Morris stays in close touch with the Republican Party apparatus in Indiana, beginning with Daniels, the governor of Indiana and a one-time Lugar staffer. Both Morris and Lugar know and are friendly with state Republican leaders, including the 92 country chairmen. During his long political career, Lugar has remained respected and admired by most Republicans, even as he has moved carefully amidst factional struggles between Indiana's economic and cultural conservatives. Since 2010, Lugar has come under attack by members of the Tea Party who find his views on judicial nominations, foreign policy, immigration, and bipartisanship too moderate for their tastes. Most analysts believe that Lugar is more vulnerable from a challenge from the right within his own party than in a general election.[21]

Morris disagrees with the common practice of writing detailed campaign plans, arguing that circumstances are bound to change as an election nears. "We know the general thrust of where we're headed, but the specifics change all the time." His campaign theory is that the primary focus should be to tell Lugar's story. He is ready to respond to any attacks leveled at Lugar. And he is always looking to try to broaden the electorate, finding new voters who might support the senator. "We never run the same campaign twice. There is no mold. The state is always changing, the issues are changing. We have to reinvent each campaign. We are trying to tell the people of Indiana a story. Not many campaigns do that anymore. The senator's story is always built around the importance of economic growth."[22]

The senator's political action committee, Friends of Dick Lugar, raises funds full time through direct mail and special events. Typically, the fund-raising for the first 4 years of Lugar's term is steady but then ramps up in the 2 years leading to his re-election campaign. Morris doesn't think political rivals are scared off by large war chests. "Money is only a tool and it's a tool to communicate," Morris said.

Morris said that it costs between $20,000 and $30,000 to produce a political ad. The Lugar team runs every commercial they create. The ads try to tell voters who Lugar is and what he wants to accomplish if re-elected. They lay a foundation for his next term. "You better establish what you're going to do. If you don't explain what you're going to do your next few years are going to be a nightmare. So we always explain what we're going to do," Morris says. In 2006, when he ran unopposed by a major party candidate, Lugar raised over $5 million and spent $3 million. The campaign produced a series of ads related to the senator's plans to work on energy issues if sent back to Washington.

Lugar's PAC outlines on its website the main issues the senator is most involved with: energy, the Nunn-Lugar program, agriculture reform, nutrition, education, and health care. It emphasizes his concern about fiscal responsibility and notes his background as a lifelong Republican, farmer, small businessman, school board member, and mayor of Indianapolis.

The Lugar team prefers not to go negative on their opponents, but it's not a passive operation. "We will answer your attack with an answer—not an attack, but an answer," Morris said. He tries to constantly put himself in the shoes of Lugar's opponents. "I know what I would do if I were them."[23]

Lugar doesn't directly solicit campaign funds, but he understands the imperative to raise large sums of money and has created a system that does so. "Lugar is not going to raise money directly. That's how he operates. He never complains about not fund-raising. He sees the fund-raising numbers constantly. But that divide between him and fund-raising is important to how he wants to run his political career," Morris said. Lugar wonders how senators can do their regular jobs if they have to devote considerable amount of time to fund-raising. "Senator Lugar is a lousy fund-raiser. He absolutely hates it. He doesn't like asking people for anything for himself," says Jim Morris, the president of the Indiana Pacers.[24]

According to OpenSecrets.org, a campaign watchdog group, Lugar raised more than $25 million from 1989 to 2010. Lugar's top contributors include Eli Lilly ($162,000), Barnes & Thornburg ($127,200), Baker & Daniels ($75,138), Indiana University ($73,040), and Cummins Inc. ($58,450).[25] But when he faced the prospect of a competitive primary in 2012, the Lugar fund-raising operation shifted into high gear and raised almost a million dollars in one quarter in 2011.

Helping this formal political operation is the senator's vast network of former staffers and political supporters, people who raise money for the senator, give him policy ideas, and take soundings of the political climate. Morris, as the senator's chief of staff, has his own network which he consults regularly to get political assessments from people back home. "Once you've worked for the senator, you are part of his network for the rest of your life," said Tinder, the federal judge who once was a Lugar staffer. "It's a large network that is totally devoted to him. Everyone feels so indebted to him, you want to help him."[26]

Sometimes the Lugar alumni are brought in on politically sensitive special projects. For example, in 2009, an Indiana judge, David Hamilton, was embroiled in a contentious Senate confirmation fight to serve on the U.S. Court of Appeals for the Seventh Circuit. A number of Senate Republicans, including the most senior one on the Senate Judiciary Committee, Jeff Sessions of Alabama, said they were troubled by Hamilton's record.

Lugar asked Peter Rusthoven, an Indianapolis attorney and a former associate counsel to President Reagan, to review these concerns and
provide him with a detailed briefing. Rusthoven examined the various
allegations and found that the most consequential were not true. He
sent Lugar a policy memo that became the basis of Lugar's speech on the
Senate floor, refuting charges about Hamilton's alleged judicial activism
and leniency in sentencing. Lugar led a public and successful campaign
to secure Hamilton's confirmation.

V

The senator has lent his name to a number of scholarships, awards,
and programs. They convey the message that Lugar is active in supporting initiatives such as educational opportunities for minorities, fitness,
good schools, clean energy, and school lunch and veterans programs.
Staffers say that Lugar enjoys attaching his name to projects and causes
that he has a long association with and that reflect his personal or policy
values. "He is not the kind of person who is interested in having an obscure road named after him. But he enjoys having things that he really
believes in bear his name," one former staffer said.[27]

Lugar's connection to agriculture is reflected in the Dick Lugar/
Indiana Farm Bureau Essay Contest, which is sponsored by Indiana
Farm Bureau. It is an essay contest for eighth-grade students who live
in the ten Indiana Farm Bureau districts. The senator's lifelong interest
in running and fitness is evident in his support of the Dick Lugar Run
and Walk sponsored by Butler University in Indianapolis. This is an
annual 5K walk or 10K run that has taken place for more than 20 years.
Lugar's passion about energy is reflected in several projects that bear
his name. There is the Richard G. Lugar Center for Renewable Energy
based at Indiana University–Purdue University in Indianapolis, which
was set up in 2007. The Lugar Collegiate Energy Network is a network
of students in Indiana who are interested in innovations in energy and
the environment. The senator also sponsors a monthly Lugar Energy
Patriot Award, which is given out each month to a Hoosier involved in
creative energy projects.

The senator's interest in food issues is reflected in the Lugar Pilot Program, a summer meals program for children, and the Richard G. Lugar School Food Service Employee of the Year award given by the Indiana Department of Education to a food service professional. Lugar's support for greater minority education opportunities prompted him to create the Richard G. Lugar Fund for Hoosier Excellence, which has raised more than $1.5 million to fund more than 250 scholarships for minority students in Indiana who stay in state to attend college. There is also the Richard G. Lugar Franciscan Center for Global Studies at Marian University in Indianapolis that encourages the study of contemporary global issues.

The senator's interest in leadership training led him to develop the Lugar Symposium for Tomorrow's Leaders. This event, described earlier, is held every December at the University of Indianapolis. Two high school juniors from each school in Indiana are invited to attend a daylong seminar on public policy issues. More than fifteen thousand Hoosiers have participated in this program since 1977. The Richard G. Lugar Center for Tomorrow's Leaders at the University of Indianapolis became the permanent home for the symposium in 2007. The senator also created the Richard G. Lugar Excellence in Public Service Series in which up to 20 Republican women in Indiana are selected for leadership training each year.

13

❧

The Statesman of the Senate

I

The question of what constitutes excellence and statesmanship in the U.S. Senate has intrigued scholars, journalists and, not surprisingly, senators for almost as long as the upper chamber has been in existence. Senator John F. Kennedy led one notable attempt to identify the great senators of the past, an exercise that compelled him to think deeply about what constitutes senatorial excellence. Kennedy chaired a panel of senators in the mid-1950s to identify the five most outstanding former senators whose likenesses would be placed in vacant portrait spaces in the Senate Reception Room in the Capitol.

Kennedy's commission struggled to define what made a senator great. Was it legislative accomplishments or could it include efforts to defeat misguided legislation? Was personal integrity a requirement or simply a hoped-for attribute? Did the senator need to be involved in national issues or could impressive accomplishments in state or regional issues suffice? How important was earning the esteem of colleagues?[1]

Near the end of his panel's deliberations, Kennedy mused that the "value of a Senator is not so easily determined as the value of a car or a hog, or even that of a public utility bond or a ballplayer." There were, Kennedy said, "no standard tests to apply to a Senator, no Dunn & Bradstreet rating, no scouting reports. His talents may vary with his time, his contribution may be limited by his politics."[2] The Kennedy commission decided to judge senators for "acts of statesmanship transcending party and State lines" and to define statesmanship to include "leadership in national thought and constitutional interpretation as well as legislation."[3]

But Kennedy acknowledged that the question of what constitutes statesmanship is a complicated one. He observed that he knew "of no man elected to the Senate in all its history who was not a 'politician' whether or not he was also a 'statesman.'"[4]

The standard definition of a statesman is a person who shows wisdom, skill, and vision in conducting a state's affairs. A well-known English proverb says the difference between a politician and a statesman is that the former looks to the next election while the latter looks to the next generation.[5]

Richard Lugar entered the Senate in January 1977 as an ambitious politician and has, in the eyes of many, achieved the status of statesman. He has been able to keep a careful eye on the next election while also thinking about the problems that confront the next generation. Lugar is widely respected and admired among his colleagues and congressional scholars, but it is more difficult to judge how effective Lugar has been in the Senate.

In assessing Richard Lugar's impact on foreign policy from Capitol Hill a few caveats are in order. First, this book has not attempted to explore his impact on Indiana politics. Lugar has been a dominant political force in his state since the mid-1970s, and he made sizeable contributions to the revitalization of Indianapolis before then, when he served as mayor. Lugar's Indiana record and legacy deserve serious study, but that has not been the subject of this book.

The senator has also been a leader on agricultural policy during his Senate career. He chaired the Senate Agriculture Committee from 1995 to 2001 and has been a member of the committee since he entered the Senate. In this book, I've considered several international aspects of his work on agriculture but have not focused on his influence on American agricultural policy. That also is the subject of another book.

Finally, this book has focused primarily on Lugar's work on foreign policy since 2006, when I began to interview him regularly and closely follow his work. Many of the issues Lugar has worked on over these years will be central to his congressional legacy, such as arms control, the Nunn-Lugar program, energy reforms, and tackling the global food crisis. While this book does not claim to be a comprehensive assessment of Lugar's long and consequential career, I believe it examines issues that Lugar cares deeply about and describes the essential qualities of Lugar's work in the Senate.

II

When evaluating Richard Lugar's influence on American foreign policy from Capitol Hill, one should begin with his considerable legislative legacy. After all, the main job of legislators is to write laws and to move bills through Congress. There is little doubt that Lugar's central legislative accomplishment is the Nunn-Lugar Cooperative Threat Reduction Program. Lugar and Nunn developed a plan to begin safeguarding and then dismantling weapons of mass destruction in the Soviet Union as it was collapsing in 1991. Seeking to secure the nuclear, chemical, and biological weapons in the Soviet Union, they faced an indifferent administration and opposition from many in Congress. The two senators were able to cobble together a modest program that was acceptable to President George H. W. Bush and Congress. That program, which has grown over the ensuing 20 years, provides U.S. funding and expertise to help the countries of the former Soviet Union safeguard and dismantle their stockpiles of nuclear, chemical, and biological weapons, related materials, and delivery systems.[6]

While Nunn played a central role in developing the program, he retired from the Senate in January 1997. Since then, Lugar has been the chief advocate of the program on Capitol Hill. He has kept the program going and even succeeded in expanding and globalizing it. Shaped by Lugar's dogged leadership on Capitol Hill, the Nunn-Lugar program has grown from an emergency response to the collapse of the Soviet Union to a more comprehensive threat reduction and non-proliferation program, to an ambitious plan to keep weapons of mass destruction from escaping the Soviet Union into the hands of terrorists and rogue regimes, to a global program to control the threat of weapons of mass destruction. The program now operates in countries beyond the former Soviet Union and is able to receive contributions from foreign governments, international organizations, and multinational entities. Lugar says that while the program continues its important work addressing threats in the former Soviet Union, new challenges are emerging, and he is eager to extend the Nunn-Lugar program into countries around the world. He envisions a day when U.S. and Russian non-proliferation teams work together to secure WMD around the world.[7]

The Nunn-Lugar program has served as the progenitor of a raft of initiatives in the U.S. government and around the world. It has been described as a rare recent example of the successful pursuit of enlightened self-interest by the United States, in which modest government resources have accomplished important goals. Some analysts describe the program as a major historic achievement, worthy of being referred to in the same breath as the Marshall Plan.

"There are not many senators who can claim that their name is on a landmark piece of legislation, that they created a program that has endured and been successful. That's a major accomplishment," said Ross Baker, a congressional expert at Rutgers University.[8] William Burns, a senior U.S diplomat who has served as the American ambassador to Russia, worked with Lugar on the Nunn-Lugar program for years and said the senator's advocacy has been crucial. "You couldn't have sustained this program without Senator Lugar's dogged approach. You couldn't have sustained the interest on the Hill. You couldn't have sustained the resources. You couldn't have worked it with the Russians or the Ukrainians or anyone else without his deep, long-term commitment because you're dealing with sensitive issues for leaders. He created it as a genuine partnership," Burns said.[9]

In a related effort, Lugar and Nunn teamed up with Senator Pete Domenici in 1996 to pass important legislation that established the country's first significant program to train local and state law enforcement officials to respond in the event of a catastrophic terrorist attack. This was an important building block for later homeland security projects.

Lugar has also played a major role in helping secure Senate approval of critical arms control treaties over the last several decades, including START I (1992), START II (1996), the Intermediate Nuclear Forces Agreement (1988), the Chemical Weapons Treaty (1997), and the New START treaty (2010). The Senate Foreign Relations Committee has primary jurisdiction over all treaties that are sent to the Senate, and Lugar has plunged into the details of arms control with trademark tenacity. "He is the go-to expert in the Senate on all nuclear weapons issues and is just as much of a leader today as he was 20 years ago," said Joe Cirincione, a nuclear expert and the president of the Ploughshares Fund. Vice President Joe Biden has called Lugar's work on arms control and nuclear security "without equal" in Congress.[10]

Lugar's legislative legacy includes major contributions to energy law. He initiated a bio-fuels research program to lessen American dependency on foreign oil. He has fought to boost fuel efficiency standards in cars and trucks and promoted conservation. He has been a leading congressional champion of ethanol, arguing that it is necessary to help wean the United States from its dependence on foreign oil. His support, however, for heavy subsidies for ethanol has prompted some to question if Lugar's adherence to free market principles is as consistent as he claims. But he has also offered politically risky energy ideas including a call to increase the federal gas tax as a way to help reduce the consumption of oil in the United States.

As the chairman of the Senate Foreign Relations Committee, Lugar played a central role in winning congressional passage of the U.S.-India Civilian Nuclear Agreement. This landmark law remains controversial as it pertains to proliferation, but it has endeavored to build a new American strategic relationship with India.

Lugar has also been a consequential senator in the often neglected area of conducting congressional oversight of the activities and programs of the federal government. Lugar's dogged and fair-minded approach to oversight has included careful examination of his own signature program, Nunn-Lugar, to make sure that it is operating effectively. The senator takes regular overseas trips to examine how the program is working and consults frequently with top officials in the executive branch who manage the Nunn-Lugar program to better understand their concerns and to help make program adjustments.

Lugar has also taken his oversight responsibilities seriously as he has examined the nation's foreign assistance programs, studied the global food crisis, assessed the nation's energy challenges, held hearings on the Law of the Sea Treaty, and probed the conduct of the wars in Iraq and Afghanistan.

Senate Historian Don Ritchie believes that Lugar's legislative and oversight legacy regarding foreign policy is important but suggests an even broader perspective on Lugar's Senate contributions. Ritchie said that it is very difficult for a president to sustain a foreign policy without the support of Congress and every president needs allies on Capitol Hill to make the day-to-day mechanics of foreign policy work. "Some senators, like Lugar, bridge gaps and make things work. It's an important role that is often overlooked. People often look at the fighting, the clashes, the blood on the floor. That makes the news. But it's not what makes the legislation or the policy work. Almost everything that happens in Congress is a compromise. One of the most important things for a president is to have people in Congress who help you avoid catastrophe. Lugar has done that for presidents of both parties," Ritchie said.[11]

Lugar has been willing to do the important but unglamorous work of making American foreign policy function. He frequently talks about the importance of constructing strong "building blocks" to undergird America's foreign policy. He has worked hard to improve the nation's diplomatic and development programs and fight for adequate resources for them. He has also served as a presidential envoy to Libya, a key election observer in the Philippines and Ukraine, a congressional observer to arms control talks, an American representative to a ceremony announcing the Nabucco pipeline, a host to thousands of diplomats visiting Washington, and a strong supporter of American diplomats and embassies.

Lugar now serves as Congress's de facto foreign minister and is usually one of the first American lawmakers that diplomats wish to meet with when they visit the United States. He has developed deep and lasting relationships with leaders of nations ranging from Albania to Georgia, from Azerbaijan to Ukraine, and especially Russia.

III

While Lugar has been at the forefront of a decades-long effort to keep the United States engaged in the world, he has also been at the center of a consequential battle within his party between the multilateralist and unilateralist factions; between those who see the country as part of a community of nations that should participate in regional and global institutions and those who believe the United States should focus almost exclusively on defending national interests. From his fierce battles with Senator Jesse Helms in the 1980s and 1990s to his more polite but still fundamental disagreements with Senator Jon Kyl over the New START treaty in 2010, Lugar has been at the center of the battle for the soul of the GOP on foreign policy. He has urged his party to support the United Nations and the International Monetary Fund and World Bank. He has not been uncritical of these institutions, but he has refused to scapegoat them or take cheap shots at them. He has not always prevailed in debates with fellow Republicans, and his views may not be in ascendancy now, but his overall worldview is seen by most foreign policy experts as the most likely to make American foreign policy successful in the twenty-first century.

Senate Republican Leader Mitch McConnell said Lugar's views are listened to by all in the Senate and that he remains a leading voice among Senate Republicans. "Dick has been among our most influential members for a very long time. And he got there for two reasons. Number one, he's very smart. And number two, he is, I think, unquestionably the foreign policy expert of the Senate. He picked an area, concentrated on it, and knows more about almost every part of the world than almost anyone else of either party. So when an issue comes up, like the START treaty for example, everyone is immediately interested in knowing what Dick Lugar thinks. And what Dick Lugar thinks makes a lot of difference."[12]

Lugar has also shown that bipartisanship in foreign policy is possible—declaring this in speeches and demonstrating it in action. He has worked closely with many Democratic lawmakers over the years, including Sam Nunn, Joe Biden, Barack Obama, John Kerry, Bob Casey, Evan Bayh, and others. And he has cooperated with administrations both Democratic and Republican. "He always tries to be constructive and to solve problems. He's quite willing to work with people across the aisle and to work with people with different points of view. He doesn't have a sharp partisan edge," said Lee Hamilton, the former Indiana congressman who chaired the House Foreign Affairs Committee in the early 1990s.[13]

Nunn also praises Lugar's bipartisan instincts. "Looking back on our work together in the Senate reminds me that each time I was involved in a major legislative initiative in the Senate, it was with a Republican partner—and many times, with the name Dick Lugar. I submit that no serious problem facing America today can be solved by only one political party. Fortunately, we still have a senator by the name of Dick Lugar who knows that."[14]

IV

With all of Lugar's achievements, there are elements of his record that have attracted criticism. Many, including some of the senator's strongest supporters, believe that he should have been more forceful in challenging the Bush administration in the run-up to the war in Iraq. As the public record shows, Lugar had many concerns that the Bush administration had not fully thought through the impending war in Iraq in the fall of 2002 and the winter of 2003. During critical hearings by the Senate Foreign Relations Committee before the war, Lugar raised hard questions, but often in a complex way that was not easy for the public to understand.

"Sometimes in international affairs you need to speak in a simple declarative way so everyone understands you," said a diplomat who has worked with, and admires, Lugar. "This is not Senator Lugar's strongest skill. Sometimes he is too opaque, too indirect, too nuanced and his statements are very hard to decode. I think this was true in the debate over Iraq. What America and the world needed was Senator Lugar to express his concerns and his reservations in strong, clear, forceful words. That did not happen."[15]

When the administration failed to provide persuasive answers to basic questions about how Iraq would be governed after a U.S. invasion and what the war might cost American taxpayers, Lugar decided not to publicly challenge the administration initially. Former senator Chuck Hagel, a colleague of Lugar's for a dozen years, says he pleaded with Lugar to be more assertive in pressing the administration on Iraq. He argues that while it is far from clear that Lugar could have stopped the Bush administration from launching its attack on Iraq, he believes

Lugar might have been able to force the administration to slow down, think more clearly, and do the kind of hard preparatory work that Lugar advocated and that was badly neglected.[16]

The U.S. misadventure in Iraq surely made the war in Afghanistan far more complex. While Lugar warned for years that the United States needed to pay more attention to Afghanistan, he supported the war in Iraq, which had the clear effect of distracting attention from Afghanistan. The two wars have consumed American resources and attention for more than a decade. They prevented the country from pursuing the kind of strategic, forward-leaning foreign policy that Lugar advocates.

Lugar's colleagues and other experts agree that Lugar did not flourish during the presidency of George W. Bush. A meticulous, fact-based lawmaker, Lugar found it difficult to relate to or have much influence on an administration whose hallmark was risky, often destabilizing, policies. There is little doubt the administration didn't quite know what to make of Lugar. "The Bush administration made a number of tragic mistakes. I think it was a tragic mistake they didn't listen to Lugar more, especially on Iraq," said Hagel. "We had a president who didn't know very much about foreign policy and, more to the point, didn't care very much. He wouldn't read. He wouldn't discipline himself. I was essentially saying they ought to get Dick Lugar in and give the president a tutorial and give this young student some information. They never did that. They didn't use him. It was a terrible, terrible squandering of a resource. And Lugar wanted to help. It was a great waste."[17]

More broadly, Lugar's approach to legislating has often been understated and deferential. Biden, who praises Lugar in most respects, argues that Lugar has sometimes been unwilling to challenge his party's leaders. "If I had to list one weakness it would be his distaste for direct confrontation. There have been times when I wish Dick would have punched back when he knew his team was wrong," he said.[18] "Dick is not a confrontational person. It's not his style. I don't think he likes confrontation. He avoids it," adds Hamilton.[19]

Baker, the Rutgers professor, said Lugar's courtly approach has endeared him to many but has often limited his effectiveness. "Lugar is a very thoughtful, statesmanlike senator. It is really tempting to describe him as the last statesman in the Senate. But he has not been a muscular or combative senator. He has avoided fights. He has been deferential to his leadership. Often, he hasn't been willing to really fight for his positions in a strong and assertive way. He is a scholarly senator and a statesman. But statesmanship is not really valued very much in today's Senate. The time of the statesman senator may have passed. We live in an era of the combative senator who can operate in the cut and thrust of a very polarized time. I don't know if the Lugar style works any more. We all hope it does. We want it to. But I don't know if it does."[20]

Marjorie Hershey says Lugar has embraced a cautious political style for his entire career. "He is a very adept senator who doesn't get too far out ahead on issues. He is cautious and careful. He has not been a risk-taking leader. Those kinds of leaders, the risk takers, don't tend to have very long political careers. The fact is that you can't be both a team player and a risk-taking leader. It is wrong to expect anyone to be both. Lugar has chosen his path and people should either accept it or reject it."[21]

Hershey says Lugar has adopted a political style that is focused on party loyalty and shaping policy from the inside. "Senator Lugar is a team player and that's been a great strength for him. He has decided that he would rather be a quiet and respected voice on the inside with influence rather than a louder voice on the outside that gets a lot of publicity but doesn't get much done. He has made a clear choice."

Lugar clearly found his place in the Senate. Like many of his colleagues, he entered the Senate with presidential ambitions. But after his failed presidential run in 1996, he threw himself into being a senator and a statesman. "I don't want to be secretary of state or vice president," he told me. "I'm an independent spirit. I'm not working for anyone. I've had this privilege for most of my life."[22]

Lugar is likely to leave his mark as a statesman of the Senate, a designation that rarely goes to practicing or even living politicians. Indiana governor Mitch Daniels says Lugar's approach to public service is deeply respected back home. "I think the senator will be remembered as a statesman, as someone we're proud of, a man who brought great credit to our state on the world stage. There haven't been too many of those. I think he will be remembered as someone who rose above politics and who enjoyed the goodwill and the electoral support from people across the spectrum. People of Indiana have been very proud that he's been ours. People here may not know all the details of his work, but they know he's someone to be proud of."[23]

Burns, the American diplomat, said Lugar has been a resource for the United States and the world. "His approach is not so much bipartisan as a genuine commitment to the country's interests. That has been his guiding star for more than 3 decades in the Senate. He has a record of accomplishment, particularly on foreign policy, that as far as I can tell, few senators in the last century can match. He represents the best of what the U.S. Senate can be. The kind of continuity and common sense that he provides is invaluable."[24]

Hagel, his former colleague, also believes Lugar's legacy will be substantial. "Dick Lugar is the most complete public servant I've met. He personifies all of what I believe are the most important dimensions of a public servant. He has great character, integrity, courage, and judgment. The breadth of his experience and knowledge is remarkable."[25]

"I never once saw him sacrifice for the good of the country, the good of the Senate, the good of a colleague, for his own ego. I can't say that about everyone I served with. He's become as admired and respected and liked as any member of the Senate. He is an immensely important part of the Senate, especially with the institution in some trouble. He's really protected the institution. Lugar is one of the cornerstones of integrity that people anchor to. Lugar has always known who he is and what he believes, where he wants to go. He's made incredible contributions to this country and this world. It's pretty hard to get out ahead of Dick Lugar and the contributions he's made."

ACKNOWLEDGMENTS

I would like to thank Senator Richard Lugar for cooperating with me on this project. The senator graciously met with me for many hours of interviews over the last 5 years. He has been willing to discuss his career, current projects, and the long-term challenges confronting the United States. While most of my meetings with the senator took place in Washington, I had the opportunity to travel with him for a week in Indiana and for 10 days during a trip to Russia, Ukraine, and Albania.

I would also like to thank Charlene Lugar for being open and engaging when we met at her home in the fall of 2010 to discuss her husband's career in politics.

Senator Lugar's staff was very helpful as I researched this book. Marty Morris, the senator's chief of staff, always responded promptly to my questions and met with me to discuss the operations of the senator's office and various aspects of Senator Lugar's career. Andy Fisher, the senator's long-time press secretary, was diligent, responsive, and reliable in setting up interviews and tracking down documents. Mark Helmke, who was both Andy's predecessor and successor as press secretary, has also been very helpful in locating critical documents and responding to questions. Chip Sinders, the senator's personal assistant, cheerfully answered questions and provided me with updates on the senator's travels in Indiana.

I would like to thank Senator Lugar's colleagues and former colleagues who took time to discuss the senator's career with me. Vice President Joe Biden was very gracious to meet with me in his office at the White House and reflect on his long association with Senator

Lugar. Indiana Governor Mitch Daniels, former senator Evan Bayh, former senator Chuck Hagel, former senator Chris Dodd, and former congressman Lee Hamilton all provided me with their perspectives on the senator, as did many others.

While this book has focused primarily on Senator Lugar's work in Washington, I have closely followed his activities in Indiana. My conversations with Brian Howey have been invaluable in gaining insights about the latest in Hoosier politics. Brian publishes *The Howey Political Report,* which is a superb newsletter about Indiana politics. I read Brian's reports regularly and checked in with him on occasion to get his assessment of the political environment in Indiana.

In the course of working on this book, I frequently relied on the excellent staff in the Senate Library to help me track down books and articles about the Senate in general and Senator Lugar in particular. My special thanks to the reference librarians who have fielded most of my inquiries: Annie Cobleigh, Zoe Davis, Meghan Dunn, Tamara Elliott, Melanie Jacobs, Nancy Kervin, Brian McLaughlin, Sara Nagel, and Natalie Sager. I also appreciate the assistance of the staff working at the library's front desk: Kara Baer, Rachel Donelson, Beverly Forrest, and Robert Nix. Thanks also to the Senate librarian, Leona Faust.

I received important assistance from the Senate Historian's Office. Don Ritchie, the Senate historian, and Betty Koed, the assistant Senate historian, have been very kind with their time and generous with their insights. I'm particularly indebted to Betty for sending me an intriguing memo on how the Senate has changed since 1977, when Richard Lugar was first sworn in.

I would like to thank my bosses and colleagues at Market News International. MNI has been a wonderful place to work for more than 20 years. Denny Gulino, the Washington bureau chief, has been unfailingly encouraging and enthusiastic about the book. Denny's management style is simple: he emphasizes his staff's accomplishments, plays down our failings, and works harder than everyone. Denny is the best boss anyone could hope for. I would also like to thank Mike Connor, the CEO of Market News, and Tony Mace, our managing editor. Both Mike and Tony have been a pleasure to work for.

For the past 15 years I've been a contributing writer for the *Washington Diplomat* magazine and would like to thank Victor Shiblie and Anna Gawel for the opportunity to write for their fine magazine. As the fates would have it, the first article I ever wrote for the *Washington Diplomat* was a profile in January of 1997 of Richard Lugar.

I feel very fortunate to have collaborated with Indiana University Press on this book. The staff at IU Press has been professional and thorough. Special thanks to Rebecca Tolen, the sponsoring editor. She has been an energetic, constructive, and insightful supporter of this book since the first time I discussed it with her.

I would also like to thank the Hoover Institution at Stanford University for providing me with several media fellowships. I took advantage of these weeklong fellowships to do research, draft chapters, and meet with Hoover fellows. These fellows, including former secretary of state George Shultz, offered their perspectives on Congress, American foreign policy, and Senator Lugar.

On a personal note, I would like to thank my parents, Joe and Terri Shaw, for their support over the years. Thanks also to my brothers, Dave and Tim, and my sisters, Susan, Pam, and Marybeth, for their friendship and good humor.

Finally, my deepest appreciation goes to my wife, Mindy Steinman. She has been supportive and enthusiastic about this project, even during times when our lives were very busy. She is a great writer, superb editor, and even a technology whiz. Her only firm request to me during the years I spent writing this book was not to "take Senator Lugar along with us on our honeymoon." By this she meant that it would be better for both of us if I did not bring the manuscript with us to Kauai. This request struck me as reasonable.

NOTES

PREFACE

1. "America's Ten Best Senators," *Time,* April 24, 2004, 29.

1. SNAPSHOTS OF A STATESMAN

1. Richard Lugar trip to Russia, August 30, 2007. Author traveled with the senator.
2. Richard Lugar speech, April 7, 2008.
3. Richard Lugar speech, December 13, 2008, Symposium for Tomorrow's Leaders.
4. Charlene Lugar interview with author, October 5, 2010; Andy Fisher interview with author, October 7, 2010.
5. Bill Hoagland interview with author, March 25, 2009.
6. Former Lugar staffer interview with author, requested anonymity, September 20, 2010.
7. Chuck Hagel interview with author, August 5, 2010.
8. Charlene Lugar interview with author, October 5, 2010.
9. Former Lugar staffer interview with author, requested anonymity, September 20, 2010.
10. Marty Morris interview with author, September 7, 2010.
11. Mark Lubbers interview with author, March 29, 2010.
12. Richard Lugar interview, campaign materials, June 5, 1994.
13. Brian Winter, "Obama's Eminence Grise," foreignpolicy.com, September 21, 2009.
14. Bob Corker interview with author, September 29, 2010.
15. Chuck Hagel interview with author, August 5, 2010.
16. Rebecca K. C. Hersman, *Friends and Foes: How Congress and the President Really Make Foreign Policy* (Washington, D.C.: Brookings Institution Press, 2000), 3.
17. Richard Lugar interview with author, August 1, 2008.
18. Don Ritchie interview with author, September 17, 2010.
19. Ross Baker interview with author, September 29, 2010.
20. Donald A. Ritchie, *The U.S. Congress: A Very Short Introduction* (New York: Oxford University Press, 2010), 28.
21. Barbara Sinclair, *The Transformation of the U.S. Senate* (Baltimore: Johns Hopkins University Press, 1989), 72; *Party Wars: Polarization and the Politics of National Policy Making* (Norman: University of Oklahoma Press, 2006), 186–187.
22. Sinclair, *Party Wars,* 229.

23. Ibid., 64.

24. Ibid., 66.

25. Adam Clymer, *Drawing the Line at the Big Ditch: The Panama Canal Treaties and the Rise of the Right* (Lawrence: University Press of Kansas, 2008), p. x.

26. Ron Brownstein, "Pulling Apart," *National Journal,* February 26, 2011, 19.

27. Ibid., 23.

28. Colin Dueck, *Hard Line: The Republican Party and U.S. Foreign Policy Since World War II* (Princeton: Princeton University Press, 2010), 307.

29. Don Ritchie interview with author, September 17, 2010.

30. Richard Lugar, "What Do We Do Now?" *Ripon Forum* 44 (Fall 2010): 11.

2. THE SENATOR FROM INDIANA

1. *Congressional Record,* March 18, 2009.

2. Richard Lugar, campaign video, June 5, 1994.

3. Ibid.

4. Richard Lugar, "Campus Clippings," *Denisonian,* May 7, 1954.

5. Richard Lugar, "A Formula For Parenting," in *What My Parents Did Right* (Nashville: Star Song Publishing Group, 1991), 143.

6. Ibid., 144.

7. Karl Lamb, *Reasonable Disagreement: Two U.S. Senators and the Choices They Make* (New York: Garland, 1998), 32–33.

8. Richard Lugar interview with author, August 1, 2008.

9. Richard Lugar, campaign video, June 5, 1994.

10. Brian Howey and Harrison Ullmann, "Dick Lugar Tells Us What Went Wrong with The Schools," *NUVO Newsweekly,* February 5–12, 1998.

11. Gordon K. Durnil, *Throwing Chairs and Raising Hell: Politics in the Bulen Era* (Carmel: Guild Press of Indiana, 1999), 9.

12. Stanley Huseland, *Political Warrior: The Life and Times of L. Keith Bulen* (Carmel, Ind.: Hawthorne Publishing, 2006), 99–105.

13. Durnil, *Throwing Chairs and Raising Hell,* 29.

14. Ibid., 157.

15. Ibid., 156.

16. Ibid., 31.

17. Huseland, *Political Warrior,* 111.

18. *Mayor Richard G. Lugar's Report to the People,* April 9, 1968.

19. C. James Owen and York Willbern, *Governing Metropolitan Indianapolis: The Politics of Unigov* (Berkeley: University of California Press, 1985), 48.

20. Ibid., 73.

21. Ibid., 89.

22. Richard Lugar, "Indianapolis Can Work Better Under Consolidation Plan," *Indianapolis Star,* January 3, 2005.

23. Richard Lugar interview with Lilly Endowment, approximately 1980.

24. Richard Lugar interview with Lilly Endowment, approximately 1980.

25. Julia Malone, "Richard Lugar's Daunting Task: Holding a GOP Majority in Senate," *Christian Science Monitor,* July 25, 1983.

26. "'84 Pressure Shape '85 Leadership Decisions," in *CQ Almanac* (Washington, D.C.: CQ Books), 3.

27. John Felton, "Lugar Moves to Put Stamp on Foreign Relations," *Congressional Quarterly*, January 12, 1985, 84–85.

28. John Felton, "In Victory for Seniority System, Helms Wrests Post from Lugar," *Congressional Quarterly*, January 24, 1987, 143–144.

29. Richard Berke, "What Might Have Been: Emotions Under Wraps, a Senator Looks Back," *New York Times*, September 12, 1990.

30. Joe Biden interview with author, February 7, 2011.

31. Rhodes Cook, "Lugar Begins Long-Distance Run for GOP Nomination," *Congressional Quarterly*, April 22, 1995, 1132.

32. Phil Duncan, "Lugar Hopes Straight Talk Will Separate Him from the Pack," *Congressional Quarterly*, July 15, 1995, 2090.

33. Bill McAllister, "Richard Lugar: A Resume in Search of Rhetoric," *Washington Post*, February 3, 1996.

34. Lamb, Reasonable *Disagreement*, 154.

35. Niels Sorrells and Milers Pomper, "Lugar's Passionate Plans for a Regained Chair," *CQ Weekly*, December 7, 2002, 3160.

36. Barack Obama, *The Audacity of Hope: Thoughts on Reclaiming the American Dream* (New York: Crown, 2006), 311–314.

37. Richard Lugar, *Letters to the Next President*, 2nd ed. (Bloomington, Ind.: Author-House, 2004), 2.

38. Lugar Doctrine, www.lugar.senate.gov.

3. THE TOOLS OF THE TRADE

1. Richard Lugar speech, September 15, 2005.

2. Richard Lugar speech, September 15, 2005.

3. Congressional Research Service, *Foreign Policy Roles of the President and Congress*, June 1, 1999.

4. Steven W. Hook, *U.S. Foreign Policy: The Paradox of World Power* (Washington, D.C.: CQ Press, 2005), 4.

5. Constitution of the United States.

6. Constitution of the United States.

7. Ralph Carter and James Scott, *Choosing to Lead: Understanding Congressional Foreign Policy Entrepreneurs* (Durham, N.C.: Duke University Press, 2009), 12.

8. *CQ Press Guide to Congress* (Washington, D.C.: CQ Press, 2006), 248.

9. Carter and Scott, *Choosing to Lead*, 100.

10. Clymer, *Drawing the Line at the Big Ditch*, 90.

11. Kay King, *Congress and National Security*, Council on Foreign Relations report, November 2010.

12. Congressional Research Service, *Foreign Policy Roles*.

13. Hook, *U.S. Foreign Policy*, 100.

14. Lee Hamilton, with Jordan Tama. *A Creative Tension: The Foreign Policy Roles of the President and Congress* (Washington, D.C.: Woodrow Wilson Center Press, 2002), 10.

15. Stephen Weissman, *A Culture of Deference: Congress's Failure of Leadership in Foreign Policy* (New York: Basic Books, 1995), 29.

16. Ibid., 28.

17. Barbara Hinckley, *Less than Meets the Eye: Foreign Policy Making and the Myth of an Assertive Congress* (Chicago: University of Chicago Press, 1994), 5.

18. Hamilton, *A Creative Tension*, 60.

19. Ibid., 34.

20. King, *Congress and National Security*.

21. Ibid.

22. Robert David Johnson, *Congress and the Cold War* (New York: Cambridge University Press, 2006), 279.

23. Hersman, *Friends and Foes*, 7.

24. Carter and Scott, *Choosing to Lead*, 3–6.

25. Colton C. Campbell, Nicol C. Rae, and John F. Stack Jr., *Congress and the Politics of Foreign Policy* (Upper Saddle River, N.J.: Prentice Hall, 2003), 57.

26. James Lindsay, "The Senate and Foreign Policy," September 9, 2010.

27. Ibid.

28. Ibid.

29. Ibid.

30. Betty Koed and Don Ritchie, "Senate Foreign Relations Committee: Committee History Series," *Unum* (Newsletter of the Office of the Secretary of the Senate), Winter 2007, 1.

31. Linda Fowler and R. Brian Law, "Seen but Not Heard: Committee Visibility and Institutional Change in the Senate National Security Committees, 1947–2006," *Legislative Studies Quarterly* 23 (August 3, 2008): .362.

32. Koed and Ritchie, "Senate Foreign Relations Committee," 1.

33. Lindsay, "The Senate and Foreign Policy."

34. Cecil V. Crabb Jr., Glenn J. Antizzo, and Leila E. Sarieddine, *Congress and the Foreign Policy Process* (Baton Rouge: Louisiana State University Press, 2000), 81.

35. Lewis L. Gould, *The Most Exclusive Club: A History of the Modern United States Senate* (New York: Basic Books, 2005), 236.

36. J. William Fulbright speech, February 5, 1971.

37. Campbell, Rae, and Stack, *Congress and the Politics of Foreign Policy*, 128.

38. Joe Biden, *Promises to Keep* (New York: Random House, 2007), 87.

39. Johnson, *Congress and the Cold War*, 246.

40. Fowler and Law, "Seen but Not Heard," 362.

41. Ibid., 369.

42. Lindsay, "The Senate and Foreign Policy,"

43. Carter and Scott, *Choosing to Lead*, 19.

44. Ibid., 14.

45. Ibid., 84.

46. Ibid., 188–203.

47. Ibid., 234–235.

48. Ibid., 245.

4. A WORLD AWASH IN WEAPONS

1. Richard Lugar office, chronology of Shchuchye project.

2. Martin Schramm, *Avoiding Armageddon* (New York: Basic Books, 2003), 167.

3. Richard Lugar speech, May 29, 2009.

4. Ibid.

5. David Hoffman, *The Dead Hand: The Untold Story of the Cold War Arms Race and Its Dangerous Legacy* (New York: Doubleday, 2009), 380.

6. Richard Lugar speech, September 15, 2008.

7. Richard Lugar office, history of Nunn-Lugar program.

8. Ibid.

9. Richard Lugar speech, January 27, 2010.

10. Joe Cirincione interview with author, April 14, 2009.

11. Brian Finlay and Elizabeth Turpen, *Cooperative Nonproliferation: Getting Further* (Washington: Henry L. Stimson Center, 2007), 56.

12. Elizabeth Turpen interview with author, September 21, 2007.

13. Richard Lugar speech, January 27, 2010.

14. National Academy of Sciences, *Global Security Engagement: A New Model for Cooperative Threat Reduction* (Washington, D.C.: Government Printing Office, 2009), 13.

15. Richard Lugar statement on National Academy of Sciences report, March 6, 2009.

16. Richard Lugar "The African Mission" report, November 2010.

5. ENDING THE AMERICAN ADDICTION TO FOREIGN OIL

1. Richard Lugar energy tour in Indiana, October 23–28, 2006. Author traveled with the senator.

2. InsideIndianabusiness.com.

3. Richard Lugar interview with author, December 21, 2006.

4. Ibid.

5. Richard Lugar and James Woolsey, "The New Petroleum," *Foreign Affairs,* January/February 1999, Foreignaffairs.com.

6. Ibid.

7. Senate Foreign Relations Committee transcript, June 7, 2006.

8. Ibid.

9. Richard Lugar speech, February 6, 2006.

10. Richard Lugar speech, March 13, 2006.

11. Richard Lugar, presentation at *Foreign Policy* seminar, May 15, 2006.

12. Ibid.

13. Richard Lugar speech, August 29, 2006.

14. Richard Lugar speech, December 18, 2007.

15. Ibid.

16. Richard Lugar statement, March 17, 2008.

17. Richard Lugar statement, May 18, 2006.

18. Richard Lugar website, www.lugar.senate.gov.

19. Richard Lugar, Practical Energy Plan, June 9, 2010.

20. Richard Lugar speech, November 27, 2006.

21. Ibid.

22. Ibid.

23. Richard Lugar interview with author, December 21, 2006.

24. Richard Lugar interview with author, February 16, 2007.

25. Ibid.

26. Richard Lugar statement, January 14, 2008.

27. Richard Lugar statement, January 15, 2008.

28. Richard Lugar energy report, July 2009.

29. Ibid.

30. Ibid.

31. Ibid.

32. Richard Lugar statement, July 13, 2009.

33. Ibid.

34. Travel schedule provided by Senator Lugar's staff.

6. THE WARS IN IRAQ AND AFGHANISTAN

1. Ronald E. Neumann, *The Other War* (Dulles, Va.: Potomac Books, 2009), 51.

2. Richard Lugar letter to President George H. W. Bush, April 18, 1991.

3. President George H. W. Bush letter to Richard Lugar, 1991.

4. Lugar Doctrine, www.lugar.senate.gov.

5. Ibid.

6. Richard N. Haass, *War of Necessity, War of Choice: A Memoir of Two Iraq Wars* (New York: Simon & Schuster, 2009), 5.

7. Richard Lugar interview with author, February 16, 2007.

8. Richard Lugar and Joe Biden, "Debating Iraq," *New York Times,* July 31, 2002.

9. Senate Foreign Relations Committee transcript, July 31–August 1, 2002.

10. Richard Lugar, "A Road Map to Succeed in Iraq," *Indianapolis Star,* August 11, 2002.

11. Brent Scowcroft, "Don't Attack Saddam," *Wall Street Journal,* August 15, 2002.

12. Thomas E. Ricks, *Fiasco: The American Military Adventure in Iraq* (New York: Penguin Books, 2006), 49.

13. Senate Foreign Relations Committee transcript, September 25–26, 2002.

14. Lugar-Biden statement, September 30, 2002.

15. Richard Lugar statement, October 3, 2002.

16. Douglas L. Kriner, *After the Rubicon: Congress, Presidents, and the Politics of Waging War* (Chicago: University of Chicago Press, 2010), 270.

17. Richard Lugar statement, October 11, 2002.

18. Sorrells and Pomper, "Lugar's Passionate Plans," 3160.

19. Ibid.

20. Senate Foreign Relations Committee transcript, July 29, 2003.

21. Senate Foreign Relations Committee transcript, September 24, 2003.

22. Senate Foreign Relations Committee transcript, April 20, 2004.

23. Ibid.

24. Senate Foreign Relations Committee transcript, May 18, 2004.

25. Senate Foreign Relations Committee transcript, April 22, 2004.

26. Richard Lugar, "Dear Colleague" letter, December 2, 2005.

27. Executive summary, *Iraq Study Group Report,* xiii.

28. Richard Lugar interview with author, February 16, 2007.

29. *Washington Post,* January 10, 2007; *Wall Street Journal,* February 27, 2007.

30. Senate Foreign Relations Committee transcript, January 24, 2007.

31. Richard Lugar interview with author, October 2, 2007.

32. Richard Lugar speech, June 25, 2007.

33. *Congressional Record,* June 25, 2007.

34. Jeff Zelney, "Key Senator Splits with Bush Over Iraq Policy," *New York Times,* June 26, 2007.

35. Senate Foreign Relations Committee transcript, September 11, 2007.

36. Ibid.

37. Senate Foreign Relations Committee transcript, September 10, 2009.

38. Richard Haass, "Rethinking Afghanistan," *Newsweek,* July 26, 2010, 32.

39. "America at War," *CQ Researcher,* July 23, 2010.

40. Senate Foreign Relations Committee transcript, February 12, 2003.

41. Senate Foreign Relations Committee transcript, February 26, 2003.

42. Richard Lugar speech, November 27, 2006.

43. Senate Foreign Relations Committee transcript, July 14, 2010.

44. Richard Lugar statement, June 23, 2011.

45. Chuck Hagel interview with author, August 5, 2010.

46. Richard Armitage interview with author, January 24, 2007.

47. Richard Lugar statement, March 17, 2011.

7. FIXING FOREIGN AID

1. Richard Lugar speech, October 15, 2008.

2. Ibid.

3. Allison Stanger, *One Nation Under Contract: The Outsourcing of American Power and the Future of Foreign Policy* (New Haven, Conn.: Yale University Press, 2009), 110.

4. Richard Lugar statement, April 24, 2008.

5. Richard Lugar statement, July 31, 2008.

6. Ibid.

7. Stanger, *One Nation Under Contract,* 63.

8. Robert Gates, Landon Lecture, November 26, 2007.

9. Richard Lugar statement, July 28, 2009.

10. Stanger, *One Nation Under Contract,* 129.

11. Congressional Research Service, *Foreign Aid: An Introduction to U.S. Programs and Policy,* April 9, 2009.

12. Stanger, *One Nation Under Contract,* 126.

13. *Embassies as Command Posts in the Anti-terror Campaign,* report to Senate Foreign Relations Committee, December 15, 2006.

14. *Embassies Grapple to Guide Foreign Aid,* report to Senate Foreign Relations Committee, November 16, 2007.

15. Richard Lugar speech, January 28, 2010.

16. Richard Lugar statement, July 28, 2009.

17. Richard Lugar statement, December 1, 2009.

18. Congressional Research Service, *Foreign Aid Reform, National Strategy and the Quadrennial Review,* February 15, 2011.

19. Ibid.

20. Kerry-Lugar statement on Pakistan, July 2009.

21. Emil Cadei, "Foreign Aid Overhaul Less Likely to Advance After GOP House Takeover," *CQ Today,* November 16, 2010.

8. COMBATTING THE GLOBAL FOOD CRISIS

1. Richard Lugar statement, September 22, 2009.

2. Richard Lugar, "The Farm Bill Charade," *New York Times,* January 31, 2002.

3. "Global Food Crisis," *CQ Researcher,* June 27, 2008.

4. Richard Lugar statement, December 11, 2007.

5. Richard Lugar statement, June 8, 2008.

6. Richard Lugar statement, October 17, 1997.

7. *A Call for a Strategic U.S. Approach to the Global Food Crisis,* Center for Strategic and International Studies Task Force report, July 2008.

8. Richard Lugar statement, July 2, 2008.

9. Richard Lugar statement, June 17, 2008.

10. Ibid.

11. Richard Lugar statement, November 6, 2008.

12. Ibid.

13. CSIS briefing, June 29, 2008.

14. Richard Lugar statement, June 29, 2008.

15. Ibid.

16. Richard Lugar statement, February 10, 2009.

17. *Global Food Insecurity: Perspectives from the Field,* Senate Foreign Relations Committee report, February 6, 2009.

18. "Global Hunger and Food Security Initiative Consultative Document," State Department, September 2009.

19. Richard Lugar statement, April 22, 2010.

20. Melissa Ho and Charles Hanrahan, Congressional Research Service, *The Obama Administration's Feed the Future Initiative,* January 10, 2011.

9. TRANSFORMING AMERICA'S RELATIONSHIP WITH INDIA

1. Richard Lugar statement, October 1, 2008.

2. Ibid.

3. Byron Dorgan statement, *Congressional Record,* October 1, 2008.

4. Richard Lugar statement, October 1, 2008.

5. Strobe Talbott, *Engaging India: Diplomacy, Democracy, and the Bomb* (Washington, D.C.: Brookings Institution Press, 2004), 27.

6. Joseph Cirincione, Jon Wolfsthal, and Miriam Rajkumar, *Deadly Arsenals* (Washington, D.C.: Carnegie Endowment for International Peace, 2005), 310.

7. Congressional Research Service, *U.S. Nuclear Cooperation with India: Issues for Congress,* October 9, 2008.

8. Talbott, *Engaging India,* 40.

9. Ibid., 45.

10. Ibid., 53.

11. Ibid., 212.

12. Congressional Research Service, *U.S. Nuclear Cooperation with India.*

13. Richard Lugar statement, November 2, 2005.

14. Ibid.

15. Nicholas Burns statement, Senate Foreign Relations Committee transcript, November 2, 2005.

16. Ashton Carter statement, Senate Foreign Relations Committee transcript, November 2, 2005.

17. Kenneth Myers III interview with author, April 14, 2009.

18. Richard Lugar statement, June 16, 2006.

19. Ibid.

20. Richard Lugar statement, June 29, 2006.

21. Ibid.

22. Joe Biden statement, Senate Foreign Relations Committee transcript, June 29, 2006.

23. Chris Dodd statement, Senate Foreign Relations Committee transcript, June 29, 2006.

24. Barbara Boxer statement, Senate Foreign Relations Committee transcript, June 29, 2006.

25. Consideration of Amendments, Senate Foreign Relations Committee transcript, June 29, 2006.

26. *Times of India,* October 11, 2008.

27. Richard Lugar statement, October. 1, 2008.

28. Sharon Squassoni, "The U.S.-India Deal and Its Impact," *Arms Control Today,* July/August 2010, 4.

29. Ibid., 4.

30. Amol Sharma and Paul Glader, "Indian Nuclear Law Blocks U.S. Firms," *Wall Street Journal,* September 9, 2010.

10. SISYPHUS ON THE HIGH SEAS

1. Scott G. Borgerson, *The National Interest and the Law of the Sea* (New York: Council on Foreign Relations, 2009), 3.

2. Ibid., 9.

3. Ibid., 12.

4. Frank Gaffney, testimony to Senate Foreign Relations Committee, October 4, 2007.

5. Ibid.

6. Richard Lugar statement, October 14, 2003.

7. Richard Lugar statement, October 21, 2003.

8. Richard Lugar, "Dear Colleague" letters, March 8–July 7, 2004.

9. "U.S. Leadership in the World and the Law of the Sea," Senate Foreign Relations Committee document, July 2004.

10. Richard Lugar speech, May 4, 2004.

11. Ibid.

12. Richard Lugar statement, May 15, 2007.

13. Richard Lugar statement, October 31, 2007.

14. Hillary Clinton confirmation hearing, January 2009.

15. Hillary Clinton letter on Law of the Sea Treaty, October 16, 2009.

16. Richard Lugar speech, September 14, 2009.

11. ARMS CONTROL IN THE TWENTY-FIRST CENTURY

1. Jon Kyl statement, kyl.senate.gov, November 16, 2010.

2. State Department transcript, state.gov, November 17, 2010.

3. Ibid.

4. Megan Scully, "Lugar: START Treaty Has Votes to Pass," *National Journal Daily,* November 18, 2010.

5. Vice President Biden interview with author, February 7, 2011.

6. Ibid.

7. Strobe Talbott, *The Master of the Game: Paul Nitze and the Nuclear Peace* (New York: Knopf, 1988), 142.

8. Richard Lugar statement, July 3, 1979.

9. Richard Lugar statement, August 7, 1979.

10. Richard Lugar statement, October 23, 1979.

11. Richard Lugar statement, August 21, 1979.

12. Richard Lugar statement, May 11, 1983.

13. Robert Byrd statement, *Congressional Record,* January 6, 1987.

14. Richard Lugar interview with author, June 18, 2010.

15. Richard Lugar statement, October 7, 1999.

16. Arms Control Association, armscontrol.org.

17. Cirincione, Wolfsthal, and Rajkumar, *Deadly Arsenals,* 210.

18. Ibid.

19. Richard Lugar statement, November 5, 2009.

20. Richard Lugar letter to Secretary of State Rice, March 12, 2007.

21. Richard Lugar letter to Secretary of State Rice, September 17, 2007.

22. Richard Lugar letter to President-elect Obama, December 22, 2008.

23. Hillary Clinton confirmation hearing, state.gov, January 13, 2009.

24. President Obama speech, Prague, whitehouse.gov, April 5, 2009.

25. Army Wolf, Congressional Research Service, *Strategic Arms Control After START: Issues and Options,* January 13, 2010.

26. Richard Lugar statement, March 26, 2010.

27. Statement of Russian Federation, state.gov, April 7, 2010.

28. Richard Lugar interview with author, June 18, 2010.

29. Dueck, *Hard Line,* 307.

30. U.S. Senate Republican Policy Committee, "START Follow-On: Dos and Don'ts," September 30, 2009.

31. Richard Lugar interview with author, December, 27, 2010.

32. Dueck, *Hard Line,* 306.

33. Emily Cadei, "Arms Dealer: How Jon Kyl Has Become the Power Broker in the Debate Over a Nuclear Arms Treaty with Russia and What That Says About Today's GOP," *CQ Weekly,* December 6, 2010, 2800.

34. Cadei, "Arms Dealer," 2803.

35. Jon Kyl speech, *Congressional Record,* May 24, 2010.

36. Ibid.

37. Cadei, "Arms Dealer," 2802.

38. Henry Kissinger, George Shultz, James Baker, Lawrence Eagleburger, and Colin Powell, "Why New START Deserves GOP Support," *Washington Post,* December 2, 2010.

39. Senate staffer interview with author, requested anonymity, October 4, 2010.

40. Richard Lugar statement, lugar.senate.gov, April 29, 2010.

41. *Treaty with Russia on Measures for Further Reduction and Limitation of Strategic Offensive Missiles,* Senate Foreign Relations Committee report, October 1, 2010.

42. Ibid.

43. Ibid.

44. Richard Lugar, "Dear Colleague" letter, September 7, 2010.

45. Richard Lugar, "Dear Colleague" letter, September 8, 2010.

46. Richard Lugar, "Dear Colleague" letter, September 9, 2010.

47. Richard Lugar, "Dear Colleague" letter, September 15, 2010.

48. "Key New START Vote Set For Mid-September," Arms Control Association, armscontrol.org, September 2010.

49. www.senate.gov/treaty.

50. Richard Lugar interview with author, December 27, 2010.

51. *Treaty with Russia*.

52. Ibid.

53. "Senate Committee Approves New START," Arms Control Association, armscontrol.org, October 2010.

54. Ibid.

55. *Treaty with Russia*.

56. Ibid.

57. "Obama Pushes for Vote on New START," Arms Control Association, armscontrol.org, December 2010.

58. Vice President Biden statement, whitehouse.gov, November 16, 2010.

59. "Obama Pushes for Vote on New START."

60. Timeline with administration meetings with Jon Kyl, whitehouse.gov.

61. "Obama Pushes for Vote on New START."

62. Richard Lugar statement, *Congressional Record*, December 15, 2010.

63. Ibid.

64. Jon Kyl statement, *Congressional Record*, December 16, 2010.

65. Richard Lugar interview with author, December 27, 2010.

66. Josh Rogin, "Kerry and Lugar Try Not to Gloat as New START Gets 67 Votes," foreignpolicy.com, December 21, 2010.

67. Richard Lugar, John Kerry speeches, *Congressional Record*, December 22, 2010.

68. Vice President Biden interview with author, February 7, 2011.

69. Richard Lugar interview with author, December 27, 2010.

12. TENDING TO THE HOMEFRONT

1. Don Ritchie interview with author, September 17, 2010.

2. Roger H. Davidson and Walter J. Oleszek, *Congress and Its Members*, 10th ed. (Washington, D.C.: CQ Press, 2006), 136.

3. Mitch McConnell interview with author, May 10, 2010.

4. John Tinder interview with author, September 22, 2010.

5. *CQ's Politics in America* (Washington, D.C.: CQ Press, 2010), 364.

6. Don Ritchie interview with author, September 17, 2010.

7. Marjorie Hershey interview with author, September 10, 2010.

8. James H. Madison, *The Indiana Way: A State History* (Bloomington: Indiana University Press, 1986), xiii.

9. James Madison, e-mail interview, September 19, 2010.

10. Jim Morris interview with author, September 20, 2010.

11. Author's observation from trip with Richard Lugar in October 2006.

12. Former Lugar staffer interview with author, requested anonymity, September 20, 2010.

13. Mitch Daniels interview with author, June 8, 2010.

14. Marty Morris interview with author, September 7, 2010.

15. Susan Brouillette interview with author, September 23, 2010.

16. Sorrells and Pomper, "Lugar's Passionate Plans," 3162.

17. Richard Lugar website, www.lugar.senate.gov.

18. Marty Morris interview with author, September 7, 2010.

19. Ibid.

20. Brian Howey interview with author, May 9, 2011.

21. Marjorie Hershey interview with author, September 10, 2010.

22. Marty Morris interview with author, September 24, 2010.

23. Ibid.

24. Jim Morris interview with author, September 20, 2010.

25. OpenSecrets.org website.

26. John Tinder interview with author, September 22, 2010.

27. Former Lugar staffer interview with author, requested anonymity, September 20, 2010.

13. THE STATESMAN OF THE SENATE

1. John F. Kennedy, "Search for the Five Greatest Senators," *New York Times,* April 14, 1957.

2. Ibid.

3. "The Famous Five," Senate Historian's Office website.

4. Kennedy, "Search for the Five Greatest Senators."

5. Chas. W. Freeman Jr., *The Diplomat's Dictionary* (Washington, D.C.: United States Institute of Peace, 1997), 277.

6. Richard Lugar interview with author, January 8, 2010.

7. Ibid.

8. Ross Baker interview with author, September 29, 2010.

9. William Burns interview with author, May 11, 2010.

10. Richard Lugar tributes, George Brown Award for International Scientific Cooperation, September 16, 2010.

11. Don Ritchie interview with author, September 17, 2010.

12. Mitch McConnell interview with author, May 10, 2010.

13. Lee Hamilton interview with author, June 25, 2010.

14. Sam Nunn tribute to Richard Lugar, September 16, 2010.

15. Diplomat interview, requested anonymity, March 17, 2009.

16. Chuck Hagel interview with author, August 5, 2010.

17. Ibid.

18. Joe Biden interview with author, February 7, 2011.

19. Lee Hamilton interview with author, June 25, 2010.

20. Ross Baker interview with author, September 29, 2010.

21. Marjorie Hershey interview with author, September 10, 2010.

22. Richard Lugar interview with author, December 29, 2008.

23. Mitch Daniels interview with author, June 8, 2010.

24. William Burns interview with author, May 11, 2010.

25. Chuck Hagel interview with author, August 5, 2010.

SELECTED BIBLIOGRAPHY

Alter, Jonathan. 2010. *The Promise: President Obama, Year One.* New York: Simon & Schuster.

Asbell, Bernard. 1978. *The Senate Nobody Knows.* Baltimore: Johns Hopkins University Press.

Baker, James A., III, and Lee H. Hamilton, et al. 2006. *The Iraq Study Group Report.* London: Vintage Books.

Baker, Ross K. 1999. *Friend and Foe in the U.S. Senate.* Acton, Mass.: Copley Publishing Group.

———. 2001. *House and Senate.* 3rd ed. New York: W.W. Norton.

Biden, Joe. 2007. *Promises to Keep: On Life and Politics.* New York: Random House.

Borgerson, Scott G. 2009. *The National Interest and the Law of the Sea.* New York: Council on Foreign Relations.

Campbell, Colton C., Nicol C. Rae, and John F. Stack Jr. 2003. *Congress and the Politics of Foreign Policy.* Upper Saddle River, N.J.: Prentice Hall.

Caro, Robert. 2002. *Master of the Senate* by Robert Caro. New York: Knopf.

Carter, Ralph, and James Scott. 2009. *Choosing to Lead: Understanding Congressional Foreign Policy Entrepreneurs.* Durham, N.C.: Duke University Press.

Chafee, Lincoln. 2008. *Against the Tide: How a Compliant Congress Empowered a Reckless President.* New York: Thomas Dunne Books.

Clymer, Adam. 1999. *Edward M. Kennedy.* New York: William Morrow.

———. 2008. *Drawing the Line at the Big Ditch: The Panama Canal Treaties and the Rise of the Right.* Lawrence: University Press of Kansas.

Cooke, Stephanie. 2009. *In Mortal Hands: A Cautionary History of the Nuclear Age.* New York: Bloomsbury USA.

Crabb, Cecil V., Jr., Glenn J. Antizzo, and Leila E. Sarieddine. 2000. *Congress and the Foreign Policy Process.* Baton Rouge: Louisiana State University Press.

Davidson, Roger H., and Walter J. Oleszek. 2006. *Congress and Its Members.* 10th ed. Washington, D.C.: CQ Press.

Drew, Elizabeth. 1978. *Senator.* New York: Simon & Schuster.

Durnil, Gordon K. 1999. *Throwing Chairs and Raising Hell: Politics in the Bulen Era.* Carmel: Guild Press of Indiana.

Fenno, Richard F., Jr. 1989. *The Making of a Senator: Dan Quayle.* Washington, D.C.: CQ Press.

———.1991. *The Emergence of a Senate Leader: Pete Domenici and the Reagan Budget.* Washington, D.C.: CQ Press.

———.1992. *When Incumbency Fails: The Senate Career of Mark Andrews.* Washington, D.C.: CQ Press.

Freeman, Chas. W., Jr. 1997. *The Diplomat's Dictionary.* Washington, D.C.: United States Institute of Peace.

Gellman, Barton. 2008. *Angler: The Cheney Vice Presidency.* New York: Penguin Books.

Gould, Lewis L. 2005. *The Most Exclusive Club: A History of the Modern United States Senate.* New York: Basic Books.

Haass, Richard N. 2009. *War of Necessity, War of Choice: A Memoir of Two Iraq Wars.* New York: Simon & Schuster.

Hamilton, Lee H. 2009. *Strengthening Congress.* Bloomington: Indiana University Press.

Hamilton, Lee H., with Jordan Tama. 2002. A *Creative Tension: The Foreign Policy Roles of the President and Congress.* Washington, D.C.: Woodrow Wilson Center Press.

Hersman, Rebecca K. C. 2000. *Friends and Foes: How Congress and the President Really Make Foreign Policy.* Washington, D.C.: Brookings Institution Press.

Hinckley, Barbara. 1994. *Less than Meets the Eye: Foreign Policy Making and the Myth of an Assertive Congress.* Chicago: University of Chicago Press.

Hoffman, David E. 2009. *The Dead Hand: The Untold Story of the Cold War Arms Race and Its Dangerous Legacy.* New York: Doubleday.

Hook, Steven W. 2005. *U.S. Foreign Policy: The Paradox of World Power.* Washington, D.C.: CQ Press.

Huseland, Stanley A. 2006. *Political Warrior: The Life and Times of L. Keith Bulen.* Carmel, Ind.: Hawthorne Publishing.

Kaufman, Robert G. 2000. *Henry M. Jackson: A Life in Politics.* Seattle: University of Washington Press.

Kriner, Douglas L. 2010. *After the Rubicon: Congress, Presidents, and the Politics of Waging War.* Chicago: University of Chicago Press.

Lamb, Karl. 1998. *Reasonable Disagreement: Two U.S. Senators and the Choices They Make.* New York: Garland.

Lindsay, James M. 1994. *Congress and the Politics of U.S. Foreign Policy.* Baltimore: Johns Hopkins University Press.

Lugar, Richard G. 1996. *Indianapolis: Crossroads of the American Dream.* Memphis: Towery Publishing.

———.2004. *Letters to the Next President.* 2nd ed. Bloomington, Ind.: AuthorHouse.

Madison, James H. 1986. *The Indiana Way: A State History.* Bloomington: Indiana University Press.

Mann, Thomas, and Norman Ornstein. 2006. *The Broken Branch: How Congress Is Failing America and How to Get It Back on Track.* New York: Oxford University Press.

Neumann, Ronald E. 2009. *The Other War: Winning and Losing in Afghanistan.* Dulles, Va.: Potomac Books.

Obama, Barack. 2006. *The Audacity of Hope: Thoughts on Reclaiming the American Dream.* New York: Crown.

Owen, C. James, and York Willbern. 1985. *Governing Metropolitan Indianapolis: The Politics of Unigov.* Berkeley: University of California Press.

Powell, Lee Riley. 1998. *J. William Fulbright, Vietnam and the Search for a Cold War Foreign Policy.* Cambridge, UK: Cambridge University Press.

Ricks, Thomas E. 2006. *Fiasco: The American Military Adventure in Iraq*. New York: Penguin Books.

———. 2009. *The Gamble: General David Petraeus and the American Military Adventure in Iraq, 2006–2008*. New York: Penguin Press.

Ritchie, Donald A. 2010. *The U.S. Congress: A Very Short Introduction*. New York: Oxford University Press.

Samuel, Terence. 2010. *The Upper House: A Journey Behind the Closed Doors of the U.S. Senate*. New York: Palgrave MacMillan.

Sanger, David E. 2009. *The Inheritance: The World Obama Confronts and the Challenges to American Power*. New York: Harmony Books.

Schramm, Martin. 2003. *Avoiding Armageddon: Our Future, Our Choice*. New York: Basic Books.

Sinclair, Barbara. 1989. *The Transformation of the U.S. Senate*. Baltimore: Johns Hopkins University Press.

———. 2006. *Party Wars: Polarization and the Politics of National Policy Making*. Norman: University of Oklahoma Press.

Stanger, Allison. 2009. *One Nation Under Contract: The Outsourcing of American Power and the Future of Foreign Policy*. New Haven, Conn.: Yale University Press.

Talbott, Strobe. 1988. *The Master of the Game: Paul Nitze and the Nuclear Peace*. New York: Knopf.

———. 2002. *The Russia Hand: A Memoir of Presidential Diplomacy*. New York: Random House.

———. 2004. *Engaging India: Diplomacy, Democracy, and the Bomb*. Washington, D.C.: Brookings Institution Press.

Tew, Kip. 2010. *Journey to Blue: How Barack Obama Won Indiana in 2008*. Carmel, Ind.: Hawthorne Publishing.

Weissman, Stephen. 1995. *A Culture of Deference: Congress's Failure of Leadership in Foreign Policy*. New York: Basic Books.

White, William S. 1956. *Citadel, the Story of the U.S. Senate*. San Francisco: Harper and Row.

Zakheim, Dov S. 2011. *A Vulcan's Tale: How the Bush Administration Mismanaged the Reconstruction of Afghanistan*. Washington: Brookings Institution Press.

Zelizer, Julian E. 2010. *Arsenal of Democracy: The Politics of National Security—from World War II to the War on Terrorism*. New York: Basic Books.

INDEX

race relations, 28
Reagan, Ronald: arms control and, 178–180; Foreign Relations Committee relationship with, 33–34; Lugar relationship with, xv, 32; opposition to the Law of the Sea Treaty, 165–166, 168–169; Reagan Doctrine, 45; Republican conservative wing and, 17
Reed, Jack, 110
Reid, Harry, 21–22, 107, 144, 174, 200
Republican Party: arms control views in, 186; historical changes in, 15–18; Indiana party opposition to Lugar, xv; Lugar as lifelong Republican, xi–xii, 20; Lugar bipartisanship and, xii–xiv; party affiliation in successful lawmakers, 4–5; rise of conservatism in, 17–19; Senate Republican Campaign Committee, 32; Unigov electoral demographic effects and, 30
Reuss, Henry, 59
Rice, Condoleezza: arms control and, 182, 183; foreign aid and, 126, 128; India cooperation agreement and, 154, 160; Iraq War and, 107, 119; Shchuchye Weapons Destruction Facility and, 2, 61–62
Richard G. Lugar Center for Tomorrow's Leaders, 5–6
Richard G. Lugar Food Service Employee of the Year award, xiii
Risch, Jim, 193, 197
Ritchie, Donald A., 15, 20, 207, 223
Romania, 92
Roosevelt, Franklin D., 22–23, 45
Roosevelt, Theodore, 45
Ros-Lehtinen, Ileana, 133
Rumsfeld, Donald, 103, 107, 181
Russell, Richard, 16, 204
Russia: Anti-Ballistic Missile Treaty, 50; Arctic territorial claims, 170; collapse of Soviet Union, 35–36, 52, 64, 180; Iraq War and, 98; Lugar expertise on, xiii; Miass River bridge construction, 1–3; Moscow Treaty, 181–182, 191–192; NATO energy security initiative and, 88–91; New START treaty, 179–203; nuclear power contracts with India, 161; Nunn-Lugar oversight trip of 2005, 1–3,

37–38; SALT treaties with, 56, 176–178, 179; Shchuchye Chemical Weapons Destruction Facility, 1–3, 61–62; START I/II treaties, 179–186, 191–192, 194–195, 198, 200; Ukraine natural gas shutoff, 82, 87; U.S. conservative views of, 19–20; U.S. foreign policy and, 121; views of U.S. arms control initiatives, 65, 68–69
Rusthoven, Peter, 215

Sarbanes, Paul, 40
Sarbanes-Oxley corporate accounting regulations, 40
Sasser, James, 178
Saudi Arabia, 13, 112
Schlesinger, James, 104, 191, 192
Schumpeter, Joseph, 24
Scott, James, 49–50, 58–60
Scowcroft, Brent, 99–100, 119, 192–193, 200
Second Gulf War. See Iraq War
Senate: area-of-expertise style in, xi–xii; committee assignment procedures, 57; earmarks issue, 205, 211–212; election cycle in, 16, 58, 213–214; election of 2006, xiv; exceptional longevity in, 204–205; hideaway offices, 10; historical changes in, 16–18; interns, 11; special foreign policy authority, 50–52, 55, 60
Senate Agriculture Committee, 19, 32–33, 35, 77, 136, 219
Senate Appropriations Committee, 56, 58, 211–212
Senate Armed Services Committee, 56–58, 64
Senate Banking Committee, 32, 40, 58
Senate Commerce Committee, 58
Senate Foreign Relations Committee: Biden as ranking Democrat, 37; Biden-Hagel Resolution of 2007, 108–109; chairmanship campaign of 1984, 32–33; committee hearings, 9, 13, 33; energy policy and, 77, 80; food policy and, 141; foreign aid studies, 127–130; foreign policy strategy and, 123–124; Fulbright as influential figure in, 54–55; Helms leadership maneuver of 1986, 34–35; historical status of, 52–58; Iraq War

JOHN T. SHAW is senior correspondent and vice president for Market News International and a contributing writer for the *Washington Diplomat.* He is author of *The Ambassador: Inside the Life of a Working Diplomat* and *Washington Diplomacy: Profiles of People of World Influence.*